Chicken Soup for the Soul®

Touched by an Angel

D0052892

Chicken Soup for the Soul: Touched by an Angel
101 Miraculous Stories of Faith, Divine Intervention, and Answered Prayers
Amy Newmark. Foreword by Gabrielle Bernstein.
Published by Chicken Soup for the Soul Publishing, LLC www.chickensoup.com

Front cover and interior photo courtesy of iStockPhoto.com/khalus (© khalus).
Photo of Amy Newmark courtesy of Susan Morrow at SwickPix.
Photo of Gabrielle Bernstein courtesy of Michele Martin.

Cover and Interior Design & Layout by Brian Taylor, Pneuma Books, LLC

Distributed to the booktrade by Simon & Schuster. SAN: 200-2442

Publisher's Cataloging-in-Publication Data
(Prepared by The Donohue Group)

Chicken soup for the soul : touched by an angel : 101 miraculous stories
 of faith, divine intervention, and answered prayers / [compiled by] Amy
 Newmark ; foreword by Gabrielle Bernstein.

 pages ; cm

 ISBN: 978-1-61159-941-1

 1. Spiritual life--Literary collections. 2. Spiritual life--Anecdotes. 3. Angels--
Literary collections. 4. Angels--Anecdotes. 5. Miracles--Literary collections. 6.
Miracles--Anecdotes. 7. Anecdotes. I. Newmark, Amy. II. Bernstein, Gabrielle. III.
Title: Touched by an angel : 101 miraculous stories of faith, divine intervention, and
answered prayers

BL624 .C45 2014
248/.02   2014946341

PRINTED IN THE UNITED STATES OF AMERICA
on acid∞free paper

24 23 22 21 20 19 18 17 16 15   04 05 06 07 08 09 10 11

Chicken Soup for the Soul®

Touched by an Angel

101 Miraculous Stories of Faith, Divine Intervention, and Answered Prayers

Amy Newmark
Foreword by Gabrielle Bernstein

Chicken Soup for the Soul Publishing, LLC
Cos Cob, CT

Chicken Soup for the Soul

for the

Changing your world one story at a time®
www.chickensoup.com

Contents

❶
~Messages from Heaven~

❷
~A Gift from an Angel~

❸
~An Auspicious Visitor~

❹
~Miracles Happen~

❺
~My Guardian Angel~

❻
~Divine Messengers~

❼
~Miraculous Healing~

8

~Answered Prayers~

9

~Divine Intervention~

⑩
~Renewing My Faith~

Foreword

Throughout my life I've had a deep connection with a world beyond the physical. I've felt the presence of loving energy surrounding me, guiding me and sometimes even communicating through me. As a motivational speaker and author, I've surrendered to this undeniable guidance to help me fully express the work I am here to bring forth. Whenever I invite this presence into my life, I always, without fail, receive intuitive guidance.

You can call this guidance whatever you want. Call it the energy of love, call it spirit, call it Higher Power, call it angels, call it whatever resonates with you most. The fact is, we all have the capacity to connect to a presence beyond our physical site. We are all being guided.

The only obstacle is the fact that we forget. From birth onward we build up a wall that separates us from the loving presence of spiritual guidance. In time we forget to call on it, and then we forget it's there altogether. We begin to rely on reason and logic and the beliefs of the physical world. We renounce our metaphysical connection and in effect we lose our greatest source of power. Henry David Thoreau said, "I think we may safely trust a good deal more than we do." This collection of powerful, personal stories will undoubtedly help you learn to trust your guides, no matter what form they take.

When I first opened *Chicken Soup for the Soul: Touched by an Angel*, I immediately felt reconnected to my spiritual presence. I felt a strong inner knowing that this book was going to be a powerful piece of work that would reignite our collective spiritual faith. While reading the very first story in the book, I got chills all over my body.

The story happened to be about someone I know and I admire

deeply who lost her son in the Sandy Hook school shooting. In the story, Natasha Stoynoff describes how her good friend, the late Norris Mailer, planned to send her a message from beyond using the word "Scarlett." When an overworked Natasha was contacted about helping a grieving mother from Sandy Hook write a book about the messages she was receiving from her son, Natasha was going to say no... until she heard the mother's name—Scarlett. And the relationship was cemented when Scarlett told Natasha that her mother was visiting and she had just finished reading a book by Norris Mailer!

I felt overwhelmed with joy to see my friend Scarlett mentioned in the book. This was no coincidence. It was guidance that I was on the right track and that I was meant to write this foreword. Spiritual guidance comes in many forms. In this case it came through the text of this book.

We all have our own ways of connecting to the spiritual realm. Maybe you connect through inner visions, or maybe you receive strong intuitive thoughts. Possibly you connect through writing, speaking or creative projects. In many cases you may receive guidance through songs, words people say or even technology. Our loving guides are working through us at all times; they are always present. We receive this guidance in ways that are authentic to who we are. We receive it in a way we will be able to believe.

This book will remind you to listen to those guides, to heed your inner voice and to pay attention to any messages that come your way. You'll read a great story by Johanna Richardson, who did that late one night when she was strangely compelled to drive right past her exit to visit her husband's grandmother instead. A few minutes after she arrived, her husband walked in, having left in the middle of his night shift as a police detective. He too had felt a sudden, unexplained urge to visit Grandma. A few hours after the visit, Johanna got a call from the nursing home. Grandma had just passed away. Imagine how glad Johanna and her husband were that they had listened to the mysterious guidance they received.

If you have felt the desire to strengthen your connection to your spiritual guidance, you are in the right place. It's likely that you were guided here. Maybe the book fell off the shelf, or a tweet caught your eye, or a random Amazon notification popped into your inbox. Smile knowing that you've been guided to a magnificent book that will reignite your faith in your guides. Allow each story to touch your soul and remind you that you are surrounded by love.

Let this book help you find power when you feel powerless. Use it as a catalyst for creating more flow, synchronicity and ease in every area of your life. As you turn each page, remember that you are never alone. Remember that you are always *Touched by an Angel*.

~Gabrielle Bernstein

Chapter 1

Touched by an Angel

Messages from Heaven

A Word between Friends

Never pass up new experiences, Scarlett. They enrich the mind.
~Margaret Mitchell, Gone with the Wind

"Scarlett" was to be our code word, our "sign" from heaven.

My dear friend Norris Mailer and I decided on this soon after we met. I had interviewed her for *People* magazine when her first novel, *Windchill Summer*, was published in 2000. It was a yarn about a Southern belle in Manhattan—she herself hailed from Little Rock, Arkansas—and as we talked of all things Southern, we discovered our mutual obsession with the film *Gone with the Wind*.

In their Brooklyn Heights brownstone, Norris showed me the prized antique Scarlett O'Hara doll that her husband, literary lion Norman Mailer, had given her. I, in turn, displayed my ability to recite all four hours of dialogue from the film—not only for the two female leads, Scarlett and Melanie Wilkes, but even minor characters like Aunt Pitty and that damn Yankee overseer, Wilkerson.

Norris was impressed. From that moment onward, her nickname for me was Miss Scarlett and mine for her was Miss Melanie (Miss Melly). It was her casting decision and why she placed me—a *Canadian*—in the starring role when she was a bona fide Southerner perplexed me. It had to do with my ability to cry on cue and flirt up a storm, she assured me, and not because Miss Melly suffers an early demise in the film. Norris herself was struggling with cancer at the time and would endure a barrage of surgeries in the years to come.

Her fragile health situation and our respective loss of loved ones revealed another mutual interest—the afterlife. Do our spirits die with our mortal bodies or do they live on? It was a topic we debated endlessly while sipping Kir Royales on her balcony. Norris was a lapsed Southern Baptist and I leaned toward agnosticism. During these chats, we'd look across the East River to the Statue of Liberty—she reminded us of Scarlett at Tara, holding up her fist and looking skyward, vowing: "God is my witness...."

We delved further into the spirit world when I began work on *After Life: Answers from the Other Side*—my first of many books with psychic medium John Edward. To paraphrase *The Sixth Sense*'s tagline—John, um, talked to dead people. We were intrigued, and attended several of John's events, yearning to receive our own "messages" from this elusive Other Side.

At first, Norris wanted to connect with her deceased father. After Norman passed away in 2007, she ached to hear from him. And somehow, in auditoriums filled with thousands of people, John always gravitated toward her, giving personal details of her life with Norman that he could not have known without some kind of supernatural connection.

"If there really is an afterlife," Norris said on the balcony one day, "we need a special code word to send to each other. Whoever gets to the Other Side first will send the word as a sign."

She looked at Lady Liberty.

"If we can get in touch, let's send the name 'Scarlett'."

"Hey, if you can get in touch," I laughed, "you and Norman have to help me write my books."

It was a deal. We clinked our champagne flutes.

Norris's health deteriorated over the next few years. In the spring of 2010, she sensed she was near the end and she gave me her precious Scarlett doll, which I positioned across from my writing desk.

"I want you to have her," she said, "to remember our code word."

A few months later, I sat at her bedside holding her hand as she took her final breaths.

After she left this world, I was looking and listening for our code word everywhere — to no avail.

"Relax," John said, offering me his sound, psychic wisdom, "you'll hear from her when the time is ripe. Nothing is a coincidence."

John was right. I stopped obsessing about it, assured I would hear from Norris when and if I was supposed to.

In the summer of 2013, I wasn't thinking of the code word at all. In fact, my mind was a jumble of tens of thousands of words while on an insanely tight book deadline — I had six weeks to produce a celebrity memoir and was working around the clock, fueled by chocolate and caffeine.

In the middle of that panic, I got a call from an editor at Hay House Publishing, for whom I'd written several books.

"We have the perfect project for you," the editor said excitedly. "The President and CEO is asking for you specifically on this. It's very special, but it has to be written quickly."

"Stop right there," I told her. "Impossible. I'm on another deadline. What is it?"

It was a heartfelt story about a mom from Sandy Hook, Connecticut, whose little boy, Jesse, was one of many killed in the horrific school shooting that shocked the nation a few months earlier. Jesse was a hero; he saved the lives of several classmates that day. Since he died, his mother had received beautiful messages from him... from heaven.

"It sounds great, but I'm too busy."

"Please. Just give her a call," the editor urged. "You will love her. Her name is Scarlett."

I hung up. It was the first time I'd heard the code word since Norris had passed. It was probably nothing, but I had to at least make the call.

An hour later I was talking to Scarlett Lewis, and she was wonderful. She described the otherworldly messages of love she'd gotten from her sweet Jesse.

"Do you believe in signs?" Scarlett asked.

"I've worked on three books with a famous psychic," I said. "I'm practically a sign expert."

"You don't happen to mean John Edward, do you?"

"Yeah. How did you know?"

"I had a reading with him yesterday! What a coincidence! You are perfect for this book. I don't want to talk to other writers. I want *you*."

I hated to dampen her spirits, but had to tell her of my other deadline.

"Unless a miracle happens, I just can't. And to be perfectly honest, I called because your name is Scarlett."

I explained about my friend Norris and our code word, and she grew very quiet. Suddenly, I heard a commotion on the other end of the phone.

"Natasha... your friend, Norris... is that Norris Church Mailer?"

"Yeah. How did you know?" I asked, for the second time in five minutes.

"My mother is here with me. She just finished reading your friend Norris's memoir, *A Ticket to the Circus*."

Pause. I closed my eyes and took a long, deep breath. This was no coincidence. *Hi, Norris!*

"Well, Scarlett," I said, "it seems I'm writing your book."

After we said goodbye, I looked across my desk at the Scarlett O'Hara doll Norris had given me.

"How am I supposed to write two books in six weeks?" I asked out loud.

A few minutes later, my phone rang. It was my current co-author, the one whose memoir I was racing to finish.

"Natasha, I'm sorry. Something's come up and I have to go out of town for six weeks. We have to put the book on hold."

I hung up the phone and looked back at my Scarlett doll.

It might have been my lack of sleep, but I could have sworn she winked.

Well, fiddle-dee-dee; maybe there's a heaven after all.

~Natasha Stoynoff

Message Received

Dogs do speak, but only to those who know how to listen.
~Orhan Pamuk

had never had a dog, and at first was wary of surprising our young sons with a chocolate Labrador Retriever puppy for Christmas—until I met that little bouncing ball of silky brown fur. Gracie won me over instantly. She was beautiful and affectionate. She had loads of personality that made her tons of fun. And boy, was she ever smart!

Her first summer with us, for instance, Gracie discovered that she could cool off by lying across an air conditioning vent in the kitchen floor. One day I thought the first floor was too cool compared to the rest of the house, so I closed a couple of vents downstairs, including one of those in the kitchen. Gracie's routine didn't occur to me until she walked over to the vent and lay down. Immediately noticing the lack of airflow, she stood up and studied the grate for a moment. I watched in wonder as she then plunged her claws into it, pulled it out, and calmly flung it aside. She settled down onto the open space in the floor and looked at me with a triumphant grin. "Okay, Gracie, I get it," I said, smiling at her ingenuity. "From now on, I won't mess with your vent." Every summer, that was her favorite resting place.

We all grew close to our furry family member. We loved her, and she adored us in return. I guess she wanted to thank us for taking such good care of her because she wanted so much to please us. She did her best to be a good dog. And she was. She was a great dog. But she was more than that—she was a great friend.

Gracie also made it her responsibility to watch over us. Though she was gentle by nature, she fiercely guarded her family and our property. One night she scared off the thieves breaking into the car in our driveway. "You really take care of your family," my older son told Gracie, giving her the pats and praise she cherished.

"Yes, she's sure here for us," my husband said.

"How does she always know what to do?" my younger son asked.

Actually, it was kind of uncanny the way Gracie sensed what was needed and when. She knew when my husband was coming home, even at unusual times, and she would "tell" me he was on his way by running to the window to watch for his approach. Sure enough, within five minutes, he'd enter our neighborhood. She knew to move slowly around the elderly grandparents. If you could use some fun, she grabbed a Frisbee, ready to play. If you wanted your space, she rested and awaited your call. If you were sick or sad, she tenderly placed a huge paw on your arm or snuggled up by your side, comforting you until you recovered. "Such a good girl," I told her. "You always know how to help." She seemed to understand everything I said.

And I always understood her. Often, when I sat in my favorite chair she parked herself directly in front of me, gave me her "hand" to hold, and stared into my eyes, as though trying to project her thoughts. Her communication came through loud and clear. I knew what every look, gesture and sound meant. Whether it was a request for a scratch behind those soft floppy ears, a reminder to freshen her water bowl, a reassurance that she loved us, or something else she had on her mind, I got the message.

For ten years Gracie added joy to our family. But one Sunday evening in mid-July, the dreaded moment arrived. Our beloved Gracie passed away, and we were heartbroken. My grief was overwhelming. I cried for days. And every time I walked into the house, I ached with sorrow. I was used to a loveable big dog, with nuzzling nose and wagging tail, running to welcome me, thrilled that I was home. Charging through the kitchen, her nails clicking on the vinyl floor as she tried to stop, she often would slide right into my feet. Her greetings had been clumsy and charming, hilarious and heartwarming, all at the same time. I missed them. I missed her terribly.

After arriving home on a hot afternoon a couple of weeks after she had passed, I poured a glass of iced tea and stood in the kitchen sipping it. When I caught sight of that vent that she'd always lain on, a tear rolled down my cheek. "Oh, Gracie," I sighed, "how I wish you were still here."

I heard the air conditioning kick in, and then something special happened. Tiny puffs of brown Gracie fur began to rise from the vent and gather into a little ball. I watched, mesmerized, as the ball of fur quickly rolled across the kitchen floor toward me, mimicking the enthusiasm that its owner had shown. Like her, it stopped right at my feet.

I picked up that small bunch of fluff, and as I smoothed it between my fingers, the heartache began to ease. Here was reassurance that Gracie's love would always be with us. Her legacy would live on in our hearts, in our memories, in the ways she had helped shape our family.

Message received, Gracie, loud and clear.

~D. Riley

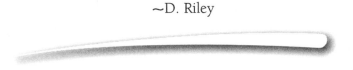

Finding Grace

What greater thing is there for human souls than to feel that they are joined
for life — to be with each other in silent unspeakable memories.
~George Eliot

When my little daughter, Grace, passed away, I was devastated, simply beside myself with grief. I didn't know what to do, where to turn. I couldn't eat or sleep. She had been through so much and it simply wasn't fair. I was so angry — with God, with the doctors, with myself — everyone. Gracie had Treacher-Collins syndrome. She had a cleft palate, was missing bones from her cheeks and chin, and her ears were little nubs with no outer openings. She had dealt with all of these problems, including surgeries to overcome them, like a trouper. At the age of three, she was a happy little blond delight and all she wanted in the world was to keep up with her five-year-old sister Katie.

Unfortunately, we discovered another roadblock. She had very little enamel on her teeth, and her baby teeth began to break down. To protect them, she needed to have her teeth capped. The only way for the dentist to work on her was to give her gas; otherwise she fought like a bear and wouldn't let him work on her mouth. At her third dentist appointment, she suddenly stopped breathing. Despite all of their efforts, they couldn't bring her back.

I was shocked. I followed the ambulance to the Emergency Room at the Catholic hospital, where they left me in a room with her. I cradled her in my arms and begged her to wake up. But that was not to be.

My sister came to the hospital right away, so I wasn't alone long, thank goodness. Finally, I had to let my baby go and walk away. I have never, ever had to do anything so hard.

People quickly gathered; family, friends, neighbors all came to offer comfort, but there was none to be found.

I became ill with a migraine, nausea, and vomiting. I curled up in my bed and closed my eyes, praying and wishing I could go back in time. Wishing I hadn't taken her to the dentist that day. Wishing she had been born without so many challenges. Wondering if the genes that caused all of her problems came from me—but no one knew the answer.

The migraine passed, but not the grief. The funeral had to be arranged—so many things to attend to! I couldn't eat; I couldn't sleep. Every time I tried to sleep, I would see her in that tiny white coffin and jerk awake. I couldn't think of anything else except my five-year-old, who still needed a mama. She was bewildered. She didn't understand why her little sister was no longer there and wanted to know when she was coming back. How do you explain that?

Then one night, a miracle occurred. I had dozed off and instead of seeing Gracie in her coffin, I found myself walking along a wooded path. The grass was thick and green. I could smell the flowers that speckled the ground. A soft breeze blew, and it felt good. In the distance I saw a tall, black wrought iron fence. As I approached, I saw people walking around on the other side. It looked like they were having a picnic. I leaned against the fence, just watching. Then I saw a child pulling a man toward me. As they drew closer, I recognized them. It was my father-in-law and Gracie! My father-in-law had passed away the month before Gracie was born. I always regretted that he never got to see her, but now I saw them together! They stopped about a foot away from the fence. Gracie's face had filled out. She looked exactly the way I pictured she would once she had all of her surgeries. She was perfect. And she looked so happy. She waved at me with a giggle. Then they turned around and walked away.

I immediately awoke with the knowledge that I had just seen two angels. My little angel was in heaven with her grandfather. She was happy and well. I had nothing to fear for her.

Some may say I simply dreamed of what I hoped to be. But I know it was no dream. And while I still grieved, it was tempered with the relief of knowing my baby was in good hands. I pulled myself together, found Compassionate Friends—an amazing grief counseling group—and went on living, something I wasn't sure I could do before.

My little Gracie passed away in 1984, and usually I can speak of her and think of her without a problem. Other days it seems like it just happened. But then I remember that dream and I know more is out there beyond this life.

~Susan Tilghman Hawthorne

The Scent of a Mother

Two things make the women unforgettable, their tears and their perfume.
~Sacha Guitry

A bottle of Shalimar sat upon my mother's dresser. Right next to it was a signed picture of Jean Béliveau. In his prime, he was the handsome star hockey player for the Montreal Canadiens. Next to her children and husband, Mom's two favorite possessions were side by side. A simple plastic frame encased the photo. The art deco Shalimar bottle by Baccarat was filled with an exotic fragrance, a blend of night-blooming flowers, vanilla and mysterious musk. The blue glass stopper was Guerlain Paris's signature. A tidy ribbon encircled the bottleneck, much like the scarves or pearls that often graced my mother's neck.

Our home was perfumed by Shalimar on a regular basis. I remember being upstairs in my bedroom when suddenly the heady scent wafted, silently but powerfully, into our rooms. I knew Mom was getting ready for an evening with Dad. Often my sister and I would watch her getting ready. Lying across her bed, we watched as she dressed "to the nines." The finishing touch was a ceremony that never varied. She dabbed on her special scent behind her ears and at the base of her throat. We always giggled when she then stroked the final dab on the most intimate of places. Our giggles turned into full-blown laughter as she said, "You never know who you're going to meet!" And out the door she swished, making a grand exit and leaving the scent of Shalimar in her wake.

We have continued to laugh through the years. My daughter recounted the first time she was introduced to my mother's wit and wisdom at the tender age of ten. Very seriously, she watched as her grandmother went through her ritual, passing on advice to the bemused little girl. Her own daughters had squealed with delight when they listened to their great-grandmother's story, passed down from their mother. And so it continues through the generations. Monsieur Guerlain unknowingly created a different kind of legend, but one of which I am sure that he would wholeheartedly approve.

Mom tried a different scent once. Her new choice was Forever Krystle, popular at the time of the hit TV show *Dynasty*. The beautiful Linda Evans played the part of Krystle, the second and "nice" wife of oil tycoon Blake Carrington. This flowery perfume was the total opposite of Mom's classic fragrance, and because it underpowered the personality of my mother, it only lasted a brief time. Forever Krystle was forever no more. Back to the beribboned bottle waiting patiently next to Jean.

My parents' fiftieth wedding anniversary marked an especially poignant time for us. A surprise party planned by her four children was a huge and emotional success. Old friends came from afar, as did family that had scattered to different parts of the world. We all watched in awe as Mom danced with our father, her great and only love of so many years. The singer crooned their special wartime song, "Yours," while Dad softly sang to Mom, "Yours till the end of life's story," with tears streaming down his face.

After my dad passed, the scent of Shalimar no longer lingered. The bottle remained untouched. Jean's picture faded. Yet both remained in their place of honor.

Now the four of us sat together, surrounding our mother as she lay quietly in her hospital bed. No scarf, no lipstick, no curls. She was more beautiful than ever.

I bent over her for one last time, and caught a subtle scent. I called my sister over and she too was amazed as the fragrance became stronger. My brother, returning from the coffee shop, was perplexed when he smelled the familiar but still unidentifiable scent. The nurse pulled open the curtain, and sternly asked, "Who has sprayed perfume in here?" My sister and I glanced knowingly at each other.

The scent of Shalimar, the scent to last through the ages, had permeated our entire surroundings. Our mother made the grand final exit, and we could almost hear her say, "You never know who you're going to meet."

~Sharlene Walker

The Mourning Cloak

*In the night of death, hope sees a star, and listening love
can hear the rustle of a wing.*
~Robert Ingersol

Spring came early to Missouri in the weeks before my mother passed away. Mom had lived a long life and was in the last stages of congestive heart failure when we moved her to hospice care. It had been a difficult process to watch her decline over the prior months. She had always been so active and alert until her stroke. It was a grueling time for our family as we undertook the tasks that accompany a move to a nursing home. It's more than the selling of a home, sorting belongings and all those other tedious chores that come with the closing of the chapters of a life. Assuming the responsibilities for a parent takes you into the uncomfortable and unfamiliar as you take the first awkward steps down that last road.

I felt exhausted, and so my husband and I began looking for a getaway near a lake some two hours driving distance from the stresses of work and family, where we could find nature and solitude and no cell phone service. It was a sunny and cool day when we toured the property we ultimately purchased. As we walked down the pathway to look at the land, a large butterfly dive-bombed me. It seemed uncharacteristic of such a gentle creature, and unseasonable for a butterfly in March. It kept circling me and then it flew away. As we talked with the real estate agent, it came back again, landing on my shoulder before flitting off again. "It must be attracted to your perfume," our agent said. But I wasn't wearing any perfume.

It was peaceful there with nature surrounding us. The butterfly escorted us back to our vehicle. At the time, I felt like it was a celestial confirmation that we'd made a good decision. We left the butterfly to watch over our new cabin and we headed north back to reality.

That was Saturday. By Monday, Mom was really weak and spoke very little when I checked on her. When I returned home from the hospice visit, I called my husband to give him an update. As we spoke, I looked out our living room's large picture window that framed the woods behind our house. A black butterfly cruised by the glass. "There's that butterfly again," I mumbled into the phone. My husband didn't understand what I was talking about, which was fine — I didn't understand it either. I was either being pursued by some phantom flying insect or slowly losing my mind.

On Tuesday morning, my brother and I went the nursing home and found the hospice nurses with Mom. She recognized us immediately and began talking rapidly. It seemed as though she had so much to say before her time ran out, but she made little sense and seemed so very tired. She told us she was fine and to come back the next Tuesday. But I knew she would have no more Tuesdays.

I was up and out of the house early Wednesday morning with laundry baskets in tow. The hospice nurses had told me that they were moving Mom to a room closer to the nurses' station, and that I should take as many of her belongings home as I could. When I arrived, Mom's breathing had a gurgling sound that was foreign to me. Was this the death rattle? I wasn't sure, but I called my brother and sister and told them to get to the nursing home. By the time I finished the call, Mom had passed away. I had never seen anyone die before. It was so quiet and peaceful. Mom had beautiful skin her entire life but never more so than at that moment. I watched as the pain and age faded from her face. Her skin became totally smooth and her body morphed into tranquil rest before my eyes. She was like a butterfly emerging from this life, spiriting onto a rebirth. The lyrics "I'll fly away, oh Glory, I'll fly away" played over and over in my mind.

Within the hour, my family gathered at my home. As we sat and talked, my brother saw the black butterfly outside our family room window. She was back again, bouncing off the glass as though she longed to join us. Back and forth, back and forth, she circled and departed. We all agreed it was a message but didn't know what it meant.

The next day, I ran out to do some quick errands. At the store to pick up dress pants for my growing six-year-old grandson, I stopped in my tracks when I saw a ladies white dress top with black butterflies. It might sound garish, but it was subtle and lovely. Since I was delivering the eulogy at Mom's memorial service, it seemed fitting. So did the black butterfly necklace that seemed to appear out of nowhere. It seemed oddly comforting, and so these items ended up on the sales counter with the pair of navy trousers I'd set out to purchase.

I did a little research before the service to learn about black butterflies. In the Philippines, a lingering black butterfly in the house is taken to mean that someone in the family has died or will soon die. In Japan, it is considered to be the personification of a person's soul, whether they are alive or dead. It is generally the first butterfly of spring. With the name Nymphalis antiopa, it conjures up the image of a nymph or fairy; or, for me, an angel. I am prone to premonitions, and attribute them to an angel who whispers subliminal messages to me. I often wonder if it's my guardian angel, the spirit of my mother's Aunt Marie, who had been a surrogate grandmother to me, or perhaps my maternal grandmother who passed away long before I was born. Whoever it was, a sense of peace and calm comes with that voice in my head.

The most interesting, and perhaps saddest, thing I learned was that this lovely black butterfly also has the name Mourning Cloak, because of its resemblance to a traditional cloak worn in mourning.

It's now spring in Missouri and my ebony-winged guardian has once again appeared in my window. I take comfort in knowing that she returns in the season of new beginnings as a poignant reminder that no matter the loss, life does indeed go on.

~Marla Bernard

Help with the Laundry

Dad, your guiding hand on my shoulder will remain with me forever.
~Author Unknown

After my dad died, my two older sisters found pennies in the most unlikely spots as they went about their daily lives. They were convinced the pennies were tokens from Dad, reassuring them that he was thinking about them and in a good place. Pennies from Heaven, if you will. I didn't find any pennies, and was despondent that they got messages from Dad and I didn't. Thankfully my daughter's summer softball season arrived. Looking for pennies from my dad took a back seat to the excitement of watching my daughter's games.

One tournament weekend, my daughter's team was playing on fields close to where my dad was born. One of my duties as an official Team Mom was to make sure the girls had clean uniforms for the following day. So after the games on Saturday, I collected all the girls' dirty uniforms and headed to the hotel laundry room.

Access to the laundry room required a hotel room key. When I walked in, I saw another team mom starting the dry cycle on her team's uniforms. We nodded politely to each other. She then sat in the chair closest to the door and watched a show on the TV mounted on the wall. I hummed as I separated dark clothes from light, sprayed stain remover on everything, and then filled two washing machines with the team's dirty clothes.

I heard a knock at the laundry room door and glanced at the other team mom sitting near the door, but she was immersed in her TV show. So I went to door, and looking through the small security window, I saw my co-team mom Robyn standing outside. Of course, I opened the door for her.

"Hey. How's everything going?" she asked, as she looked around the long, narrow room.

"Just fine. I'm going to put the quarters in, start the machines and watch television while they run through the cycle."

"Okay," she said. "Do you need quarters?"

"No, thanks," I replied patting my back pocket. "I'm pretty sure I have enough."

Robyn left and the door shut firmly behind her. I walked back to the washing machines at the far end of the room and dug in my pocket for quarters. I came up three quarters short of the eight I needed.

Rats, I thought, as I remembered the pile of quarters I had left sitting on the nightstand in my room. I turned to the other team mom and held out a wrinkled dollar bill. "Do you have change for a dollar? I don't have enough quarters for both machines after all."

She shook her head. "No, I'm just about finished here and I've used all my quarters. Sorry."

I quickly opened the laundry room door, leaned out and shouted down the hallway. "Robyn, I do need some quarters after all. Do you have any?"

Robyn spun around and headed back to where I stood. She handed me four quarters.

"Thanks a lot, sweetie," I said. "Sorry to be such a ditz."

Smiling, she waved and left.

After the door closed, I walked back over to the two washing machines. I fumbled a little as I stacked the quarters in my left hand then reached out with my right to load them into the little slots. That's when I saw the eight shiny, bright quarters that filled every slot on the two machines.

I smiled and turned to the other team mom engrossed in her TV program. "Thank you so much for putting the quarters in the machine for me."

She looked at me and asked, "What do you mean? I didn't put any quarters in the machines. I don't have any more, like I already told you."

"But here are eight quarters lined up in the slots, four in each machine," I said.

The woman got up, walked over to the machines and peered at the quarters neatly in the slots. Then she looked me in the eye and said, "I told you, I don't have any quarters and I certainly didn't put them in the machines." She sat back down.

Puzzled, I started the wash cycle, then walked over and sat down next to the other team mom. My mind raced as I tried to figure out what had happened. "So while I was talking with my friend at the door, you didn't get up, walk over and put the quarters in the machine?"

"No. No, I did not," the woman said.

"Well, how did the quarters get there then?" I asked.

She didn't reply. She got up and opened the dryer that had just buzzed. Silently, she took out the clothes, folded them, and turned to leave. As she turned the handle to open the door, she said, "I want you to know that was the weirdest thing I've ever seen happen."

Now I'm not saying my dad put those coins into the slots on the machines, but I also can't figure out how they actually got there. Quarters from Heaven? Perhaps.

~Darlene Sneden

Butterflies

Grieving is a necessary passage and a difficult transition to
finally letting go of sorrow — it is not a permanent rest stop.
~Dodinsky

t had been a rough year for us. Within a month's time, I had surgery for breast cancer and my husband, Jeff, had surgery for prostate cancer. Luckily, his follow-up tests showed no further signs of the disease and he didn't require more treatment. I, however, received chemotherapy and radiation for six months. When my first MRI was scheduled for a year after surgery, I was in a state of panic. Not only was I still recovering from the treatments, but also beyond frightened about having to start the process all over again… or worse! Once again, we were lucky. My MRI was clear. I'm not a crier, but I did cry when I received the news. So much emotion in such a short period of time just couldn't be contained any longer. But our relief was short-lived.

Three days later, my niece, Cathy, called. My sister, Nancy, was in the emergency room. She hadn't been feeling well for several months but always seemed to have an excuse as to why. This time, however, there were no excuses. She'd been so ill that her daughters Cathy and Karen had taken her to the ER. The diagnosis shocked us all. She had leukemia and lymphoma. Once again, we began our cancer-fighting vigil.

For the next year, Nancy spent time in and out of the hospital. At home, Cathy left her job and did most of the caretaking, with Jeff and I taking the afternoon "shift." A stem cell transplant was her best option for survival. After numerous setbacks, she was finally able to have the procedure. While she was very ill after, everything looked good. It seemed that, like us, she was in remission. She came home, tired but feeling hopeful about the future.

Unfortunately, that future lasted for less than a month. Leukemia struck again. This time, there was no treatment. Her heart and lungs were too weak for more chemotherapy. The best treatment available hadn't worked. She was sent home for the last time with many medications to make her as comfortable as possible, but with nothing that would fight the disease. She would soon die. Eventually, the wonderful people from hospice took over all of her medical care along with providing a support system for the rest of us. My nieces Cathy and Karen, and Cathy's daughter Carissa, took turns staying with her at night while her husband Ted tried to get some rest so he could continue working and pay the bills. We continued with our afternoon duties.

Things seemed to improve for short periods of time, but the inevitable happened. After a particularly difficult weekend, we received a call from Ted telling us that Nancy had passed away around six that morning.

The family soon gathered. We cried and laughed and were silent, lost in our own thoughts. I'd lost my sister and my best friend. Cathy and Karen had lost their mother. Carissa and seven-year-old Christian had lost their grandmother. Ted had lost his wife. My sons, Eric and Greg, had lost an aunt they'd been very close to. And on it went.

Several days later, Cathy had to pull herself together enough to go to the grocery store. With a seven-year-old, life gets a push in returning to some normalcy. I agreed to go with her—to get myself out of the house and hoping I could support her a little.

"Are you still sad, Mommy?" Christian asked as Cathy dabbed her eyes.

"Yes, Christian," Cathy replied. "I'll be all right. Just for right now, I'm still sad."

"What would make you happy?" Christian asked with all the innocence of a child.

Cathy thought for a few seconds. "I don't know. Maybe a butterfly," she replied. It was too early in the season for butterflies to be out in profusion, but at least it gave Christian something to look for that would make his mother happy.

We walked around the store in a trance. Even little Christian was visibly upset, as he'd been very close to his grandmother and now hated seeing the other members of his family so sad. We finally completed our shopping and were getting into the car when Christian yelled, "Look!" He pointed to the parking space next to us.

There, to our shock and surprise, was a light blue Volkswagen bug. It was covered with painted, white butterflies of all shapes and sizes. Cathy and I just stared. Then a sense of peace came over us. Was this what we'd been looking for? Had we needed a sign that Nancy was, indeed, all right? We didn't know for sure, but at that moment some of the sadness lifted. We'd been given butterflies.

~Jane Lonnqvist

Mom's Goodnight Kiss

A mom's hug lasts long after she lets go.
~*Author Unknown*

On December 10, 2007, the bottom fell out of my world. My mom died—a sad end to her nearly twenty-year struggle with rheumatoid arthritis.

Mom was smart and funny, kind and beautiful. She charmed everyone who met her and, even through her illness, worked tirelessly to find forever homes for cats and dogs. Not a week goes by that I don't meet someone who knew Mom, and they always say the same thing: "I was just thinking about your mom the other day." Then they'll tell me a story of her thoughtfulness or compassion or humor. What a legacy she left, remembered so often, so fondly, and so well by so many!

But a little over a month after we lost her, all I could think about was how much I missed her. We'd talked on the phone several times each day for years, saw each other several times a week, living just a few blocks apart. The hole in my life was enormous, raw, and exhausting. I was lying on the living room sofa a few days after what would've been Mom's seventy-third birthday. I wasn't asleep, but not fully awake either.

Suddenly, I felt a firm, steady pressure against my mouth. It was so strong that I could feel my lip pressing into my teeth. I opened my eyes, wondering what it was. When I reached my hand to my lips, I knew. It had been Mom kissing me goodnight, just as she'd done when I was a girl.

I smiled through my tears. I didn't tell my husband, who sat across the room. He'd say I'd been dreaming. So I kept it close to my heart, and felt comforted more than words can say.

The next day, my whole family gathered at Mom's house for the sad task of sorting belongings. I found myself alone in Mom's bedroom with my sister-in-law, Elizabeth. She's a spiritual and philosophical person, so I shared my experience with her. "I know it was Mom kissing me goodnight," I concluded. We hugged and cried a little.

Later that night, back at the home she shares with my brother, she told Tom the story. Only then did he tell her the very same thing had happened to him, the same night, around the same time! He'd been in bed, somewhere between waking and sleeping, when he had felt a surprisingly strong pressure on his mouth.

"I could really feel it, pushing against my teeth," he told me when we talked.

He hadn't mentioned it to anyone either, not knowing what to make of it.

But I'm certain it was Mom, reassuring us she was okay, proving there's a life beyond, bestowing one more gesture of her unending love.

In the days and years since, I've thought often of that kiss and have selfishly wanted more, of course. But the memory never fails to soothe my grieving heart and always makes me smile.

Amazing when she was here with us, Mom is amazing still.

Love never dies.

~Kate Fellowes

The Day Nanny Died

We cannot banish dangers, but we can banish fears. We must not demean life by standing in awe of death.
~David Sarnoff

Nanny's body barely created a bump in the bed as she lay under the hospital sheets. I stood with my brothers and sisters alongside my mother as we gathered around her bed. The doctor held the do-not-resuscitate order in his hand. Mother was letting her go. Nanny's body could take no more. For the second time, she was paralyzed by a catastrophic stroke that affected her entire right side. We were there to say goodbye. My mother intended this to be a beautiful moment before she slipped away. But as it turned out, Nanny wasn't quite ready to go.

Nanny struggled to sit up and speak to my mother. A garbled sound came out. Nanny's irritation showed as her good hand flew in the air, waving wildly for Mother to move closer. She did. Nanny tried again. But with the right side of her face motionless, nothing she uttered was decipherable. Frustration showed on the left side of her face. She fell back in defeat.

Horrified, I cringed. Only sixteen years old, little things like school and dogs and elevators produced fear and trepidation in me. Withering bodies clawing for life scared me for real. Someone dying was a nightmare I had not encountered. Gillian, our dog, had died. Hit by a car. But he hadn't struggled. He hadn't cried.

I glanced around and saw my distress reflected in my siblings' faces. Death was in the room. I was frightened.

I watched as Nanny's good hand reached out, like a claw, and grasped my mother's arm. Mother leaned in as Nanny tried to speak again. A horrible rattle came out. She was drooling. Gone was my lovely, elegant grandmother who had played cards with us and taken us on fantastic cruises. In her place was someone I didn't know.

I tried not to recoil.

Mother grabbed a tissue and moved to wipe the drool off Nanny's face.

Suddenly, Nanny's voice cleared. She sat up, unhindered. All signs of her stroke were gone, but she was still clearly annoyed. She flapped Mother's tissue away and wiped her mouth herself.

She spoke. "Anita, I need you to listen. I'm trying to tell you where I hid Aunt Bess's diamond ring."

My jaw dropped. Now, Nanny was known as a great hider. She stashed dollars in jelly jars, rings in the sofa and her silver tea set under the bathroom sink. Everyone knew that. My mother was quite confident they would never find all the things she had hidden. Mother had spoken of "Nanny's stash" many times in frustration. She had tried to get Nanny to tell her where things were, but Nanny had always shooed her away, saying she would tell her when she needed to know.

Now, here Nanny sat, lucid and functioning, talking about her hoard. So bizarre. I swear, if Elvis Presley had walked in and serenaded us, I wouldn't have been more surprised.

My mother was shocked too, her eyebrows raised almost to her hairline. And she hadn't moved an inch. I watched as the tissue in mother's hand fluttered to the floor.

"Yes, Mother?" my mother said.

"I've placed Aunt Bess's ring in *Gone with the Wind*. I hollowed out the book." Nanny giggled, seeming pleased. "The book is on the third shelf in the library, left side."

Stunned, Mother nodded.

Nanny's giggle transformed to an expression of loving impatience as she turned and addressed an empty spot at the end of her bed. "Herman, I am not ready yet. Give me a minute."

Herman was my grandfather, her husband and the love of her life. He'd died seven years ago, so I was surprised to hear her addressing him. Confused and still flustered, I looked to see if he was standing there. He wasn't, at least not that I could see, but I couldn't help but smile. I couldn't recall a time when Grandpa wasn't trying to hurry her up. He called Nanny "DD," short for his "Delayed Darling." She'd laugh and say she was never late for anything important. An inside joke. Everyone knew the only time she'd ever been on time was the day she married Grandpa. He told her he was not standing before the congregation and waiting for her. So she'd promenaded down the aisle before the flower girls and her bridesmaids, causing gales of laughter from all those who knew her well.

I always hoped to have a marriage like theirs.

Nanny turned back to my mother. "And you found my bracelet?"

Mother nodded again.

"Just a minute," Nanny said to the end of the bed.

"And the silver coins?" Nanny asked. Her voice had passed bossy and was right on its way to vexed, exasperated and demanding. Nanny shot my mother a look meant to burn. I'd seen that look before. Nanny believed that a quick switch on the butt made children more attentive. I was glad I was not in the hot seat with my mother.

Nanny's hoard of silver dollars flashed before my eyes. Great memories. Nanny used those coins as gambling money to teach us to count. We played 21, like in Las Vegas. By the time I was six, I could count better than anyone I knew. I loved those coins. I hoped mother had found those. I looked at her in time to see her nod.

Nanny looked relieved.

Nobody spoke. But everybody's eyes flashed around the room trying to assess if anyone else was seeing this… this… bizarre something we were experiencing.

By the look on everyone's face, everyone was.

"Good." Nanny lay back on the bed and closed her eyes. A contented look settled on her face. For a minute, she said nothing. Then she spoke again. "Okay Herman, I'm ready."

And she died. Right then, that very instant.

Silence. Then wild chatter filled the room as everyone started talking at once. A glint, something like an errant sunbeam, hit the window and caught my eye. It sparkled and then vanished. I wondered for a second, but dismissed the thought.

The doctor alone remained silent.

Finally, my mother turned to him and asked, "Did you see that?" She sounded rattled. "Have you ever seen anything like that before?"

"Yes," he said, taking a deep breath and letting it out slowly. "I see this more often than you'd think."

I looked back at Nanny, knowing she wasn't there. I'd watched her life pass to... to... I didn't know where. But, wherever Nanny and Grandpa had gone, they were together and happy.

Later, as we drove home, I realized one more thing. I was not afraid of death anymore.

~Karen Ekstrom

You Only Need to Tell Me Twice

I think miracles exist in part as gifts and in part as clues that there is something beyond the flat world we see.
~Peggy Noonan

was exhausted. The weeklong trip to introduce our newborn son to our Southern relatives was taking its toll. Now that the baby and my husband were taking their naps, I sat on the couch and could not keep my eyes open either. Unfortunately, our toddling two-year-old daughter was not sleepy at all.

It was a beautiful day in the hills of West Virginia. Grandparents and aunts sat on the back porch enjoying the soft rustling breeze, the chirping birds, and the sound of the distant flowing creek.

"Would you mind watching Abigail for a little? I'd like to take a nap," I asked the chatting group on the porch.

"Sure. You take a rest," encouraged the well-meaning relatives. I had forgotten they had not looked after a two-year-old for some years.

I was in deep sleep when I was roused by an audible voice: "Go get Abigail." It was an urgent but gentle command, and I was not afraid at all.

I sat up quickly to take stock. The baby was peacefully sleeping. The aunts were watching Abigail. No one was around to talk to me. It must have been a dream. I nestled again into the comforting cushions and went back to sleep.

Again a calm but serious voice ordered firmly, "Go get Abigail."

This time I did not hesitate. I had heard the voice of an unseen being twice, and I did not need to be told again. I jumped from the couch and ran out the back door and onto the peaceful porch.

"Where's Abigail?" I cried.

Gray heads swayed to survey the yard. "She was here a minute ago."

I leapt off the porch into the yard and headed straight to the sound of the rushing water. It took only minutes to reach the swollen banks that bordered the back property. There on a sun-warmed slab of rock was Abigail peeling off her socks, preparing to step into the beckoning, shimmering flow.

"Thank you," I said to God, tears streaming down my face.

"Here let me help you," I said to my little girl, settling her securely on the creek's edge.

Now safely under my supervision, I let her dangle her little toes in the cool stream. We picked violets, threw them into the water, and watched them wind away from us.

No one needed to be admonished this minute. For now, we all just needed to be thankful.

~Laury Davis

Touched by an Angel

A Gift from an Angel

Bryan's Last Gift

We long for an affection altogether ignorant of our faults. Heaven has accorded this to us in the uncritical canine attachment.
~George Eliot

t was a dreary March day, and the black clouds that emitted torrents of sideways blowing rain were nature's commentary on the way I felt. As I sat in my big chair until late in the afternoon, the thunder boomed and brilliant displays of lightning occasionally lit up the living room. I fell into a deep sleep but was awakened by a huge thunderclap and the ringing of my doorbell.

Who could this be? I was annoyed at having to stir from such a peaceful sleep. I hoped it wasn't one of the neighbors, inviting themselves over for small talk. Having always kept to myself, I didn't know any of them very well. And now, after my stroke, was not the time to make new friends. I hated having to act polite as they yammered on about the weather, or their kids, or my health.

I made out a familiar silhouette at the doorway, and was pleasantly surprised to see it was my son, Bryan. I couldn't get the door open fast enough. After my stroke I moved a bit slower, but he was uncharacteristically patient while standing at the doorway in the driving rain. Oddly, he hardly looked wet at all. He stood there smiling like a six-year-old with something to tell.

I opened the door to receive the biggest hug that I'd had in years, with all of the exuberance that had been absent since he reached his teens. No hug had ever felt so good!

I pulled him in and had him sit down. He said he would, but he had to go out and get something. In a flash he was back. Accompanying him was a small dog—not a puppy, but not an adult. It was a cute dog, kind of. As I'm not a dog person, dogs can only be so cute—they are, after all, only dogs!

"You know I don't like dogs," I said, protesting.

The dog looked at me, sniffed at my feet, and proceeded to sniff his way through the rest of my living room. I did not like the idea of a dog walking around my house, but if that's what it took to have Bryan here for a while it was worth it.

Bryan and I talked and talked while the weather outside raged and the dog lay at our feet.

"What's his name?" I asked as I ventured to pet the dog's silky fur.

"It's a she, and she doesn't have a name yet—I was hoping you'd come up with a name."

"Me? You know I don't much care for dogs, let alone name one."

"Let's give her a good name," Bryan said. He gave me the same look he did as a little boy whenever he really wanted something special. I sensed this was important to him.

It seemed like "we" began the naming process, but it ended up being just "me." I settled on "Happy" because she looked like she was smiling.

"And besides," Bryan said, "that's the way she makes me feel." It was clear that Bryan loved the dog, and the dog clearly loved Bryan. They made quite a pair.

So it was settled.

The storm raged on as we talked of times past and looked at old pictures, many of which I had not seen in years. Bryan served as my guide, pulling out dusty old photo albums that were older than he. I relived memories, and fought to remember names, faces and episodes of my life. The journey was amazing. I caught myself petting this little dog that had managed to sit so close beside me that I couldn't help but touch her. Happy was warm and silky with deep brown eyes, almost identical to Bryan's, and she obviously appreciated my touch. I saw a gentleness in her eyes and a desire for companionship that I did not know in my present condition. I allowed her to continue to lie on my feet. It somehow felt natural.

I went to the kitchen to prepare dinner for us. Bryan continued to thumb through the photo album. In the middle of cooking, Happy came in the kitchen. She lay under the table, out of the way, and watched me. I found myself talking to her as I cooked and moved about. She simply watched, and occasionally cocked her head in curiosity.

When dinner was almost ready, I went into the living room and heard Bryan talking… to Happy.

"She's really going to need a friend…."

I didn't know who he was referring to, but I thought it slightly strange that he sounded so serious. I announced dinner and Bryan bounded into the kitchen with the ferocity of a hungry kid, and right on his heels was Happy. We ate what I do believe was one of my finest meals. We sat afterward looking out the living room window and quietly enjoyed the remnants of the storm. Right before the last rays of the sun faded, a muted rainbow appeared, barely clear enough to see.

Happy lay at Bryan's feet, relaxed, but attentive.

I must have dozed off, because the next thing I knew, Bryan was on his feet and announcing he had to leave. He told me not to get up and said he'd lock the door on his way out. I must have been sleepier than I thought, because I didn't get up from my chair. In my half-sleep state, I continued petting Happy's silky fur with her licking my hand in return until I heard the door close. Then I jolted awake, worrying I'd missed giving Bryan one more hug. And, even more importantly, that he had forgotten the dog. How could he have been so absentminded as to leave Happy behind?

I quickly got up and attempted to catch Bryan before he left. But when I opened the door, I saw no sign of him or any vehicle he could have come in.

There was nothing.

Happy stood on her hind legs and looked out the picture window for a while, letting out a long, low whine. Then she came to my side and rubbed her head on my hand to get me to pet her. The look in her eyes told me what I had just realized—my Bryan was gone.

Two days later, two men came to my house to inform me that Bryan had died in an accident four days prior. I found it unnecessary to tell them that their chain of events was not accurate. It was impossible, because Bryan had visited me and left Happy just two days before. I didn't bother to tell them that, because you had to know Bryan to understand. Bryan had always been a most thoughtful boy who would do the least expected thing, and when it counted most! He visited me, bringing sunshine on one of my darkest days, and left me the gift that I needed the most. Happy has been at my side from that moment on.

I cannot say how Happy has changed my life, but the change is obvious and lasting. I get up earlier, and go outside daily, whether I want to or not, to walk my friend. I walk farther and faster than ever. I get more exercise and sleep deeper. Happy and I play together, chasing squirrels and balls. We go to the dog park, where we occasionally take treats to share with other dogs. Happy is the ringleader of doggy-play while I sit and chat with other proud parents of happy dogs.

I now gladly interact with my neighbors, and talk to strangers and children alike. I feel the morning sun on my face, and hear the birds singing in distant fields. I see beautiful flowers, and imagine patterns in clouds. I smile! Happy and I have made friends and acquaintances that I would have never made by myself.

I have once again begun to see the world as a living mosaic of colorful wonder—all thanks to a friend called Happy, made all the more special because she was Bryan's last gift!

~Roberta Marie Easley

What a Pal

Only in the agony of parting do we look into the depths of love.
~George Eliot

My best friend in high school and I refused to be called "boyfriend" and "girlfriend." And instead of saying, "I love you," we said, "What a pal," running it all together as one long word—whatapal. When we said it fast enough it sounded like "waterpail," which became our secret word to express that no matter what else happened, we had each other. Sometimes I called him "What a fella," (said fast it became Waterfalla) although we never could find a good variation on "What a girl," so we let that idea go.

We spent a great deal of time in the park and searching different routes to familiar places. We often took my Collie, Duff, with us. Jeff and I walked next to each as we headed down the street from my house. Duff would begin our adventures walking a few steps ahead of Jeff, wagging his tail, head held high, smiling his dog smile. Then he'd gradually slow down until he was walking beside me, with Jeff a few steps behind us.

"You like Duff better than me," Jeff would lament, feigning insult. "You'd rather walk with him than me."

"No, he likes me better than you like me," I'd joke back. "See, he wants to walk beside me. He's not ashamed to be seen with me."

Our walks were leisurely. We'd stop often so Jeff could take photos.

He and his camera were never apart. Duff and I were never impatient. We had all the time in the world.

While our time together was happy and carefree, as idyllic as a tender movie about young love, our time apart was full of strife. We both felt trapped, powerless in situations beyond our control. We didn't know where we fit in the world. Shortly before high school graduation, Jeff shot himself. My world collapsed. We had talked about suicide many times and had promised each other that if one of us ever killed ourselves, the other one would not be sad. We vowed if there was any way we could come back to the other, we would.

But talk and the brutal reality of suicide are worlds apart. We had no idea of the finality. The ache. The loneliness. The endless "what if's" that had no answer.

Jeff left me his camera, which helped me navigate the overwhelming sorrow and loss. Through the lens, life was bearable. I could still find beauty, see joy. Even if the beauty and joy were not my own, I knew they existed.

Time passed.

I went to college, worked, fell in love, said "I do," and had two sons. I inherited my parents' love of Collies and had three Collies during my adulthood, including one my children grew up with. With my Collies beside me, I worked on my dreams of becoming a writer and on Jeff's dreams of becoming a photographer. Like Jeff, I was seldom without a camera.

Through all the twists and turns of my life, I spoke to Jeff, especially when I was alone taking pictures. I'd tell him how much he'd like shooting whatever it was I was photographing. I'd focus the camera on landscapes, flowers, the lines of old people's faces, architectural details, leaves blowing in the wind and imagine Jeff seeing them along with me. I knew his spirit was with me.

But two springs ago, while on a three-day photography trip in a remote area of Oregon, a strong feeling washed over me that it was unfair to hold on to Jeff. He had left the physical world more than three decades earlier and perhaps by keeping him alive in my heart I was preventing him from going on to what lies beyond death.

I held that thought driving along the winding back roads of Eastern Oregon, the sun sinking closer to the horizon. I got a room in the only motel in the tiny town of Heppner, a place I'd never been before. As the moon shone through the windows of the modest room, I said a tearful goodbye to Jeff, to someone who had filled the role of best friend long beyond his death.

My marriage had ended ten years earlier in divorce and I'd chosen to focus on my children rather than jump back into the dating game. Now my children were grown. While we talked often and they came home for vacations, my time with them was limited to days here and there. Geronimo, our family Collie, had died at the age of twelve the previous winter. I had never felt so alone.

When I returned from my trip, I checked Collie rescue sites on the Internet. I wasn't sure about getting another dog, since I worked long hours, but I thought perhaps an older dog wouldn't mind. He could sleep the days away and have plenty of energy for evening walks catching tennis balls. I'd checked the rescue sites in Oregon, Washington, and California before without any luck. Maybe this time I'd find my way to a new pal. But once again, there were no good matches.

Frustrated, I typed "Collies for sale," "Collie needing home," and "Collie breeders" into Google, following every link. My heart skipped a beat when I found a listing for puppies in an Oregon newspaper I'd never heard of before. Deciding there was no harm in at least getting more information, I called the number.

The price was quite high. "It's just as well," I told the breeder. "I work too much to give a puppy the attention he'd need."

"I have a three-year-old male," she replied. The price was reasonable.

I asked where she lived. In Heppner — the town I'd been in when I said my goodbye to Jeff. "What's his name?" I asked, stunned at the coincidence.

"On his papers, he's Whatafella." I caught my breath and held on tight.

I drove the 250 miles to pick him up the next day. He stood by the fence expectantly, as if he knew I'd be coming for him. We became best friends before the ride home was over. He walked by my side without a leash. He waited patiently for me to come home at night, recognizing the sound of my car from the first day. And at night, no matter where he was when I fell into bed, he got up, trotted over to me and put his paw on my arm before he settled down beside my bed. None of my other dogs—all of who loved me and whom I loved in return—had ever done that.

He accompanies me when I set off to take pictures and sits beside me when I write. He reminds me I'm not alone and that in this world the possibility for connections with others is never far away. His presence reminds me that life is more mysterious than we can imagine and the possibilities for happiness are endless.

It is impossible not to believe that this Collie—who I named Casper—was not Jeff's parting gift to me. He knew I loved Collies. And he didn't want me to be alone.

Love transcends many things in ways we cannot begin to imagine. Casper is living proof. What a pal.

~Nancy Hill

The Gift

No, I never saw an angel, but it is irrelevant whether I saw one or not.
I feel their presence around me.
~Paulo Coelho

My husband's beloved grandmother was a very nurturing person who had been raised on a farm. She was roundly plump, with white hair and kind eyes. She never had a harsh word for anyone, did not believe in spanking children, and could cook and bake like a dream. Her rhubarb and gooseberry pies were family legends. When in her presence, you knew you were loved. Babies adored her and if any of us had a colicky or fussy infant, all that Grandma had to do was cuddle the baby against her ample bosom and it immediately became content and drifted off to sleep. She was loved by all.

When she was in her nineties, her daughters placed her in a nursing home that was a distance from where we lived. My husband and I both had demanding jobs and worked long hours. But we made the effort to visit Grandma every weekend, if not more frequently.

One night, I had been at work completing a special, complex project and I was exhausted. I had been at the office about sixteen hours and it was quite late when I left. As I drove down the darkened freeway on the long commute home, I could hardly wait to get to bed. Suddenly, out of nowhere, I was startled by an overwhelming need to see Grandma. What an odd notion—I was not only tired to the core, but it would be after 11:00 p.m. by the time I would reach the nursing home, far too late to visit and certainly not appropriate visiting hours. I dismissed the feeling.

As I continued my drive, that overpowering need to see Grandma abruptly came again, this time even stronger. How foolish, I thought. Yet the feeling persisted and it became an imperative. As the off-ramp to home neared, I fully intended to turn onto it. Instead I found myself pushed forward, driving right past it. I arrived at the nursing home a little after 11:00 p.m. Feeling a bit foolish, I had to ring a bell to gain admittance.

When I got to Grandma's room, she was sitting on the side of her bed, awake, with the light on. "Land's sake, look who's here!" she declared with a bright, surprised smile. She was delightfully pleased and so was I; the anxious feeling of being pushed suddenly fell away and was replaced by an enveloping warmth.

As I hugged Grandma and sat down beside her, she asked me how my husband was. As I replied, I heard a noise in the doorway and looked up. There stood my husband! I was as surprised and shocked to see him as he was to see me. A police detective, he too had been working on a project and was on an extra shift. His project site was about an hour away from the nursing home. He had asked special permission to take three hours for a personal matter and said that he would make up the time. As he came forward and hugged me, he softly whispered that he felt like an idiot, but that he had suddenly been driven by an urgent need to see his grandmother. Despite realizing the inappropriateness of the hour, the need was so strong and so insistent that he couldn't ignore it.

We three sat close to one another, held hands and talked, reminiscing about days gone by and memories that brought smiles all around. It was a wonderfully sweet visit.

It was soon the wee hours of the night and time to leave. We promised Grandma that we would be back to visit the following day. She plaintively asked, "Can't you stay just a bit longer?" We couldn't. My husband had to make his long drive back to work and make up his time, and I had my long drive back home. We said, "I love you," and kissed Grandma a fond goodnight. Once outside, my husband and I marveled at how each of us had come to make such an unusual visit at the same time so late at night, and had both felt a strong presence compelling us to do so.

Only a short time after I arrived home, the telephone rang. It was an RN at the nursing home. The voice on the other end of the line informed me that after we left Grandma went to bed and fell asleep. When someone went into the room to check on her later, they found she had passed away. It seemed so unbelievable; I could hardly process it.

My husband and I were stunned and heartbroken. But we were also deeply grateful that we had just been with her and had one more chance to say, "I love you." We still speak of that night; how both of us, independently, had the same highly unusual guided experience.

We later learned we were fortunate that the night staff let us in to visit Grandma, as they have a strict policy against unexpected late-night visitors. It seems that even the nursing home staff felt compelled to help enable our visit.

Our experience was not one of a visitation with halo and wings. But whatever happened that night — however it came to be — it continues to leave us filled with awe and wonder.

However it happened, whatever angel insisted and compelled us to make that final visit with our beloved grandmother, we are eternally grateful for that benevolent blessing. Grandmother's name was Berta Angelia, her life reflecting the "angel" in her name. I like to think that as she left this earth our compassionate angel greeted Grandma and was gently and lovingly guided to her ultimate joyful destination.

~Johanna Richardson

Desert Angel

*The prayer that begins with trustfulness and passes on into waiting will
always end in thankfulness, triumph, and praise.*
~Alexander Maclaren

My husband John and I were doing what we liked best—traveling by motor coach out west. Miles of deserted highway lay ahead. Our eyes played tricks on us as the scorching sun transformed the hot pavement into shimmering ripples of water. Our throats felt extremely parched.

"Let's take a break and get a cool drink from the cooler," John suggested. That's when we heard a loud boom, and the motor coach careened off the road.

"Are you alright?" John shouted, jerking the gearshift into park and then reaching for my hand.

"I'm fine, but I don't think our tire is!" I glanced out the side mirror to see pieces of rubber blowing across barren clay.

With wobbly legs, we climbed out of our "home away from home" for a closer inspection.

"What do we do now? It's been hours since we've seen a station, let alone a single soul on this lonely highway!"

Silently, John retrieved his cell phone from a trouser pocket. After several futile attempts to get a signal, he snapped his phone shut.

"We need to ask God to send highway angels to rescue us," I murmured.

I took John's hand in mine as we made our way back inside the motor coach in search of the cooler. After several long chugs of water we bowed our heads, asking God for help. I kept my eyes tightly closed, pressing the cold water bottle against my forehead.

Suddenly, I felt John's finger poking me in the ribs. "Take a look behind us…"

The vision of a tow truck pulling up behind us seemed too impossible.

"Need any help?" the tall driver shouted, approaching the driver's side.

"We sure do! Do you have any idea where we can find a tire for this thing?" John asked.

"Doubt if we have the right size at the station for a motor coach this big, but I seem to remember a motor coach tire or two lying around. I'm on my way to answer an emergency call though. If you folks can hang on, I promise to return as soon as I help the family on up the road a piece."

"Please don't forget us!" I cried, as John waved the driver on his way.

We did our best to remain calm by planning the following day's itinerary.

An hour later we spotted the same tow truck barreling in our direction. The vehicle had barely come to a complete stop when the driver hopped out like a rabbit. He grinned from ear to ear. "Sorry it took so long. I went back to the station to see about your tire. You aren't going to believe this… we had one single motor coach tire left at the station. Follow me!"

Reaching into the bed of the truck, he hoisted a huge tire into the air. It bounced to the dusty ground with a thud.

"It can't be!" John cried, recognizing the exact size tire needed. Slowly, the two men maneuvered the huge tire to the rear of the motor coach. In no time at all they managed to change it.

"There are no words to express our appreciation," we said in unison. The driver gave us a wave before disappearing in a cloud of dust.

Eventually we discovered a nearby campground. After a good

night's rest, we awakened to sunshine and the smell of bacon and eggs from a nearby campfire. Over coffee, we rehashed the previous day's miracle.

"You know, I'd really like to find that tow truck driver's station and speak to his superior. He needs to be commended, as well as rewarded for his kind deed."

John agreed, and we quickly gathered together the remnants from breakfast.

Soon we were on the road again, making our way in the direction the driver had said the station was.

We'd driven an entire hour when John slowly shook his head.

"I just don't understand it. We've come too far and there's not a single station in sight. How could that be?" He pulled the motor coach off the road.

I reached out, taking my husband's hands in mine. Together we bowed our heads in prayer. Only this time, we prayed in silence.

No words seemed necessary. The angels had already spoken, loud and clear.

~Mary Z. Whitney

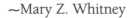

A Mysterious Adviser

There is a guardian angel who's walking by your side who'll help in life's decisions if you let her be your guide.

~Author Unknown

During difficult times in my life, my maternal grandmother has occasionally visited me. She died the year I was born, and she's been my guardian angel for the last thirty-two years. She first appeared to me when I was twelve and facing great danger and her spirit has continued to watch over me, shielding me from harm and unwise decisions.

A few years ago, I was struggling to decide whether to leave my low-paying job that I liked for one that would double my salary. During the interview for the prospective job at a law firm, I began to feel uneasy. At that same time, I had a vision of my grandmother in the corner of the office. The interviewer, an attorney, offered me the job on the spot with some great perks. She offered to pay my tuition to get a paralegal certification; she promised a quarterly and Christmas bonus; she offered to give me a corporate credit card; and the list continued. I kindly told her that I needed a few days to consider the offer. In an effort to persuade me, she took me to lunch in her new fully loaded BMW 7 Series, indicating that I could have a car like hers one day with a little hard work and dedication.

That same night and the following night I had trouble sleeping, pondering whether I should take the job. The attorney had called and left me a voicemail about accepting her offer. What was I going to tell her?

When I finally nodded off the second night, my grandmother visited me in a dream. She told me to heed the instructions that would be given to me, because all that glitters is not gold.

The next day, I was shopping at a market downtown where I normally would not shop. I must've looked puzzled because a salesclerk asked if I needed any assistance. "Yes," I said. "Can you direct me to the laundry detergent?"

"It is on aisle seven; down on your right," he said.

As I glanced at his name badge that read "Sebastian" I thanked him.

"You have the most intoxicating smile that lights up this entire store," said Sebastian.

"Thank you," I said with a big smile on my face.

I was wearing a T-shirt that bore my employer's logo and slogan, which got Sebastian's attention.

"Do you work for that company?" Sebastian asked.

"Yes, sir I do."

He indicated that it was an excellent company to work for. He told me that before his youngest son and wife had to transfer, his son was an employee for the company. To my surprise, he had worked under my manager. Sebastian emphasized how his son admired and respected the manager because of his fairness and congeniality.

"That is a good place to be," Sebastian said. "You are in a good position. Don't go anywhere else and don't be fooled by outside influences. God is where He wants you to be for this season."

"Wow, thanks!" I said as I walked away in amazement.

That was the confirmation from my guardian angel—my grandmother—and I rejected the job offer.

About two months later I was having a casual conversation with one of my girlfriends whom I hadn't spoken with in a while. My girlfriend shared that her cousin, with whom I was also acquainted, had started working at a law firm and having a difficult time with the boss. The attorney was apparently too controlling and very demanding.

Although her cousin was making "good money," she had no quality time with her family. She constantly worked through her lunches and ate dinner while working late hours. Her boss called her consistently during the evenings and on the weekends. The boss was a workaholic who put her family second to her career and wanted her employee to do the same.

My girlfriend went on to say that her cousin constantly called her, complaining and sobbing about her unhappiness with the job. I later learned that her cousin was working for the same attorney I had interviewed with a few months earlier. But even before I knew that, after hearing that story, I knew that I had dodged a bullet and felt compelled to say thank you for the spiritual guidance that I had been given.

I took a drive downtown to the market where Sebastian had helped advise me about my job dilemma. I asked the manager if Sebastian was working that day or when he would be back on the schedule. The manager gave me a puzzled look and told me there wasn't anyone on the payroll with that name. I told him I had shopped at the store a few months ago and wanted to thank Sebastian for his assistance. I even gave a brief description. The manager emphasized he'd been the store's manager for five years and no one named Sebastian had ever worked there under his management.

~Kimberly Nichelle

Proof Positive

Faith is a knowledge within the heart, beyond the reach of proof.
~Kahlil Gibran

"'m sorry, but your prenatal test came back positive for Down syndrome," the nurse told me over the phone.

"Um, okay," I mumbled.

"I've made you an appointment with a specialist for two weeks from today."

"Um, okay, thanks," I stumbled.

"Have a nice day," she said and hung up.

I set down the phone and cried. I vaguely remembered having a blood test, but the doctor said it was designed to rule out a variety of disabilities. I was only twenty-four, so I didn't think I'd have anything to worry about. Obviously, I was wrong.

I called my husband at work and told him about the phone call. Then I called my mom and sobbed. Mom, always the problem solver, got on the computer and researched the prenatal test I'd taken.

"Honey, the test is just a screening test," she said. "It doesn't mean the baby has anything wrong at all. It just means they want to do further testing."

"But why didn't the nurse explain that?" I cried. "She made it sound like the baby definitely has Down syndrome."

"She probably thought you knew about the test already."

"Mom, this is my first baby and I don't know anything about anything."

"Don't get all upset," Mom said. "It's most likely nothing."

"Yeah, but what if it's something?"

The two weeks until the appointment with the specialist stretched before me like an eternity. I could hardly eat or sleep. All I could do was pray and worry about the health of my baby.

Five days after the nurse's phone call I went to my monthly obstetrical appointment. I sat in the waiting room, praying that my doctor would assure me that I had nothing to worry about.

A nurse I'd never seen before called my name. I smiled at her and stood up.

"Hi, I'm Amanda," she said. "You're here for your ultrasound, right?"

"No, I had my ultrasound two weeks ago. Today is just a checkup."

She glanced at the chart in her hand. "It says here that you are supposed to have an ultrasound before your regular appointment today."

"Is it because of my test results?" I asked, suddenly nervous.

Amanda smiled. "Let's just take a look at your baby, okay?"

She led me upstairs to the ultrasound room. I lay down on the table and she squirted the jelly on my stomach.

"So I know that certain body parts can measure differently if something is wrong with the baby, right?" I said, hardly breathing.

"Let's not worry about that right now," she said kindly. "Let's just watch the little guy."

My eyebrows shot up. "It's a boy?"

"Let's just watch the little guy—or girl," she said. "Babies are precious, no matter what their gender."

Or their disability, I thought sadly.

Without speaking, she ran the wand over my stomach as I watched the screen. The baby moved almost constantly and I was mesmerized by what I saw.

This ultrasound was so different from my first one. During the first one, the technician seemed to be in a hurry. She had certain pictures and measurements she needed to take, and she was all business to get her job done.

Amanda was in no hurry at all. She seemed to sense that I needed to just see my baby, to watch him or her move, and to know that, at least for now, he or she was all right.

"Would you like to know the gender?" she asked quietly.

I shook my head. "Just tell me nothing is wrong."

She smiled gently. "This baby looks perfect to me, and even if something is wrong, you'll think he's perfect too. Moms always feel that way about their babies." She squeezed my hand. "I promise."

Tears filled my eyes as her words sunk in. She was right. I realized I no longer cared if my baby had Down syndrome. He was perfect, just as he was. I loved him, and no diagnosis could make me love him any less. Just as God loved me despite my many problems and imperfections, I would love this baby, regardless of any medical challenges.

I felt a peace come over me, and I knew that things would be all right, no matter what the appointment with the specialist revealed.

"Thank you, Amanda," I said through my tears. "You have been so kind to me."

Gently, she wiped off my stomach and helped me up. "I'm glad you're feeling more peaceful. Hopefully, you'll sleep better now."

Had I told her I hadn't been sleeping? I couldn't remember.

I went back downstairs to the waiting room. Minutes later, my usual nurse called me back. As I stepped onto the scale, I said, "I really like the new nurse, Amanda."

She frowned at me. "Who?"

"Oh, I guess she's an ultrasound technician, isn't she?"

But the nurse shook her head. "There's no one named Amanda in our office."

"Of course there is. She just did my ultrasound."

The nurse looked at my chart and shook her head again. "You weren't scheduled for an ultrasound today."

"But I just…" I started and then shook my head. "Never mind."

When I got home that afternoon, I pulled the ultrasound photos from my purse. These photos were proof of what I already knew. I wasn't alone. God loved me and He cared about what I was going through. God was watching over my baby and me.

He'd even sent one of His angels to prove it.

~Diane Stark

The Rose

Flowers are those little colorful beacons of the sun from which we get sunshine when dark, somber skies blanket our thoughts.

~Dodinsky

"The surgery went well. Your husband will be in the recovery room for several hours. You should go home and get some rest."

The surgeon patted my arm and stood to go. When the waiting room door swung shut behind him, I released an exhausted sigh. Six agonizing hours earlier, I had kissed my husband's forehead as he was wheeled to the operating room where the surgeon would remove a large, cancerous tumor from his colon.

We never suspected that John's routine colonoscopy would turn out to be anything but. The initial cancer diagnosis was followed by days of soul-sucking stress as we waited for test results, appointments with specialists, and calls from the hospital's scheduling department. So far, the prognosis was cautiously optimistic. The tumor appeared to be contained, in spite of its size. According to the surgeon, we were incredibly lucky.

I stood and stretched. Maybe I'd take his advice. A quick trip home would allow me to take in the mail and pick up a few things I needed for my stay in the hospital. As I drove home in the dazzling Florida sunshine, I inhaled the salty air and tried to exhale the anxiety that had overwhelmed my life for the past week.

I was dragging myself up the walk to my front door when a splash of color caught my eye. On the scrawny branch of a rose bush we had given up as lost, I saw a bloom the size of a saucer. How could I have missed that on the way out this morning? I shook my head, thinking that I must have been too preoccupied with the impending surgery to notice. Still…

I bent to get a closer look. The bush was as dry and scraggly as ever, but the rose was flawless. Each petal was the color of the roseate spoonbills that waded in the nearby lagoon and was tipped with a buttercream yellow. The flower seemed to glow from within. As I stared at it, I had a sudden image of my mother-in-law's face. John was the center of her life. Nothing brought her more joy than seeing her son happy. She also loved roses and coaxed the most amazing blossoms from her tiny patch of garden. She even wore rosewater cologne.

I've heard it said that the sense of smell triggers the strongest memories. These particular roses gave off a fragrance almost identical to that cologne. When the bush was new, John would cut the roses and bring them inside. He said the smell made him feel as if his mother was somewhere in the house instead of resting beside her husband in the mausoleum at Eagleton Cemetery.

On a whim, I decided to bring the rose to the hospital. It might be good for John to have this small touch of home. I took the pruning shears from the garage and clipped the prickly stem. Then I tossed the rose onto the back seat of the car and went into the house.

By the time I pulled back into the hospital parking lot, I'd forgotten about the rose. I gathered up my things and was about to close the car door when a breeze caressed my face, carrying the scent of roses. What did I do with that flower? Then I remembered. I reached into the back seat, picked up the rose, and hurried into the building.

John was asleep when I opened the door to his room. I slipped inside, careful not to wake him, and dumped the rose, my purse, and my overnight bag onto the futon where I would sleep. Then I pulled a chair up to the bed and sat down, taking my husband's limp hand. I stared at his sleeping face until my eyes grew heavy. At the edge of sleep, I thought I heard my mother-in-law's voice. "Don't worry," she said. "Everything will be fine." A feeling of peace enveloped me, driving away all the doubt and fear that had taken root in my heart.

I was startled awake when a nurse with a stethoscope draped around her neck pushed through the door. She sniffed the air. "It smells really good in here," she said. "What perfume are you wearing?"

"It's not my perfume," I answered.

After the nurse left, I filled a glass with water for the rose. I was surprised to see that it hadn't wilted. I poked the stem into the glass and placed it on the bedside table. John stirred in his sleep. "Ma?" he whispered, the ghost of a smile curving his lips. I leaned over and kissed his cheek. "Don't worry," I said. "Everything will be fine."

In the days that followed, John amazed everyone with his rapid recovery. Every so often, he would take the rose and inhale its fragrance as if breathing in some life-giving essence. By the end of the week, he was well enough to be discharged. His test results showed no evidence of cancer, and the oncologist said he wouldn't even need chemotherapy.

As we prepared to leave the hospital, I noticed the rose on the bedside table. My first impulse was to leave it there since we had so many other things to carry. But the bloom looked as fresh and perfect as the day I picked it, so I wrapped the stem in a wet paper towel and carried it out to the car. John held it under his nose all the way home.

Once we were settled in, I put the rose in a crystal bud vase that had belonged to John's mother and set it on the dresser in our bedroom. The scent perfumed the air as we slept. The next morning, I awoke to the sound of John singing in the shower. I smiled at the wonderful normalcy of it all. Everything would be fine.

Suddenly, a fluttering movement, like the wings of a butterfly, caught my eye. I glanced at the dresser in time to see the last rose petal join its companions on the bedroom floor.

"Goodbye, Mom," I whispered. "And thank you."

~Jackie Minniti

A Patchwork
of Hope

A quilt will warm your body and comfort your soul.
~Author Unknown

n February 2005, my daughter Julie and son-in-law Mike died in a motorcycle accident. I was stunned and grief-stricken, but the heartache my young grandchildren suffered after losing both parents was unimaginable.

While my husband Walt and I struggled to make sense of it all, family and friends asked, "What's going to happen to the kids?"

In the middle of making funeral arrangements, Walt and I vowed to do whatever it took to raise ten-year-old Cari and six-year-old Michael. After petitioning the courts, we became our grandchildren's legal guardians.

The first few weeks were a blur as we struggled to stitch together the ragged pieces of our lives. A grief counselor advised us to keep Cari and Michael's routines as normal as possible to help them feel loved and secure. Rather than having the children change schools in the middle of the year, I moved into their home. At mealtimes, I prepared dishes their mom used to make; one breakfast favorite was Julie's hot cinnamon rolls.

And each night, I read bedtime stories before we folded our hands and remembered their mom and dad in prayer. Then each morning we recited the Guardian Angel Prayer, just as I had with Julie when she was a child:

Angel of God, my Guardian Dear,
To whom God's love commits me here,
Ever this day, be at my side,
To light, to guard, to rule and guide.

After hugging and kissing Cari and Michael goodnight, I tucked them into their beds underneath one of their mom's quilts.

As a teenager, Julie began collecting quilts after I won an embroidered blue-and-white one for her at a church picnic. Over the next twenty-plus years, I won several for her at local socials, fairs, and festivals. Those hand-stitched quilts had a special place in my daughter's home — and heart.

Months after the accident, we moved Cari and Michael into our home, along with their furniture, clothes, toys, and other belongings. We didn't have space to fit everything, but we made room for Julie's collection of quilts. In each of my grandkids' new rooms, their beds were covered with one of their mom's brightly-colored quilts, which I rotated each season.

When Cari turned twelve, she announced she wanted to paint and redecorate her room. I asked which of her mom's quilts she wanted to use after we were finished and was surprised when she told me she wanted a quilt of her own.

Realizing she was almost a teenager with her own tastes and style, I hugged her and said, "Sweetie, we'll go shopping to find one you like."

"I don't want one you can buy in a store," she said. "I want you to win one for me like you did for Mom."

Choking back tears, I said, "That won't be easy, but I'll try."

I became a woman on a mission, buying chances and raffle tickets, wishing for good luck, with no success.

By late 2009 I'd almost given up hope when I entered the mega-raffle at our parish's fall craft fair, a huge countywide event Julie and I had attended each November. The raffle featured a dozen giveaways, including the top prize everyone coveted—a queen-sized, hand-stitched patchwork quilt.

Because the craft fair fell on what would've been my daughter's fortieth birthday, I couldn't bring myself to go. The memory of attending past craft fairs with Julie would be too painful. Instead, I bought my chances in advance.

While admiring the handiwork on display in the parish gymnasium, I printed my name on the tickets. As I dropped my tickets into the huge wire barrel, I whispered a prayer to my guardian angel, "Angel of God, my Guardian Dear...."

The day of the craft fair not only fell on Julie's birthday, it also coincided with opening day of deer season, so Walt and Michael went hunting. Cari was spending the day with a friend.

My sisters Kathleen and Bridget and niece Angie tried to convince me to go the fair with them. Knowing I wouldn't be good company, I declined and moped around the house, missing my daughter more than ever.

Shortly after five o'clock, the phone rang.

"You won a raffle prize," a weary voice said. "We'll be here for about half an hour if you want to pick it up today."

When I arrived at the Parish Center, I spotted a woman sitting behind a long table. Nearby sat the big barrel crammed with thousands of raffle tickets.

When I identified myself, the woman pointed to a large black plastic bag. "Congratulations," she said.

"What did I win?" I asked.

When she answered, "the quilt," I burst into tears of joy.

Staring at the giant container crammed with tickets, I couldn't believe how fortunate I was that mine was the one drawn for the big prize. And I felt especially lucky to have won the quilt for Cari on her mom's birthday.

Then it dawned on me. Winning the quilt for my granddaughter on my daughter's birthday wasn't a coincidence. And it wasn't because of my good luck; I had help from an angel.

Cari's quilt is a homespun beauty, unlike any other in her mom's collection. Scraps of fabric in various colors, shapes, and patterns—once part of something else—had been carefully pieced together and transformed into a loving creation.

The patchwork quilt is a one-of-a kind work of art that provides comfort, warmth, beauty, and hope—a guardian angel's answer to a grandmother's prayer.

~Donna Volkenannt

A Miraculous Second Chance at Friendship

A friend knows the song in my heart and sings it to me when my memory fails.
~Donna Roberts

Kimberly came into my life when I was the single mother of a middle-school son and the owner of a thrift store. New to west central Ohio, blond and in her early twenties, Kim would occasionally stop by my secondhand shop to chat. We instantly connected and spent lots of time together over the next decade. I was a bridesmaid at her wedding and watched her start her family. Then, when she moved out West, we lost touch. That is, until the phone call came almost a decade later.

"Kimberly's in the hospital. It's cancer. The doctors aren't giving her much hope," a mutual friend called to tell me. Kim had moved back to Ohio by then. The following day, I drove over a hundred miles to be at her side during her first chemotherapy treatment. It was as if we had never been apart.

By then, I had remarried, and almost miraculously, we soon moved only ten miles away from Kimberly. This allowed us time to reconnect, and to share our families with each other.

Over the next couple of years, I watched helplessly as Kimberly bravely endured countless treatments trying to fight the deadly disease.

Occasionally, my husband and I took her wonderful children out for an evening when she was in the hospital.

At the beginning, Kim made a promise that her life would not be about the cancer, but about the living. That's why whenever we got together we talked tirelessly, like two best friends on borrowed time. I would pick her up and we would go to lunch and giggle like schoolgirls, despite her oxygen tank and growing tumors.

Then about a month before her passing, I happened to watch the classic movie *Beaches* on TV. It's about best friends going through the same thing as Kimberly and I. In the movie, Hillary, played by Barbara Hershey, is terminally ill, and C.C., a famous singer played by Bette Midler, rushes to be at her side.

When C.C. sings the song "Wind Beneath My Wings," it portrays her admiration and undying love for her courageous friend. The lyrics say, "Did you ever know that you're my hero?" Silently, I prayed that seeing that movie wasn't heavenly preparation for losing my own best friend, who grew weaker each day.

She was hanging on, wanting to be with her husband and children. I had never seen such great faith. Even when doctors said there was no more that could be done, we continued to pray for the miracle she desperately wanted.

Then it seemed as if she let go and began reaching for Heaven. One evening, I sat at her bedside holding her hand, as tears of gratitude for our second chance at friendship ran down my cheeks.

At eight the next morning, the phone call came. My beautiful blond friend had breathed her last earthly breath. The morning after Kimberly's funeral, I woke up feeling so empty. I listlessly dragged myself to my Pilates class. Leaving the gym, I noticed a garage sale sign on the corner. It was a perfect autumn day. The sun was shining, the sky was vivid blue, and the trees were covered with colorful fall leaves. Still, my heart was unbearably heavy. I didn't feel like going to the sale, but it was as if some unseen presence led me there.

While absentmindedly looking over the merchandise, I spied a musical water globe, the kind my elderly father collects. Inside was an angel dressed in an aqua and lilac robe with long golden hair. The angel was lovingly embracing a small child, and her white-feathered wings were covered with iridescent sparkles.

The globe was only two dollars. Impulsively, I paid for it. Later, when I wound the musical key, it began to play the tune "Wind Beneath My Wings." Instantly, I realized it was no coincidence that I had gone to that garage sale or purchased that globe.

That same afternoon, one of the movie channels showed *Beaches* again. This time, I sobbed as I watched it, allowing myself to begin grieving my dearest friend's loss. Yet, I was also joyful as I realized that God had sent me a garage sale angel to remind me that Heaven is real, and that Kimberly would be waiting there.

The globe now sits in a prominent place in the glass cabinet in my living room. After a decade apart, I am so thankful that my heroic best friend and I remained inseparable until the very end, and that I now have the angel to remind me of her every day.

~Christina Ryan Claypool

A Breakfast Blessed

The wings of angels are often found on the backs
of the least likely people.
~Eric Honeycutt

just wanted to toast my stupid bagel. Inspecting the industrial slicer through a fog of exhaustion and heartbreak, it might as well have been designed in outer space. I had been trying to cut the bagel for a few minutes. In my state of anguish, such a simple act was just too complicated. I felt nauseated all of a sudden and knew the past few days were finally welling up within me, ready to burst. So instead, right there in the breakfast line of the Long Beach Memorial Hospital cafeteria, I leaned on the counter, put my head in my hands, and sobbed.

How had I gotten here? It seemed a lifetime ago that I was dropping my kids at tennis lessons before driving to Orange County to teach musical theater to at-risk teens. My six-year-old son Braden had been lethargic and fragile during our trip to Yosemite the month before but had seemed to rally afterward. Altitude sickness? I had wondered, but barely gave it a second thought as we resumed our regular routine and Braden's strength returned. Yet in the middle of the week — a Wednesday I'll never forget — the tennis instructor stopped me to report her concern that Braden was sick. He had been to the bathroom multiple times throughout the day and didn't seem himself. I thanked her and said I would have him checked immediately. Taking him straight to the doctor and believing I'd get a prescription for a bladder infection, Dr. Percer's words stopped me in my tracks.

"We found a lot of sugar in your son's urine," he said quietly. Alternate waves of cold and heat washed me over. "I'm sorry?" I asked. Surely I had heard him wrong. "There's quite a bit of sugar in Braden's urine sample," he repeated. "We don't have an up-to-date glucose monitor in our office, so we need to get him to the hospital right away." Type I diabetes. The words felt like a death sentence.

The next few hours were a blur. There was the phone call to my husband's office, me working hard to keep my voice and hands steady for the sake of the children. Braden's sister, Colleen, asking fearfully in her small nine-year-old voice, "Mama, is it contagious?" Drew and I packing slowly for the hospital, hoping to avoid the inevitable diagnosis. The team of doctors and nurses descending upon us as we got Braden to his room, poking, prodding, and pricking him as he became more and more panicked. It felt as though I was living my very worst nightmare, yet no matter how hard I tried to shake it off, I couldn't rouse myself.

Three days later, after another sleepless night of constant blood sugar checks, insulin shots and taking of vitals, the nurses changed shifts and our original admitting nurse, Laura, came into the room. Taking one look at me, she said, "You need to eat. Braden's sleeping. Go down to the cafeteria and take a break from all of this. I'll watch him until you get back." I told her I couldn't bring myself to leave him. "You need to get away for a few minutes. Carry your breakfast back up here if you want, but get out of this room and take a breath." That was how I found myself face to face with this bagel-slicing contraption. And how I found myself, broken and alone, weeping uncontrollably over a hospital tray.

I felt a movement beside me and looked up to find a woman wordlessly taking the bagel off of my plate and effortlessly arranging it in the cutter. With one quick movement, she cut my breakfast bagel in half. She looked at me and asked, "Toasted?" I could only nod in affirmation. She put her hand on my shoulder, guiding me down the stainless steel counter. "Cream cheese?" she asked. Again, I nodded.

"Butter?" she asked. I shook my head. She took two little Philadelphia cream cheese containers and placed them on my tray.

Once the bagel was loaded up, napkin, knife and even a spoon gathered for my yogurt, she carried my tray with hers to the cashier and paid for everything. I didn't have the strength to speak but knew that my tears, now of gratitude for her simple act of grace, spoke volumes. She looked deep into my eyes, squeezed my arm warmly, and said, "It will get better." I inhaled and looked down at my tray, trying to compose myself enough to utter a word of thanks.

Only a moment passed before I glanced up again, yet when I did, she was nowhere to be seen. I looked left and right, in front of me and behind, expecting to see the back of this Good Samaritan walking away, but there was only the bustle of hospital life. A feeling of peace washed me over and I knew for certain in that public moment of despair, thinking I had no one to lean on and wondering how I would persevere, I had been divinely blessed. God had sent an earthly angel to shore me up at my lowest, to envelope me in His care.

It's been eight years since Braden's diabetes diagnosis. There are still days that are a challenge, and dealing with the blood sugar of a teenage boy can feel like a science experiment gone awry. But all in all, he is in good health. We as a family have adjusted to a life of glucose checks and insulin shots, counting carbs, and treating highs and lows. We're so proud of him for somehow managing most of it on his own.

More than these physical feats, however, we feel abundantly blessed in our hearts. We have the support of our friends and family. We have access to the latest medical treatments and our insurance covers a huge percentage of Braden's prescriptions. But most importantly, from the very start we have felt the guiding hand of our Father on this challenging journey. He's brought us peace and solace in our sadness, answers to questions in our confusion, and he's placed amazing people in our lives to help guide us.

Yet none of these gifts have been more memorable than the time, one particularly desperate morning eight years ago, He sent an earthly vessel to perform a random act of kindness to a woman in need. Truly, this stranger was my angel, helping me trust in His plan as she sustained me with His comfort and grace.

~Cynthia McGonagle McGarity

Touched by an Angel

An Auspicious Visitor

Dropped from
Heaven

Dogs are miracles with paws.
~Attributed to Susan Ariel Rainbow Kennedy

had just come home from the hospital. As I stepped out of the car, I was assaulted by a pair of huge paws and a wet, lapping tongue. In less than a minute, I was sitting on the driveway, receiving the biggest tongue licking of my life! My heart immediately belonged to that dog. In spite of our search for his owner, no one claimed him. It was like he had been dropped from heaven, and maybe he was.

Sam did more than change my life; he became my guardian angel. My convalescence from a serious illness was supposed to take place at home, under the care of my husband, a first class petty officer in the U.S. Navy. Louie had been given thirty days emergency leave from his ship for the sole purpose of caring for me. I was so thankful as Louie cooked, cleaned, and took care of our two young daughters.

My doctor had spoken to Louie's commanding officer, personally explaining my illness and need for constant care. The commander assured my doctor that Louie would get the leave. All that my husband had to do was check out from the ship Monday morning. So when Louie left for the ship, we were both certain that he would be home by noon. I could take care of myself for a few hours, and I could use that time to get to know my new puppy.

Mid-day came and went, and Louie did not come home. Then

it was two o'clock. Perhaps he had to finish up things. Four o'clock arrived. Then five, and six, and seven. Finally, the phone rang. It was Louie. He was on the ship, and it was leaving. His emergency leave had been canceled, and he had only a moment to call and say goodbye. My husband was sick about it, but he had no choice in the matter.

What many civilians do not understand is that emergency leave for a service member is at the commanding officer's discretion. So, sick wife or no sick wife, Petty Officer Lewis was ordered back to duty. The ship went out to sea, and I was alone.

I don't remember much about that week. I was sick, helpless, and afraid. My young children did the best they could for me. Neighbors came and went, but the only thing I remember is Sam. He never left my side. I stayed on the couch, except to go to the bathroom. I don't know if I ate or drank. But I can still feel the pressure of Sam's body leaning against me, and I can still feel the scrape of his tongue on my face. He hovered near me every moment. At one point, when I began to lose consciousness, Sam barked wildly and licked my face, bringing me to. He made me laugh, and I clung to the reality of Sam.

God took care of everything. I needed someone, and God sent me Sam. In time I recovered, and our family was reunited. Sam remained a member of our family for years. Though it's been nearly twenty years since I last hugged that blessed dog, Sam will always be a part of my heart. I'm certain that Sam is frolicking in some snowy part of heaven, looking forward to seeing me again.

~Jaye Lewis

An Angel in Uniform

Everyone entrusted with a mission is an angel.
~Moses Maimonides

"You have a phone call," a woman in the aisle whispered. She motioned for me to follow her. The theatre-type seat thumped when I stood. My stomach cramped as I worked my way through the row of preachers' wives.

"Thelma took the call," the woman whispered to me. "She said it's a sheriff."

The District Superintendent's wife? Oh, God, what happened? What did Gary do? I rushed down the hall to the church office and reached for the phone. "This is Kathy Crawford."

"Is the Reverend Gary Crawford your husband?" a deep voice asked.

"Yes."

"Mrs. Crawford, I'm sorry to inform you, but I arrested your husband. He's being held for drunk and disorderly conduct, resisting arrest and assaulting a police officer. I believe he planned to commit suicide."

Why had I left home? Why didn't I tell anyone how fragile I thought Gary appeared? Why didn't I confide in the District Superintendent when he preached in our church only two weeks before? Gary looked to everyone like he felt better than in the spring when he said he wanted to die.

Too numb to cry, I handed the phone to Thelma. She wrote down the pertinent information and hung up the phone. "Give me a minute, Kathy, I'll call my husband. We'll figure out what we need to do."

Twenty hours later, I walked into the courthouse.

When I told the desk clerk my name, he said, "The deputy sheriff wants to speak with you, Mrs. Crawford." He motioned for me to follow him.

"Have a seat. The sheriff will be here shortly." When the door shut behind him I felt more alone than I had in years.

The glare of the August sun shone through the bare windows. The furnishings looked like something from *Perry Mason*—a stark interrogation room with old wooden chairs and a long, scarred walnut table in the center. The room smelled of sweat and tobacco. I could imagine a criminal sitting at the table, but not myself. Never could I see my preacher husband at the table. Help us, Father.

"Mrs. Crawford." I jumped when I heard the deep voice. "Sorry we have to meet like this. I'm the sheriff who arrested your husband. Have a seat, please."

My eyes filled with tears when my sleeve caught on the jagged edge of the table. No one should face this problem—preacher's wife or not.

"Before we go into the courtroom I wanted to prepare you for what your husband faces." The broad-shouldered uniformed man seated himself across from me. "Reverend Crawford attacked me, which in any court of law is a felony and means at least two years in prison."

My head felt like it might explode. Oh Lord, how would I tell our children? Our grandchildren? Why didn't He help Gary before this happened?

"Mrs. Crawford, I rarely drive a road that far off the beaten path, but I was cruising. I felt like my week had been sixty hours long and I'd seen my share of conflict. I was tired and I hoped to finish the day without incident. Only something glinted in the sunlight. I don't know why, but it alarmed me enough to call for backup, just in case." He paused and then added, "Mrs. Crawford, I believe God sent me down that back road to help your husband."

My face felt frozen while the sheriff described his rescue efforts.

"Mr. Crawford screamed at me and then yelled for the dog to attack me. Fortunately, a bunch of college boys were swimming further down the river. They helped calm the dog.

"When the boys pulled the dog aside, Mr. Crawford came at me in a fit of rage. I knew there was something different about your husband. Even though he fought like a wildcat, he never once cursed." The officer looked sixty pounds heavier than my husband and several inches taller. "He kept yelling, 'Shoot me. Just shoot me,' and then he ripped my uniform."

My husband is a strong man, but never combative. He boxed in his teens, but never as an adult. I didn't think him capable of a fight like the man described. Gary taught our children to live in peace. The scene sounded like something from a movie, not from the Crawford family.

"One of the students held the dog while four others helped me wrestle your husband to the ground." The sheriff reached his hand across the table to touch my clenched fists. "Mrs. Crawford, I'm a strong believer in Jesus Christ, but rarely do I mention God when I'm working. Still when we finally pinned Gary to the ground, I felt the Lord urging me to sing. In all my years I don't recall ever doing this before. I lay spread-eagled across your husband's body and sang 'Jesus Loves Me This I Know.' That's when the wild man gave up the fight."

Tears streamed down my cheeks.

I heard a door open. "Sheriff, the judge is about ready."

"We'll be right there." The officer pushed the box of tissue my direction. He waited while I composed myself.

"Did your husband battle depression? Talk about suicide?"

"Yes. He told many others last spring. For a couple of months he seemed better, but lately... I couldn't help him."

"I don't know what will happen in the courtroom, but remember God loves your husband. He sent me down that road and showed me how to rescue him. I believe Reverend Crawford was determined to kill himself. When his Biblical training, his love of God wouldn't let him, he pushed me to do the job for him."

The uniformed man pushed his chair back and motioned towards the door. "Don't lose sight of hope. Your husband isn't a criminal; he is ill and mental illness is treatable."

The judge reviewed Gary's case and said, "Because you don't even have a speeding ticket, Mr. Crawford, this court is dismissing the felony charges."

Gary received a year of probation and the judge suggested Gary seek professional counseling.

Two days later I heard a sermon from Proverbs 13:12 (NIV): "Hope deferred makes the heart sick, but a longing fulfilled is a tree of life." A message from God to assure me He knew where my husband was and He knew what we'd both need in the months to come.

Gary entered a mental hospital for a month, finished his probation and two years of counseling. It took years, but God restored joy to Gary's heart and healed his mind.

Although shattered and scared, I stood in awe of God who worked miracles — He sent His rescuer, an angel in uniform.

~Kat Crawford

Angelica

All God's angels come to us disguised.
~James Russell Lowell

When my wife Anne and I were dating and working in Boston's financial district, my older sister Elizabeth, a medical relief worker, invited us to join her and a man named Andy Ortega on a short-term service trip. The trip was hosted by the Mexican Medical Ministries—an organization that Andy served at the time. We were part of a volunteer team from the United States, made up of people from California, Massachusetts, Minnesota, and Rhode Island. Our role was to entertain the children of a remote village on Mexico's Baja peninsula while a house was built for the village doctor.

At first, we were overwhelmed by the poor sanitary conditions and the impoverished lives in this migrant-farmer village. Some families lived with as many as ten children in one-room mud-brick huts. Yet as the days passed, we were touched by how rich they were in what we felt mattered most—faith, family, fun, and a sense of community—despite how poor they were in what perhaps mattered too much to us.

Having been so distressed and distracted by the conditions, Anne silently asked God to help her see these children how He sees them—beautiful and pure regardless of how filthy and disheveled they looked. Otherwise, she didn't know how she would get through the week.

Just minutes after Anne's silent prayer, a girl who was about four years old came running up to us, introducing herself in broken Spanish as "Angelica." She grabbed Anne's hand and begged her to sing to her and play with her. Anne, who is tone deaf, claims to this day that she can't sing. Yet, how could she say no to this sweet little girl whose innocent love brought Anne immediate joy? So Anne sang, and played, and sang!

The two of them spent lots of time together that week. At the close of each day, when Anne would ask to walk Angelica home, Angelica would insist that she could walk herself home, following her brother. Anne would watch her follow that little boy into their house until the door shut behind them each night.

Sooner than we wished, the time came for us to say goodbye to our new friends. We could not wait to finally meet and thank Angelica's parents and siblings for allowing her to spend so much time with us. We wanted them to know how special Angelica had become to us.

Yet that Friday, as we prepared to go back to the United States, Angelica was nowhere to be found. We called out her name repeatedly as we walked through the small village. Finally, we spotted the little boy who was Angelica's brother. But when we asked him where his sister was, he simply responded in Spanish, "I do not have a sister, only brothers." We then went to his house. The parents told us they not only did not have a daughter, but also knew of no girls in the entire village named Angelica. We checked with the village doctor. Sure enough, nobody by that name lived in the village.

Who was Angelica? We'll never know, but that little community sure seemed to be blessed, so we have our suspicions!

~Jim Solomon

The One Who Stayed

We are each of us angels with only one wing,
and we can only fly by embracing one another.
~Luciano de Crescenzo

got rheumatoid arthritis in my early thirties and as it progressed, I was increasingly debilitated. After a while I couldn't live with the pain shooting down my back, groin, and leg. The orthopedic surgeon looked at the X-rays and described my hip exactly the way it felt to me. "It's like trying to fit a square peg in a round hole," he said. RA had destroyed the ball and the socket. But he offered some good news. "There's a ninety-nine percent chance a total hip replacement would eliminate the pain." With those odds, I scheduled my surgery that day.

The day after surgery, I stood with my new hip and knew I had gotten my life back even though I faced a long recovery with a lot of precautions. I was told not to lift my leg too high, cautioned not to bend over, and taught how to swivel to get out of bed. At no time in the first three months was I to bend from the waist more than ninety degrees. That was my healing time. The muscles surrounding my hip replacement needed time to strengthen. "It could slip out of joint and you don't want that to happen," my nurse said. "It's extremely painful." I would follow the rules to the letter. I had had enough pain.

Five days after the surgery I was home and doing well. My physical therapist went through the rundown, showing me what exercises to do to get my muscles back in shape. I loved the smooth motion of an artificial joint and gladly went through the routine several times a day. I regretted having waited so long to get it replaced.

In six months, I was back for my checkup. I walked in with no assistance. My surgeon was as happy as I was. "How long will my new hip last?" I asked.

"It should last a lifetime."

"Do I have any restrictions?"

"I'd advise you not to cross your legs or play competitive sports." I had to laugh at that one. I couldn't play sports if I had too.

When he stood to leave, I thanked him and gave him a big hug. "See you back in three years."

Nine months later, I was at the emergency room entrance in excruciating pain. It was the last place I had expected to be that hot July morning. Three attendants unfolded me from the passenger seat and brought me inside, doing all they could to keep from adding more hurt to my damaged body.

A few hours earlier, my husband Eddie and I had decided to spend the day sightseeing in the country. We stopped to see a friend and look at a canoe he had for sale. Since he wasn't home, we only stayed a few minutes, but long enough to for me to bend over to pick up a paper I had dropped in his driveway. That's when my hip implant rolled out of joint, sending me crashing to the ground. Although I knew immediately what had happened, I was never so shocked. I had made the same movement hundreds of times since my doctor released me with no problem.

I screamed for my husband to help me, trying to tell him where I was hurt. I couldn't use either hand. My left one was swelling like a softball and I couldn't move my right arm from the shoulder down. He gently lifted me off the ground and worked me into the car inch by inch as my left leg hung precariously sideways. For what seemed like an eternity, I prayed and Eddie drove eighty miles per hour. We were in an area where there was no cell phone service and we were fifty miles from the nearest hospital.

Despite the long drive, my arrival time couldn't have been better. My surgeon was just finishing in the operating room and would take me right in. But first I would have to go to X-ray to see what was going on. I begged the three people in radiology not to move me onto the hard table, but it was no use. "It has to be done," they all said, but promised to get the pictures quickly. "Yell if you have to. We'll understand."

On the count of three, they lifted my 100-pound body off the stretcher amid my screams. I pleaded for someone to put a pillow under my leg. I couldn't stand to stretch it out. It felt as if it was tearing loose from my body. Then, from somewhere in the dark room, I heard a soft, calm voice: "I'll stay with her." The other two radiologists went to stand behind the shield while a woman stayed and held my leg up off the table in its awkward position until the X-rays were over and I was wheeled into surgery. I never saw her again. My hand was set, my shoulder put back into place, and my dislocated hip put back together again. Three days later, I went home to begin my recovery.

As the days went by, I couldn't get the lady in the X-ray department off my mind. Why had she done that for me? I was just another patient not unlike the ones she saw every day. Why would she risk her own health to help a stranger? But the magnitude of her compassion had impacted my life like nothing before. Every time I tried to tell the story, the words stuck in my throat. Somehow, I had to let her know. The least I could do was say thank you.

I contacted the hospital and tried to get a name with no luck. I couldn't provide a good description, only that she was rather petite with shoulder-length hair, about thirty-five to forty, and was on duty at the time of my X-rays. No one on duty that day came close to my description. They didn't have a clue who it could have been. And besides, no one was supposed to stay in the room while I was having the X-ray.

At that point, I tried to explain it away. Maybe her job would have been in jeopardy for ignoring hospital policy or, for whatever reason, she wanted to remain anonymous. All those things made perfect sense.

Nevertheless, five years later, I haven't forgotten her. I realize there are some things that can't be explained. All I know is that when I was in unbearable pain, a soft-spoken lady stayed with me, doing all she could to help despite the fact that she shouldn't have been in the room with me and that no one else saw her. I will never know her name, but to me, she was an angel from heaven.

~Linda C. Defew

I Call Myself Bob

When angels visit us, we do not hear the rustle of wings, nor feel the feathery touch of the breast of a dove; but we know their presence by the love they create in our hearts.
~Author Unknown

watched the weather through the window of the small bookshop where I worked with a sense of dread. When my shift was over, I intended to drive over the mountains of Tennessee for my best friend's wedding. The bride-to-be had called earlier in the day and warned that a winter weather advisory had been posted and authorities were predicting icy roads and dangerous travel. She urged me not to make the trip, but as her closest friend not attending wasn't an option. After I told her that a little storm wouldn't stop me, she cautioned me to be careful and promised to keep me in her prayers.

The trip through the winding mountain roads was slow going but beautiful. Large, wet snowflakes flew through the air and my wipers worked valiantly to keep my windshield clear. Large clumps of snow sat upon the boughs of the trees. As the sun fell behind the frost-tipped peaks, the temperature dropped and the roads became slick and icy.

I had virtually slowed to a crawl as traffic thinned. Although I was one of the few people left on the road, I was determined to reach my destination. I clutched the steering wheel with both hands, watched the dark road attentively and prayed for God's guidance.

I came to a point in the road where a sharp turn led into a steep descent. Even though I was traveling slowly, the icy pavement and steepness of the road was too much for my two-door compact car. My loss of control started with a small fishtail that led to a full spin. The nose of my car was pointed in the wrong direction before it slid onto the shoulder of the road and simply dropped over the side of the mountain.

My car rolled at least once before it came to a stop in the upright position against a stand of trees. The airbag had inflated and now dangled from the steering wheel like a deflated balloon. Blood trickled down the side of my face and my left hand throbbed painfully. The driver's side door wouldn't open, even when I rammed it with my shoulder, and the seatbelt was jammed, effectively trapping me inside the car. I fought a sense of hysteria by chanting a prayer aloud.

I became aware of a tapping on the passenger window. A man pulled the passenger side door open and crawled carefully inside. "Hey," he said gently. "Are you okay?"

I was so relieved to see this man. I swiped the tears from my cheeks. "I think so. I think I'm okay. I can't get my door open though. I'm stuck. I need to get out of here," I said, feeling the sense of panic return. "Can you help me?"

"No, I'm afraid I don't have the right equipment to get you out of here and back up to the road. Your car came pretty far down the side of this mountain. A family that was traveling behind you saw you go over and they're calling 911. It won't be long now; help is on the way."

"I hit some ice and lost control. I can't believe it. There was just nothing I could do to stop it. I've never had an accident before," I rambled.

"Well," he said kindly, "you started with a doozy!"

I smiled in return. "Yeah, I guess I did."

"Since we have a few minutes, allow me to introduce myself," he said extending a hand. "I call myself Bob."

Our voices mingled softly in the stillness of the night. Bob was such a comforting presence. I was filled with a sense of peace. Despite the frigid temperatures outside, the interior of the car was comfortably warm. I realized that I was no longer afraid.

"Well, Vicki," he said after a time, "it looks like help is on its way."

He pointed ahead where the faint rays of flashlights could be seen through the darkness. "I'm going to get out of their way and let them do their job."

Panic filled me. "Please don't leave me."

"Oh, I'm not going far. I'll be watching. But these guys don't need another body to worry about. You hang tight and they'll have you out of this car in a jiffy."

I grabbed his hand. "Thank you… for staying with me, for keeping me company until they came."

He squeezed my hand. "It's been entirely my pleasure. God bless you."

True to his word, the rescue squad arrived shortly after he left. They used the Jaws of Life to free me from the tangled wreckage, loaded me onto a stretcher and hauled me up the mountain. As they loaded me onto an ambulance I looked around for Bob.

"Bob sat with me in the car until you arrived. He said he'd wait for me."

The firemen exchanged wary glances. "Ma'am, there's no way someone could have been waiting in the car with you. We couldn't even reach you without safety lines and crampons. Both doors were too damaged to open without the Jaws. There's no way anyone went in or out of that car before we arrived."

I sought to make sense of what he was saying. Then I noticed a family of four huddled together by their car. "Wait! He told me that a family was calling for help I bet they saw him!"

A fireman led the family to me and I thanked them for calling for help. I asked if they had seen Bob. "There wasn't anyone else here. No one except the emergency crew has come up this road since you went over. You're just lucky we were here tonight and saw your car go over the side. If we hadn't, no one would have known you were down there!"

I believed them. However, if it had all just been a dream, how had I known that it was a family that had seen me go over the side of the road and called for help? How could I have imagined that so accurately?

A few weeks after the accident, I received a photo of my car taken by a road crew tasked with bringing it back up the mountain. The picture plainly shows the passenger side door mangled against a huge tree trunk. I believe the firemen were right when they said that no earthly body had been with me that night, but I firmly believe a heavenly presence had been! The passing of the years has not lessened my memory of Bob. He was a real and solid presence in that vehicle with me. He held my hand and promised that I would be safe. I will never forget that accident or the time I spent with an angel named Bob. To this day I believe that my angel is doing just what he promised: watching over me.

~Vicki Kitchner

A Touch on My Shoulder

Angels descending, bring from above,
Echoes of mercy, whispers of love.
~Fanny J. Crosby

The emergency room doctor tapped my daughter's knee with a little hammer, but didn't get the usual involuntary knee jerk in response. Nor did Bethany's foot flinch or toes curl when her reflexes were tested. Perplexed, the doctor shook her head. She continued to poke and prod. Bethany didn't respond in any way.

"I've never seen anyone this debilitated before," the doctor admitted.

Swallowing the lump in my throat, I looked down at my beautiful twenty-three-year-old red-haired daughter lying helplessly on the examination table. She appeared to be paralyzed. She couldn't move her fingers or toes, her arms or legs. She couldn't even turn her head. Bethany's eyelids were frozen in a half-shut position that made her look even more pitiful. What was wrong with my dear girl?

At the beginning of the examination, the doctor had asked the usual questions: "Is she allergic to any medications? Does your daughter take illegal drugs? Did she mix alcohol with prescription drugs?"

"No, not Bethany," I replied with certainty.

Normally healthy and very active, Bethany had recently been

honorably discharged from the Army after serving her country for four years as an Arabic linguist. She had come down with the flu over the holidays. When three weeks passed, and she still wasn't well, I became concerned.

I called her every day. "Are you vomiting? Coughing? Do you still have body aches and pains?" I pressed. "Maybe you should go see a doctor."

"I'm just so tired," Bethany replied wearily. "And there's a strange tingling sensation in my feet and hands. But don't worry, Mom. I'm bound to get better soon."

But she didn't get better. The tingling sensation got even worse. A numbing paralysis spread to her arms and legs. One afternoon, she called. "Mom, come get me. There's something really wrong."

My heart lurched. I barely recognized my daughter's strained, feeble voice, but I did detect the note of panic in her tone.

"I'll be right there," I assured her. "I'm on my way."

My friend Nancy and I made the drive to Albuquerque in record time. When we arrived at Bethany's apartment, we found that she was barely able to walk or lift her arms. The tingling numbness had spread throughout her body. My daughter moved stiffly like a robot. She was extremely pale and barely able to open her mouth to speak. Something was terribly wrong.

"We've got to get her to a doctor," I told Nancy. But once again, Bethany insisted that she would be all right. She believed she was simply dehydrated and weak from hunger. She couldn't remember the last time she'd eaten a sensible meal.

"Mom, just take me home," she pleaded.

Against my better judgment, I did so. It took all of my strength and Nancy's to assist Bethany down two flights of stairs and into the truck.

Two hours later, Bethany was in the ER at our local hospital.

"She may have Guillain-Barré syndrome," the doctor told me, after looking up something in a thick medical tome. "It's a rare disorder—the sensory nerve myelin becomes damaged. I've never seen a case, but she's got the symptoms."

As there was a serious possibility that Bethany's lungs would soon be paralyzed, the doctor decided to have her transported by ambulance to the university hospital in Albuquerque.

I had just enough time to call my husband, who was in Chicago on business, and ask my friends Nancy and Jennifer to put Bethany on their church prayer chains. The two-hour ride in the back of the ambulance seemed the longest of my life. Stunned by the sudden turn of events, I tried to pray, but my words were an incoherent jumble.

Glancing down at my helpless daughter on the stretcher, I agonized: What if she died on the way to the hospital? I'd never felt so alone and frightened in my life.

By the time we arrived, it was nearly 2 a.m. The doctors and nurses in the emergency room immediately took blood samples and performed a spinal tap. I blinked back hot tears when Bethany—as floppy and limp as a Raggedy Ann doll—did not respond to any of their poking and pricking.

"You'd better sit down," one of the nurses told me. "You look exhausted."

I dropped heavily onto a tall stool outside the door of the examination room. I did feel weak, and realized that I hadn't had anything to eat or drink in more than twelve hours. I was trembling too—from hunger and nervous anxiety. I had never felt so powerless and miserable.

It was then I felt a warm, reassuring hand on my shoulder. A deep comforting voice said, "Everything will be all right."

In an instant, my body stopped trembling. I felt calm. My stomach stopped churning. Heaving a sigh, I turned to thank the kind wellwisher, but no one was behind me. In fact, there was nothing behind me at all—just a blank wall. No door, no corridors, no windows.

But I was certain that I had heard a voice close to my ear. I had felt the warm pressure of a hand upon my shoulder. I got goose bumps when I realized that an angel of God had spoken to me. I believed in angels, but I'd never ever expected one to speak to me. Nevertheless, I believed what I'd been told. How could I not?

When my anxious husband arrived the next day, he found me

smiling and composed, sitting next to our daughter's bed. He almost cried when I lifted Bethany's eyelids so she could see her dad.

I repeated the message the angel had given me. Bill raised an eyebrow, but my calm, unwavering assurance was convincing. I was filled with "a peace that surpasses all understanding." If the Lord had gone out of His way to send me a message, I certainly wasn't going to doubt Him.

The doctors, having indeed diagnosed Bethany's condition as Guillain-Barré syndrome, recommended an experimental treatment of intravenous immune globulin. We were cautioned that she would be in intensive care for three to six weeks, and would require months of physical therapy. We were warned that she might even be paralyzed or partially paralyzed for the rest of her life.

But Bethany astonished everyone with her rapid recovery. She was released from the hospital after only one week and required no physical therapy at all.

"It's amazing!" the doctors declared.

"It's a miracle," I told them.

That was more than a dozen years ago. Bethany soon married and had a beautiful baby boy. She remains healthy and even participates in the occasional half-marathon.

We've met other people with friends and family members suffering from the paralyzing effects of the Guillain-Barré syndrome. They always marvel that Bethany has recovered fully.

But I knew she would. An angel had told me, "Everything will be all right."

And it was.

~Shirley R. Redmond

The Best Man

There's no other love like the love for a brother.
There's no other love like the love from a brother.
~Terri Guillemets

"Let's not have a best man then," I whispered softly to him. "A wedding ceremony doesn't necessarily need a best man."

"I just don't know who could fill his shoes."

My fiancé's only brother had died suddenly in an accident at the age of twenty. The two brothers had been best friends. It had been over fourteen years since his death. Yet, no one could take his place at our upcoming wedding.

"Moments like these are the hardest," my future husband had explained, "when there's a happy occasion and I just want to call him up to share the good news.... and I can't."

We decided that my three brothers would serve as ushers but the role of best man would remain vacant. To honor my fiancé's brother, we would have a moment of silence during the ceremony and a best man's boutonniere would be laid at his grave afterwards. My fiancé had silently agreed to all this. But, I could sense he felt his brother's absence more deeply than ever.

The afternoon of our wedding, I took my first step onto the rose-petal-strewn path that led to my future husband. The ceremony was taking place in a garden and he stood waiting for me under a tree. My three brothers stood next to him in a perfect row. They smiled as

I approached. I then noticed that my first brother, standing next to my groom, was off his mark. We had practiced several times during rehearsal the night before, each of us standing on a taped X denoting our spot. I suspected that due to nervousness, my brother had forgotten where to stand.

As I joined my soon-to-be husband at the head of the garden, I nodded my head to my brother, motioning for him to stand at his designated spot. He gave me a confused grin and a thumbs-up.

I mouthed, "Move over."

He whispered, "What?" It was a bit louder than he intended. Giggles filled the crowd.

I decided to ignore it. Who cared if our line was a bit disjointed? I had bigger fish to fry. So, I joined hands with my groom and joyfully became a married woman.

It wasn't until several weeks after the wedding that we understood the significance of the seemingly trivial circumstance. My husband came home with our wedding proofs. Like any other excited newlywed couple, we thumbed through them giddily. Then we came to the photos of our ceremony.

My bridesmaids stood in a nice neat row, right next to the bride. However, there was a visible gap between my husband and my first brother. The space was large enough to accommodate another groomsman. It looked as if someone was missing from the lineup. It looked like the best man had walked away.

I touched the photo with my fingertip. "Why is my brother standing way over there? And what's that?"

The lighting in the garden had been dappled that day. Patches of sunlight were strewn here and there. But there was one small, very distinctive sunny patch that caught my eye. It had emerged from between the leaves and illuminated the spot on the grass where the best man should have stood. It shone on the grass to my husband's right, marking the spot for a very special unseen guest.

"I guess someone made the event after all."

My husband may not have been able to pick up the phone to deliver the good news of our engagement to his brother. He may not have been able to address that particular wedding invitation. No text or e-mail was ever sent. However, somehow, a very special VIP had found his place of honor right next to the groom.

Everything was just as it should have been.

~Michele Boom

The Doctor

Angels deliver Fate to our doorstep — and anywhere else it is needed.
~Jessi Lane Adams

My dad paced the hallway, wringing his hands in despair. He had called the doctor's office and left another message with his answering service, but there had been no reply. My mom sat next to me on my bed trying to soothe my forehead with a cool cloth after another bout of vomiting had left me weakened and feverish.

The knock at the front door brought a man, medicine bag in hand, bundled against the winter's cold. It was the 1950s, and doctors made house calls. He introduced himself, explaining that he was filling in for our regular family physician that evening. My father quickly brought him to my room. After an exam, he announced that my appendix had ruptured and they needed to get me to surgery immediately. He told my parents to drive me to our local hospital and he would meet us there.

I was wrapped in blankets and loaded into the car, my younger brother in the front seat with my dad and my mother by my side in back. I remember the anxious look my parents shared as they drove to the hospital. When I arrived, the doctor was waiting.

My parents had walked through the same hospital doors just months earlier after the death of my older brother. A car had hit him while riding his bicycle home from school. Now, I saw the look of fear on my parents' faces as they watched me wheeled into the operating room.

Over the next few days, I would wake for short periods of time inside an oxygen tent only to see my mom or dad in a chair by my bed. A couple of days after the surgery, our regular doctor came into the room. The look he exchanged with my parents was one of shock and disbelief.

I would learn many years later that our family doctor had just returned from a trip and was given my dad's old messages. There was no doctor on call that night by the name given to us. No one from our small town hospital had heard of him either. He had told the staff that he had just joined our doctor's family practice and was filling in for him that evening. My parents, our doctor, and the hospital tried to find the man who showed up on our doorstep that blustery night to save my life. They never did.

~Catherine Kopp

The White Owl

Don't look for God in the sky; look within your own body.
~Osho

t was a low time for me. Matt, my husband of almost thirty years, had died after battling cancer for seven years. Our four children were all married now and had left, the last two just a couple of months before we lost their dad. I felt like I was not needed anymore. For the first time in my life I lived totally alone in our big farmhouse, the closest neighbor half a mile away. The three miles to the village were gravel road, lined here and there by trees and bushes, and not always passable in bad weather. From there it was twenty miles of open highway to the city of Winnipeg.

I was lonely. That winter I joined a widow support group in the city, which met once a week. Driving home from a meeting one night it had started to snow. The visibility was not too bad on the highway, but by the time I had reached our gravel road the snow got heavier, coming down thick and slow, almost like a curtain.

Suddenly a large white owl flew straight across my windshield, almost touching it, totally blocking my view. My heart almost stopped. I couldn't believe the size of that bird! Automatically my foot hit the brake pedal. The car slowed, coming to a complete stop just by Remi's bridge.

Before me on the narrow bridge stood three deer, motionless, mesmerized by the lights of the car—a doe and her two young ones, a fascinating picture with snowflakes reflecting the brilliant light. For a moment they kept staring, then sauntered off past the car and disappeared into the bushes.

I sat there, stunned and shaking, awed by the beauty and wonder of the moment as I burst into tears. The owl had been our family emblem, since our family name means owl tree.

It slowly dawned on me that the snowy white owl flying across my windshield had been my guardian angel warning me to slow down. At the speed I had been driving, I would have been unable to stop in time. I would have hit the deer and crashed into the stone sides of the bridge.

A warmth spread over me like a cozy blanket—I was not alone!

Thank you, my guardian angel!

I realized I still had a life to live, that God must have something in mind for me to do yet. I promised myself I would try my hardest to scramble out of my pit of sadness.

Slowly I drove the last half-mile home with new hope in my heart for the future.

~Anne Ullenboom Van Humbeck

A Night to Remember

There are angels all among us, sent down from up above,
to offer guidance and protection and unconditional love.
~Author Unknown

"Wow! Best concert ever!" my friend, Judi, raved. It was July 6, 1967. We had just attended a performance by Simon and Garfunkel at the Winnipeg Auditorium, an intimate concert hall in the heart of downtown Winnipeg, Manitoba. Of course, the concert was amazing—just the two men and a guitar and the most incredible harmonies ever.

"Please, please, can we stay to see if they sign autographs?" Judi had begged after the echoes of the last encore had died away.

Never going to happen, I thought, but why not? Imagine my shock when, not ten minutes later, out popped Simon and Garfunkel by the back entrance, pens in hand, to sign anything presented them by the eager handful of fans, including my penny loafer. Judi got a kiss on the cheek from Simon and I got a hug from Garfunkel. Life was complete!

We waved as they hopped into their black limo, and just stared as it disappeared into the evening traffic. We could not believe what had just happened! We pinched ourselves and started home.

"Want to check out Memorial Park?" Judi suggested. Memorial Park was an oasis of grass and trees in the center of the business and government area of this capital city. In the 1960s it was a favorite haunt of the local hippies who would gather, guitars in hand and flowers in their hair, to serenade one another and ponder the political and musical happenings of our American neighbor.

That night, several different groups were sprinkled amongst the treed areas of the park. We meandered from group to group, savoring the music of some and scampering discretely away from the less harmonious ones!

"What do you think is going on over there?" I pointed to a small group huddled together under some trees in the direction of the concert hall we had left earlier. We decided to investigate. Imagine our surprise to find Simon and Garfunkel nestled amongst the twenty or thirty musicians there. Apparently, they had heard about Memorial Park and had wanted to investigate themselves. Two blocks from the Auditorium, they had ditched the limo and snuck back to the park. Picking this one well-secluded group, they begged the musicians not to spread the word of their arrival and plunked themselves on the grass. They would not play or sing themselves, but told the group they had come to hear them sing. We quietly slipped into the group, and time stood still as these two marvelous, gracious men leaned back and savored the local talent and a few moments of anonymity. Then they were gone.

Finally, I glanced at my watch. "Oh, no! It's after midnight!" I wasn't that worried about my curfew, but more terrified to realize my local bus, the Ness Express, had stopped running at midnight. The closest bus stop now was two miles of dark streets away from my house. We raced to the transit station. I madly hugged my co-conspirator and hopped on my bus while Judi ran to find hers.

By the time the bus pulled up to the stop, it was really late and really dark. I hunched my shoulders and tried to look invisible as I started the long walk home. Just when I began to celebrate the dearth of traffic, the lights of a car slowly approaching from the rear picked me out in the shadows. I was instantly terrified. Why had that car slowed down and why was it now inching along behind me? I sped up, looking for an escape route. I heard the car stop about twenty feet behind me and a car door open, but I was too terrified to glance back.

At that moment, I felt pressure at my elbow and looked up. A very tall, broad-shouldered man had taken my arm and was walking beside me. Instinctively I knew he was not there to harm me. He did not say a word but did not leave my side. After a few moments of hesitation, I heard the driver mutter a few not-nice words, get in his car, and slam the door. He turned the car around, gunned the engine, and took off in the other direction.

"Thank you, thank you so much!" Tears of relief streaming down my cheeks, I turned to thank my rescuer. He had vanished.

As remarkable as the concert had been, as impossible as hiding amongst the trees with Simon and Garfunkel had seemed, that night has been emblazoned in my memory forever for a different reason. It was the night I learned that angels really do walk among us.

~Randy Joan Mills

Chapter 4

Touched by an Angel

Miracles Happen

Saving Mallory

For every soul, there is a guardian watching it.
~The Quran

"Welcome to Phoenix, ladies and gentlemen. Please remain seated with your seatbelts fastened until we come to a complete stop at the gate and the captain has turned off the seatbelt sign."

Welcome to Phoenix my behind! I didn't want to be there. I wondered if I just stayed seated with my seatbelt fastened if they would fly me back to Orlando.

Glenn and I had come to Phoenix to be with his youngest daughter, Mallory, when she had surgery. The month before, doctors had discovered that she had a brain AVM. I had never heard of an AVM until a few months earlier when I had listened to Dr. Jill Bolte Taylor's TED talk about her experience when her AVM exploded. We had brought her book, *My Stroke of Insight*, with us. I knew the same thing could happen to Mallory if it wasn't repaired; nevertheless, I didn't want to be in Phoenix.

For one thing, Glenn's ex-wife and her husband would be there and they made me uncomfortable. Secondly, and more importantly, I would have to spend time sitting around a hospital. I hadn't been inside a hospital since the night I lost my son, Jay. I had a sense of foreboding and my stomach felt tied in knots. I couldn't convince myself that anything good ever happened in hospitals other than babies being born. We collected our bags and proceeded to the hotel and from there, the hospital.

On the day of our arrival, Mallory was to have an embolization to prepare the veins and arteries around the AVM for surgery. When we arrived, we headed to the waiting room. Ex's husband met us at the door.

"They had to rush her into surgery. The embolization caused the AVM to burst and she was bleeding into her brain. They weren't prepared to do the surgery today. This doesn't look good."

We were stunned, not understanding what this meant.

Ex looked spent. Her eyes looked teary, red and beyond worried. Even though we didn't care for each other's company, the mother in me wept for the mother in her.

Were Glenn and I going to lose a second child? Could we survive as a couple if we did? I began to shut down, my mind going to my safe place where I didn't have to face what was happening. I sat on the sofa with Glenn, Ex and Ex's husband. They whispered worriedly, but I didn't hear. I had, in a sense, managed to leave Phoenix.

● ● ●

Glenn and I had married just as Mallory and Jay were approaching their terrible twos. Jay loved playing Mallory's knight in shining armor, defending her from terrifying bugs and other dragon-like creatures. But when it came to playtime, he preferred his older stepbrother, Nick. At five, Nick was a font of knowledge for a two-year-old. Still, Jay felt the need to care for Mallory. We should have known that he would be looking after her in that murky between-worlds state where she was.

"You can go in to see her now," announced the nurse.

Ex, Ex's husband and Glenn started toward the door in a rush. I couldn't blame them for their eagerness to see their daughter. I lagged behind; my stomach clenched looking at all the medical equipment I passed in the hallway. I fought to keep from vomiting, dragging my feet and dreading the moment I would see her.

My fear was justified. She looked dead. The ventilator maintained her breathing but tubes were running into and out of every part of her. Machines beeped and hissed. Her color was gray and her eyes were open and fixed. It was all I could do to keep from turning around and running out of the hospital. In my mind's eye, I saw Jay lying there—dead.

Sitting quietly, I tried to distance myself as much as I could but I couldn't stop looking at her. Was she there? Was she really in there? In my mind, I pleaded with her to wake up.

I stayed as long as I could but soon became exhausted. The flight had been long and then the shock had taken its toll on me. I excused myself and went back to the hotel. I was not helping at the hospital and I needed to try to talk to Jay on the other side.

After resting, I began to meditate. I relaxed, drifted, and then went to our meeting place. I meet Jay in a special place. It is a hillside meadow: bright, colorful and filled with grasses and flowers. There is a dense forest at the bottom of the hill and a stream. Jay took me there once when I was under hypnosis. There is a beautiful university made of glass or crystal on a hill nearby. Jay says I am not allowed to visit there until I cross over.

Jay met me at our usual place but quickly took me to another place I had never visited. It looked like a waiting room for teenagers—poorly lit and with large sofas and several other young people there. That's when I noticed Mallory sitting beside Jay! My heart felt like it had stopped. I thought she had died and that was the reason she was there!

"Jay, why is Mallory here with you?" I asked, my voice filled with dread.

"She is just hanging out, Mom. She is going to be okay. She'll go back when it's time."

Hope filled me. I so hoped that this vision was real! It seemed as real as talking to a flesh and blood person. Mallory didn't speak directly to me. Maybe it was because she didn't belong there. Can it be that you can't speak to people in the physical realm when you are between worlds?

I ended my meditation and rushed back to the hospital to tell

Glenn. Naturally, he was unimpressed since, at that time, he didn't believe in spirit communication. He was so worried about Mallory that nothing would reassure him except for her to wake up. In my heart, I felt she would be okay.

Thus began our long vigil. There were so many surgeries, CT scans, MRIs, everything that they could think of to do. Nothing seemed to help.

Each day I would meditate. I would meet Jay in that dim place and Mallory would be with him. They seemed to be relaxed and enjoying each other's company.

After a week, I returned to Orlando to take care of things at home but I continued to meet with Jay and Mallory each day. Glenn stayed in Phoenix most of the time, hoping for signs of improvement.

We endured six weeks of this limbo. The doctors only gave Mallory a five percent chance of survival. It looked dismal. At least I knew that if the worst happened, if Jay was wrong and Mallory didn't make it, she would be with him and they would be fine. The rest of us would fall apart.

One day, when it began to look like this suffering would go on forever, I began to meditate. I went to the dim room and Jay was still there. I looked around and saw other teenagers but didn't see Mallory.

"Jay, where's Mallory?"

"She has gone on about her business, Mom," he calmly replied, then got up and left the room.

My eyes snapped open. Puzzled, I didn't know what to think. I fretted over what it could mean for the rest of the day. Late that afternoon Glenn called. "She's waking up!"

Mallory's recovery was long and difficult. She didn't leave the hospital for several more weeks. She had to have physical and occupational therapy. It was a tedious process. When she finally went home, Glenn and I traveled to see her.

When we picked her up for dinner, she looked so thin and frail. She was in a wheelchair and had a hard time speaking. But in view of all she had been through, she was lucky to be alive. We had dinner and then decided Glenn would drop me by my mom's house while he took Mallory home. I had gotten out of the car, hugged her goodbye, and had turned to walk away when I heard her.

"Marilyn…" she said weakly.

I turned and went back to her.

"I just have to tell you—Jay brought me back."

"What?"

"He brought me back. When I was waking up he was there with me. He was saying 'Mal, wake up now… Mal, wake up.' He brought me back."

"Thank you so much for telling me," I managed to choke out.

I hugged her again and ran inside with tears streaming down my face.

It was just like Jay. He was still taking care of Mal.

~Marilyn Ellis Futrell

Lost and Found

Miracles happen to those who believe in them.
~Bernard Berenson

When it comes to being brave, my grand-dog Nessie is no prizewinner. She lets the cat have first dibs at all table scraps. She's never once barked at the postman. Squirrels have taken over her back yard because she dares not chase them up a tree.

Loud noises are what scare Nessie most. She trembles whenever a truck backfires. She goes nuts during thunderstorms. And she's terrified of fireworks. Knowing that Nessie hates Independence Day, my son James and his wife Natalie are always careful to keep her safely inside the house during the firecracker-crazy days of early July.

But one year, assuming that fireworks season was over after the Fourth had passed, they left her outside in the fenced back yard when they went to dinner with friends. Big mistake. They returned home to find spent bottle rockets littering the street beside their house. Nessie, who wasn't wearing her collar and ID tag, was gone. Their black dog had disappeared into the black, black night.

It would take a miracle to bring her home.

James called his dad and me before sunup the next morning to tell us the sad news. "Can you come help us look for her?" he asked. Of course we could.

On foot, on bicycle and by car, we searched the area in an ever-widening circle. We talked to friends. We talked to strangers. We hung posters on telephone poles and placed a LOST DOG ad in the newspaper. Nessie's picture was posted and shared countless times on Facebook. We checked daily with the kind folks at the animal shelter to see if a dog matching Nessie's description had been turned in. Every time James received a phone call from someone saying they'd spotted a scared-looking black dog with no collar, we followed the lead. All to no avail.

Days passed. And Nessie did not come home.

Inevitably, the what-if's began. What if she'd been hit by a car and flung into a ditch where no one but the buzzards would ever find her? What if she couldn't find food and water and was wasting away? What if she had a new owner who thought it okay to chain a dog to a tree in the hot sun? There was no end to the horrible possibilities that sprang from our tortured imaginations. When we tried to talk ourselves into believing that a nice family had found Nessie and taken her into their loving home, we failed.

It was after midnight, more than a week after Nessie went missing, when James's phone rang. The caller said he'd been feeding a very friendly and very hungry black dog for a couple of days.

"Female?" James asked.

"Yep."

"About fifty pounds?"

"Looks to be."

"Ummmm," James stammered, his heart beating hard. "Does she, by any chance, have four white feet and a white tip on her tail?"

"She does."

"Don't get too excited," James told Natalie. "This guy lives clear on the other side of the county. We didn't even put up signs that far away. And we've had our hopes dashed too many times."

But this time was different. The dog was, indeed, Nessie. Who was overjoyed to see James and Natalie when they pulled into her rescuer's driveway. The happy outcome that so many people had hoped and prayed for had finally come to pass.

But how?

Nessie wasn't traffic-savvy. Why hadn't she been hit by a car the very night she escaped into the darkness? How could she have travelled more than ten miles and crossed dozens of busy streets and not have a scratch on her? Her coat wasn't matted or dirty. Her ribs weren't showing. How had a dog who'd been pampered all her life managed to find food and water and shelter for more than a week?

And what about the man who found her? He wouldn't have known that the dog who appeared on his front porch was someone's beloved pet unless his buddy had stopped by that evening. A buddy who happened to have seen a LOST DOG poster only because he'd run out of gas and spotted the poster while walking to a service station. A buddy who just happened to have a pen in his pocket when someone or something whispered to him that he ought to scribble the phone number down on his hand.

It was after midnight when Nessie's rescuer made the phone call. What if he'd decided it was too late and that he should wait until morning to call? Would Nessie have headed on down the busy highway in the pitch black dark, trying to make her way back to James and Natalie?

Some folks who have heard this story just shrug and shake their heads. Some contend that we simply got lucky. Others theorize that the stars somehow happened to be lined up just right the night Nessie was found. But we know better.

We know that nothing short of a miracle brought our dear, sweet Nessie home.

~Jennie Ivey

33

Angels at the Intersection

*I am convinced that these heavenly beings exist and that
they provide unseen aid on our behalf.*
~Billy Graham

attend a small church about sixty miles from my house. During the hour-long drive, I have time to disconnect from my daily routine as a round-the-clock caregiver for my aging mom and prepare to spend time in the presence of the Lord. On the way home, I often reflect on the wonderful sermons and teachings each service brings, and offer prayers, thanks and praise. It's my chance to have quiet time with God.

Almost the entire trip is through the countryside, so it's a scenic drive in the daylight hours but pretty dark and lonely at night. At the midpoint, there's an interstate exit with the usual gas stations and fast food spots that light up the horizon.

One night, after a particularly emotional week—feeling isolated as a caregiver, and questioning my value not only to my mother, but also to the world at large—the angels were gathering, on high alert. As I drove toward the brightly lit intersection, the unthinkable happened.

Suddenly, with no warning at all, a white airport transport van made a left turn directly in front of my car. It was impossible that the driver didn't see me. In those critical seconds before impact, as time seemed to unfold in slow motion, I could see the faces of the people riding in the van. They seemed to be just as shocked as I was. I had pressed the brake to the floor and was sliding into the van. Based on the trajectory, I knew that in seconds my car would be embedded in the center of the van. I thought about dying. I felt acceptance. I wondered who would take care of my mother. Myriad thoughts raced through my mind. I closed my eyes and braced for the impact... waiting for the sound of metal and glass. The only words I had time to utter were "Lord Jesus."

But there was silence. I opened my eyes just in time to see the white van go past while my car continued forward. It was as if unseen hands had literally pushed the van through the intersection and out of my way in the nick of time. Before I knew it, I was through the intersection and continuing my moonlit journey down the back roads. Then it hit me.

I'd had a couple of close calls before, and they left me shaking with fear. Once or twice I had to pull off the road to regain my composure. But this time, there was no such residual panic. My pulse wasn't racing; my heart wasn't pounding. I was at perfect peace. I was smiling. I was driving along as though nothing had happened. And that took me as much by surprise as the sight of the van passing in front of my car.

Only divine intervention could explain the fact that I made it home that night. That's when I knew that I was valuable, not only to my mother, but to God. That's when I knew that no matter how insignificant I thought I was to others, my life still had meaning and purpose.

I'm pretty sure I sang the rest of the way home—grateful for God's protection, and blessed by a sense of renewed hope, the opportunity to share the story with the ones I love, and the chance to make a difference in the lives of others.

~Jan Walker

34

Miracle in Tow

We cannot pass our guardian angel's bounds, resigned or sullen; he will hear our sighs.
~Saint Augustine

Late one night, my husband and I were traveling home from a trip with our infant son in tow. We were on the back roads in a place called "Irondale." If that name conjures images of desolate landscape laden with chunks of iron, then that pretty much fits the name. I thought of how terrible it would be to break down in such a place. There were no houses for miles, streetlights were few and far between, and it had been hours since we had passed another car.

And then the drive shaft dropped from underneath our ugly old car. We were stranded in the middle of nowhere.

However, this was just one more occurrence in a series of unfortunate events. So almost methodically, we gathered our son in his carrier (realizing our slim chances of hitching a ride at such an hour) and began walking toward home.

Minutes later, seemingly out of nowhere, a tow truck pulled alongside us. Its cheerful driver hopped out and began preparing our car for tow. He allowed the three of us to pile into the cab of his truck, and we made small talk as we traveled the dark roads. How lucky we were that a tow truck just happened to pass during our time of need. Suddenly, it occurred to me that we had no money to pay for this service. Trying to remain inconspicuous, I scraped the bottom of my purse for dollar bills and loose change as my husband continued light banter with the driver. Finally, I managed to gather a random amount—something like $7.56. My heart raced and my palms were sweaty. What happens when you don't have enough money to pay for the services? Would they take the car? They could certainly have it!

As we pulled into our apartment complex parking lot, I asked the driver how much we owed. He said, "Oh, let's just make it $7.56," and he winked at me! He had no way of knowing the exact amount I had gathered from the bottom of my purse! In fact, I had purposely kept my hand inside my purse in an awkward attempt to disguise my frantic search for money.

When we stepped out of the wrecker, I glanced at the sign on its door: Rainbow Wrecking. I made a mental note to call the company to report the driver's commendable actions. However, I could not find that particular wrecker service among the other towing companies in the phone book. When I dialed 411 for information, I learned no such listing existed.

Angel? I don't know. Maybe it was. But I definitely believe that God, our Source, puts others in our lives as resources during times of tribulation. Perhaps sometimes those resources are not as "human" as we believe them to be.

~Cynthia Zayn

Undercover Angels

Never drive faster than your guardian angel can fly.
~Author Unknown

t was a steamy summer night in Boston. After attending a party in the city, I lingered in the restaurant parking lot with a group of college friends. I beamed with pride as they admired my first car, a Pontiac LeMans, its newly painted gold metallic finish shining in the streetlights. With promises to get together soon, I bid them goodbye and headed onto Interstate 93 toward my home just south of the city. The highway was dark and deserted. I turned up the radio to keep me company and glanced at the clock—1:00 a.m. Chastising myself for staying out so late, I sped up to 75 mph, trying to hurry home.

By the time I saw the twisted metal bumper lying on the highway it was too late to hit the brakes. My body froze. The screech of the LeMans driving over the metal sounded like a freight train. I heard the loud "pop" of a blown tire and then a rhythmic banging as the car lurched from side to side, the back of the car pounding against the roadway. Terrified, I clutched the steering wheel. With a fear I had never known before, I screamed out, "God help me! I don't know what to do!"

At that moment the car, still bucking wildly, turned and drove off the interstate on a sharply curved exit ramp. The steering wheel spun through my clenched fingers. The headlights illuminated the guardrail as it flew past me. I strangely felt as if I were on an amusement park ride. I had no control of the car and could not stop it. Suddenly, my body slammed back against the bucket seat as the car came to an abrupt stop. The LeMans had parked perfectly on the side of a divided highway. I sat in stunned silence, my heart pounding and body shaking. My thoughts ran wild. I was alive! How did I get off the interstate? Where was I?

I looked around and recognized the area as a rough part of town known for gang activity. Concern for my safety snapped me out of my mental fog. I scrunched down in my seat and looked around. A nearby strip mall and fast food restaurants were in darkness, obviously closed at this late hour. The street was quiet.

I breathed a sigh of relief. In the days before cell phones, my only hope was to find a pay phone and call for help. I spied a phone booth on the opposite side of the divided roadway. I'd have to make a run for it. Carefully, I looked in all directions again, pulled on the door handle with shaking hands, and bolted from the car.

To my shock, I almost ran into a dark-haired man who was standing right in front of me. A younger man stood to his right. Startled, I jumped back, my heart pounding with fear. The man smiled and said reassuringly, "Don't be afraid. I'm a hockey coach and this is one of my players. We were coming from a game and saw what happened. We followed you off the interstate." He turned toward his car that was now parked behind mine. My mind raced. I knew they had not been there when I opened the door! His voice remained calm. "I have a daughter your age," he said. "We are going to fix your tire for you." Being an avid Boston Bruins fan, I started to relax. Although wary of these strange men, there was something about his demeanor and the hockey reference that put me at ease.

"Do you have a spare tire and jack?" the coach asked with a smile. My mind drew a blank. My brother Vinnie, a mechanic, had always taken care of the family's cars. "I don't know," I said sheepishly. I walked to the back of the LeMans and opened the trunk but couldn't find a jack. The sight of the car's mangled rear tire and bent rim made me shudder. How would I ever get home? Panic rose in my chest. The coach said calmly, "Go stand by the front of the car and we'll take care of it for you." A feeling of peace came over me when he spoke. I sensed he could be trusted and did as he instructed. "Stay right there. There's nothing to worry about," he said.

The younger man never spoke, but walked to the rear wheel of the car and squatted out of view. I saw his shoulders and upper arms moving back and forth, but there was no sound. After what seemed like a minute, the coach said cheerily, "All done." "You mean, it's fixed?" I said in disbelief. "Yep, come and take a look." He smiled and shut the trunk with a slam. To my surprise, the LeMans was ready to go with four good tires. "But... how?" I stammered. The car was never even jacked up.

Without explanation, he walked to the driver's door and opened it for me. "Now go right home," he said. I assured him I would and thanked them both profusely. They stood there smiling. With a sigh of relief, I got into the car and turned to wave, but they had disappeared. I looked into the rearview mirror. Their car was gone!

My mind raced as I tried to think clearly. Only a second had elapsed! This was impossible! Had I been visited by angels? I had never thought about angels before, but knew something miraculous had just occurred. "Thank you angels," I said aloud as I drove slowly home.

The next morning, I told my brother Vinnie what had happened. He walked around the LeMans inspecting the vehicle. "It's unbelievable," he said. "The new paint job doesn't even have a scratch." In the trunk were the pieces of the mangled tire and smashed rim. "You must have been going pretty fast; there's nothing left of this wheel," he said. "Where did this happen again?"

"Just before exit 12 on Interstate 93," I explained.

He looked at me with eyebrows raised. "There is no way you could have driven off that exit with this wheel," he said.

Leaning into the trunk, Vinnie shook his head as he examined the strips of shredded rubber in his hands. He looked up with a puzzled expression. "The temporary spare I put in the trunk is still in here," he said. "Where did you get the tire they put on? It looks brand new." I ran my hand over the treads of the new tire and said a prayer of thanks to God for sending his angels to rescue me.

~May Carlson

Roadside Assistance

God understands our prayers even when we can't find the words to say them.
~Author Unknown

t was pouring rain when I left my office for lunch. I'd driven to work on an empty tank of gas that morning, as was often the case on payday. My commute was thirty miles one way. I worked as a secretary for a technical college and payday came once a month. I was a single mom with two children, so stretching my salary out over a whole month was a challenge.

That rainy morning, as I emptied the last box of cereal and drove to work on fumes, my emotions were almost at the breaking point, threatening to keep me from going to work. At all cost, I had to go in to at least get my paycheck.

I was burned out and feeling very insignificant to God. We weren't starving, and we had clothes to wear and a roof over our heads. I was thankful for my job, but I was exhausted. I just wanted a break from having to count every single penny and having to hope the car would keep running or one of the kids wouldn't get sick. This particular morning I felt forgotten by God and wondered if He even saw me or knew I existed.

With my paycheck in one hand and an umbrella in the other, I dashed out of the office for my hour-long lunch break. I earnestly prayed that my car would make it to the bank, which was less than a mile away. My next stop would be the gas station next to the bank. This was back in the early 1990s, before the days of direct deposit and debit cards, which meant I had to go to the bank first to deposit my check and get enough cash out to cover gas and other immediate expenses.

The road in front of the building where I worked was a busy four-lane road that I needed to turn left onto. As I waited for the traffic to clear, my stress level rose. I feared my car would sputter out its last drop of gas right in front of the college. Then I'd have to ask for help and my co-workers would find out just how broke I really was.

Finally I was able to pull out and head in the direction of the bank. "Please, please, please just get me there," I said to myself. I breathed a sigh of relief as the bank came into view. I was going to make it.

There was a sharp right curve in front of the bank where I needed to turn left and cross two lanes before turning into the parking lot. As I approached the sharp right curve and prepared to turn left towards the bank's parking lot it happened. P-p-p-u-t, p-p-p-t. "No! Not now! Not here!" I pressed my foot on the gas pedal yelling, "Come on, come on!" I turned the steering wheel as I coasted just enough to come out of the sharp curve and into the two oncoming lanes of traffic. Puhthunk. The car completely shut off.

Disbelief and panic took over as I looked straight ahead and saw cars crossing the busy intersection ahead and coming straight towards me. I put the car in neutral, jumped out into the rain and started to push. "God no! Please help me!" I attempted to push with the driver's door open and my right hand on the steering wheel. The big Oldsmobile didn't want to budge.

Suddenly through the rain I heard a man yelling, "Get in, get in!" I looked behind me and saw a small, slender man at the rear of my car with his hands on the trunk. He was motioning for me to get in the car, yelling over and over, "Get in, get in!"

I jumped into the car, thinking that this little man who weighed less than I did was not going to be able to push this big, old car with me in it. I had no choice but to do what he said as the oncoming traffic was getting closer and not going to stop. I mentally prepared myself for a serious collision. Suddenly I felt the car move forward. I turned the steering wheel, cleared the two oncoming lanes and coasted safely into the bank parking lot. I even ended up parked straight in a parking space. As relief and gratitude swept over me, I quickly jumped out of the car to thank this man for helping me. He had quite possibly just saved my life and anyone who would have hit me.

I expected him to be right there since he'd just pushed the car into the parking lot. When I didn't see him, I turned and looked in the other direction. No one was there. I looked across the street in both directions and all around; he was nowhere. The only thing I saw were two lanes of cars whizzing past me.

The whole event seemed to move in slow motion, but transpired so fast I didn't have time to really think about what had happened. Where did he come from? Where did he go? I was bewildered beyond words and suddenly felt something larger than human intervention had just taken place.

I've read that God commands His angels concerning us. I couldn't reason with myself or explain what happened. I thought that maybe my rescuer didn't want to get wetter and once he saw I was safe, simply ran off in the other direction to seek shelter. I couldn't stop thinking about the incident the rest of that day and finally accepted that my small, slender hero was an angel.

God used what happened that day to show me that He was with me, and I wasn't invisible to Him or forgotten. I felt cared for and protected. It didn't matter that I had to go back to the office with damp hair and clothes.

Twenty years later, I still remember the fresh touch from God I felt that day. So far, that was the most memorable lunch hour I've ever had! I don't know where that angel is today, but I hope he knows that I'm still telling his story and thanking God for sending him to me that dreary, rainy day.

~Terri Webster

Belayed

*It comes down to whether you believe in seven miraculous escapes a week
or one guardian angel.*
~Robert Brault

My sister Lynn, her best friend Rosanne, and I were nearing the end of our one-week summer camp. The day's outing was to the Bowl and Pitcher rock formations inside Riverside State Park in Washington State. The Bowl is a huge roundish boulder. Next to it sits the Pitcher, a much taller cylindrical formation. The pair guards the winding Spokane River.

Having feasted on a picnic lunch, the 100 or so high school campers anticipated the evening campfire: hot dogs and hamburgers complete with a sing-a-long and s'mores. But now we had free time—a peaceful little interval to nap, read, or explore the trails. Friends gathered to chat at the weathered picnic tables or split off in clusters to hike. Lynn curled up in the shade with a book. Roseanne and I, opting for a hike, headed for the rock formations. The Pitcher towered above us. "Let's climb to the top," I suggested. Roseanne was game, so up we went—no ropes, no gear—freestyling in tennis shoes and shorts.

For years, I had, unbeknownst to my family and friends, climbed rock formations along other portions of the river—sites that eventually became training locations for amateur climbers bedecked with harnesses, helmets and sturdy shoes. I would later giggle, watching the saddled students clamber up sheer faces that I had conquered with the wind in my hair and caution as an afterthought.

Roseanne and I pulled ourselves up to perch on the top of the Pitcher. Settled on the jagged edge, we reveled in the grand scene. Knots of hikers reconnoitered the trails like spies. The sparkling river roiled and coiled below. More giant boulders dotted the landscape. The sun shone on us while we planned our next adventure, examining the vista of enticing possibilities.

A group of hikers passed below, like ants in colorful hats. One of them pointed up at us. We waved. They waved back and then darted off. In a matter of minutes our afternoon plans changed.

The ants returned with two camp counselors who cupped their hands around their mouths and yelled at us. "You two get down here right now!" We'd reigned long and well on our peak, so we complied without protest. Roseanne headed down first and I followed, carefully choosing foot and hand holds. About a third of the way down I couldn't find a place for my right foot to grip. My handhold was a thin ledge about fingertip in width. The left toehold was also slim. As I searched for a supportive niche, my body leaned backward. I was losing my grip!

Roseanne must have noticed that I was in trouble, because I felt her hand supporting me between the shoulder blades. Firmly, yet patiently, she guided me back toward the rock and kept me steady. I didn't dare upset my balance by so much as turning my head to glance in her direction. I didn't even dare to speak! Once my toehold was secure I turned to thank Roseanne, but she was not there. I spotted her at least ten feet below me, deeply concentrating on her own descent.

As soon as our feet touched soil, we were scolded. "Do you have any idea how dangerous that was?" "You set a poor example!" "We were so frightened for you!" We were summarily confined to within fifty feet of the fire pit for the remainder of the outing.

I told no one about the hand on my back, but I never forgot it.

~Barbara Crick

One Miracle After Another

It only takes a thought and your angel will be there...
for although you may not see them, you're always in their care.
~Author Unknown

was living in Emporia, Kansas and attending Emporia State University to finish my degree. My son Jeff and my daughter-in-law Gina resided in Kansas City, an hour and a half away. It was an exciting time because Gina was about to give birth and I was "on call" to travel to Kansas City to help out.

I was studying for two final exams when the phone rang at 10:00 p.m. one Sunday night.

"Hi, Mom, it's me," my son announced. His voice was somewhat elevated and his words spilled out at a fast pace.

"We're here at the hospital," he continued nervously. "Gina's contractions have started and the doctors are telling us she will have the baby tonight! Can you come now?"

I did what any mother would do and responded as calmly as I could. "Of course, I'm on my way!"

I could hear the heavy rain outside pelting my apartment windows. There was also thunder and lightning. I hurried to the car through high winds. I was afraid to drive in this weather, but I had to get to the hospital. I prayed: "God, I am so overwhelmed. Please send your guardian angels to make this journey with me and to help me through this time."

The streets were empty. It was almost impossible to see through the downpour, even with the windshield wipers on high. As I inched onto the highway, I was surprised when a semi-trailer suddenly appeared out of nowhere in front of me. I felt a calmness come over me as I began to follow these lone red taillights on the open highway to Kansas City.

Amazingly, two hours later, the semi-trailer turned off the highway and drove right past the hospital where Jeff and Gina were having their baby. As I turned into the parking lot, I looked over my shoulder to catch a passing glance at the semi only to find it had disappeared as quickly as it appeared. I had arrived at my destination, white knuckles and all, thanks to my heavenly guide.

Then I noticed it—after a frantic search throughout my car, my purse hadn't made the journey with me. After a brief interlude of verbal venting, I mentally retraced my steps. I remembered placing my purse on the hood of my car while fumbling to unlock my car door in the torrential rain. I had taken off with it riding on top of the hood in the storm. Only God would know where that black purse could have landed! As I rode up the hospital elevator to Gina's room, I was overwhelmed again when I remembered I had just cashed my paycheck that afternoon, and all my credit cards and personal information were in my wallet.

Baby Gabriella decided to take a break and postpone her arrival, so I placed a quick call to the Emporia Police Department relating my story and the missing purse.

"Are you telling me that you drove to Kansas City without a driver's license?" the stern officer on the other end barked. I guessed he hadn't been listening to the tumultuous part of my story!

"Yes, but I didn't know I had done that," I blurted back. "I had to hurry to get to Kansas City for the birth of my granddaughter and I accidentally left my purse on top of the car. All my money and credit cards are in it. It had to have fallen off in the rain and it could be anywhere!" No point trying to sound distressed—it came easily.

After giving me a friendly ribbing about driving to Kansas City without a license, the police officer informed me that a man had come in earlier that night and said he'd found my purse and for them to let me know. Before they were able to thank him or get his name, he was gone. Another officer went outside to get his name, but he was nowhere to be seen. Guess he didn't know that angels don't leave calling cards.

It was morning before Gina delivered our beautiful Gabriella. Jeff and I, not wanting to be found asleep when the event took place, decided to stay awake all night. Since I had been studying for exams the night before, too, I was running on four hours of sleep in two days. Though I took several pictures of our new baby and family, I'm not sure if the pictures were blurry or I was! With exams waiting, I said my goodbyes. Exhausted mentally and physically, I reluctantly headed for home. Unlike the day before, the sun smiled down on me as if to join in the celebration of new life. I became part of a caravan of several semi-trailer trucks and cars heading down the two-lane interstate toward Emporia.

The last thing I remember was passing Beto Junction, a popular truck stop midpoint in my journey home. Suddenly, I was jolted awake and saw that I was heading for the center median at a high rate of speed. I had fallen asleep at the wheel. I turned the wheel to go in the opposite direction and zigzagged several more times on the highway until my car began to overturn. As I braced myself, my car suddenly halted its mid-air roll. It fell back on the pavement on all four tires and sped headfirst into the ditch.

Two semi-trailer trucks and five cars stopped to assist me. Miraculously, I walked away without a scratch and my car only needed to be realigned. But it was the testimony of the first two truckers I will never forget.

One flabbergasted trucker told me, "It was just like someone suddenly stopped it in mid-air and pushed it back down on all four tires."

Another shook his head. "I've never seen anything like it!"

"It was an angel," a voice from the crowd exclaimed and an unsolicited number of heads quietly nodded in agreement.

We all agreed we were standing in a heavenly construction zone.

We had seen angels at work. They had been on call themselves, and had been with me throughout the journey.

~Patti Ann Thompson

The Lifeguard

One thing you can say for guardian angels: they guard.
They give warning when danger approaches.
~Emily Hahn

The warm, soothing sun was turning my skin a golden brown. I lay stretched out on a lawn chair by a swimming pool, relaxing, my family playing happily nearby, thinking how blessed I was. My chair was by the pool's shallow end so I could keep a close eye on my daughter—the youngest of my bunch. From this vantage point, I could see the length of the pool to the other end where my two older children played with their cousins.

Splash! My middle child, eight-year-old Robert, hit the water again in another backflip. He was having fun. He swam to the edge and hurried up to do yet another backflip. The condo pool where we were vacationing didn't have a diving board so Robert's backflips were from the edge of the pool on the deep end. He had done this many times. But I could tell as his feet left the ground that this was different. This time he was not close enough to the edge.

What happened next is forever etched in my memory. I can see it again now, as if it were yesterday. It plays in my mind in slow motion. Robert jumped up and flipped his body in midair. But as he came down into the water, the back of his head hit the side of the concrete pool.

Smack! The sound was awful! His head jerked forward and he sank into the pool.

I stood up and screamed, "No!"

My brother-in-law Teddy saw and heard it too. Before I could even begin to run in Robert's direction, he was out of his chair making his way there. Teddy was closer to the deep end anyway, and I was frozen in fear.

Just as Teddy got to the edge of the pool, Robert's right hand and arm surfaced. He seemed to be floating up in a sitting position with his right arm extended upward, his hand held in a tight fist. Teddy didn't even have to reach down in the water because by the time Teddy made contact, Robert's hand was above the water. Teddy grabbed that extended arm and pulled Robert safely out of the water.

Blood poured from Robert's head. I suddenly came to life and sprang into action. Grabbing a towel, I wrapped his head and yelled for someone to get my husband as quickly as possible. In a few seconds, John arrived. He picked up Robert in his arms and loaded him in the back seat of our car. I rode in the back seat too, cradling Robert's head in my arms. Robert was awake, alert and talking, for which I was thankful.

At the Emergency Center, X-rays were taken, his head wound cleaned and stitched. We were told his skull had not cracked, so to take him home and watch him carefully for the next forty-eight hours. That's how it all happened. I remember it clearly!

However, Robert told me an entirely different story a few days later.

According to Robert, he felt his head hit against the side of the pool and he was in immediate and severe pain. He sank to the bottom. He can vividly remember sitting on the bottom of the pool, opening his eyes under water and looking up.

That's when he saw the hand. It extended down in the water to get him. He was glad to see it and assumed it was an adult member of his family reaching in to rescue him. Robert reached up and grabbed hold of the hand and then felt his body being pulled up to the surface. Since it was his Uncle Teddy who pulled him out of the water, he assumed it was Teddy's hand he had been holding on to all along.

Teddy and I know differently. Teddy never reached his arm down to the bottom of the pool. How could he? A human arm is not long enough to stretch to the bottom of the deep end of a swimming pool. But that's what Robert is certain he experienced. He remembers sitting on the bottom of the pool and feeling the concrete below him. And he clearly remembers grabbing hold of an outstretched hand extended to him. Just as he also remembers being pulled up—his body lifted upward without any effort on his part. I, and others, certainly saw him come to the top of water with his right arm extended and right hand fisted as if he were holding onto something or someone.

I have only one explanation—his guardian angel reached a holy hand down into the water and rescued my child.

That was nearly twenty years ago. My son is grown now. Today when summertime rolls around and I'm enjoying vacations with my now-grown family, when I relax on lawn chairs and with my family enjoying themselves nearby, I can't help but remember that incident. And I know that yes, I am very blessed indeed!

~Harriet Michael

Divine Heat

For He will give His angels charge concerning you...
they will bear you up in their hands.
~Psalm 91:11,12

Heat shimmered over the large flagstone plaza in Mexico City. Trying to entertain my two toddlers, Ben and Andy, was getting tedious. Their dad and I were taking turns browsing in the tourist shop that adjoined the plaza. It was my turn to be outside with the boys. Ben had just turned three years old. Andy was one year old—walking, but unsteadily—like a typical toddler.

In the heart of a bustling city of nine million people, the plaza was relatively deserted with just a few pedestrians. Nobody lingered in the heat. Even the *paleta* (popsicle) vendor tucked himself carefully under the shade of his cart's umbrella. The ubiquitous smell of cornmeal and diesel fuel filled the air and the tall buildings surrounding the plaza pleasantly muffled the cacophony of the city.

We lived in Chiapas, the southernmost state in Mexico, working for a relief organization. Andy had been born there, and we had finally made the two-day drive to Mexico City to get his Certificate of Birth Abroad at the American Embassy. We were doing a little shopping before we started the long drive home.

Squat stone walls surrounded flower and tree beds on the plaza. Very low, the walls were perfect for little boys to climb on, balance on, walk on, and jump off. I tried to keep us squeezed into a little sliver of shade, but the boys were too active. Over and over they scrambled on the little walls. Andy wobbled after his big brother, up and down, back and forth. Sometimes I would walk with him, his chubby fist clutching my finger. Sometimes he wanted to do it by himself, while I stood close by. So far, so good.

What was taking my husband so long? The wait became more monotonous. The boys were getting wound up and bored. They left the little square where we were seated and moved on to the next one a little further away from me.

Tired of trying to confine them to our little area, I asked myself, "What's the worst that could happen?" I remained where I was but watched them carefully, more concerned about sunburn than falls. When they tired of the next square, they moved on to the next. And then the next. I never took my eyes off them.

Andy moved farther away and climbed up on a new wall by himself, putting one unsteady foot in front of the other, walking like he was on a balance beam. I watched, amused, for a moment or two. Suddenly, my "mom radar" went off. There was something not quite right about this, but the danger wasn't clear. Languid from the heat, I got up and moved slowly toward him to check things out. "You're so overprotective," I chided myself. After all, if he did fall, it seemed unlikely he'd be hurt.

Then, everything happened at once. Andy tripped and started to fall. His arms and legs spread out like he was doing a belly flop—like he was flying. It appeared that he was going to land on the other side of the wall, not on the flagstone. Abruptly, I realized that I didn't really know what was on the other side of the wall. I assumed it was a flowerbed, and the fall would be tiny. But my level of concern ratcheted up a notch and I started moving faster.

A rush of something—wind? an angel?—surged ahead of me. The subdued, tremulous heat waves that I had been watching all afternoon focused themselves into a swirl, a force with real presence. It pushed toward Andy, surrounded him, and held him up. Andy hovered. Yes, he simply hovered in the air. No slow motion falling, no twisting, no crying—he just hovered. The force was quietly holding him, like a hoist beneath his tummy, waiting…

The concern I had felt turned into terror. I sprinted, inclined myself over the wall, and stretched out my arm toward Andy. As I leaned, I could see beyond—below, really—and my stomach lurched. It was a void—a two-story drop to an underground parking entrance below. Cars were whizzing into the garage. One car slowed, its terrified driver and passenger looking up in horror at Andy suspended in the air above their car.

I scooped Andy safely back from his hovering space and my adrenaline-infused legs collapsed beneath me on the flagstone plaza. I clutched him, shaking all over. The glimmering air descended around us as if to check us over. Seeing the baby safely in Mom's arms on solid ground, it playfully tousled my hair as if to say "goodbye," and dissipated back into its slow lazy dance over the plaza.

Just then, my husband came out of the store. He hurried over to where we sat huddled in a heap. "What's wrong?" he asked, his brow furrowed. How could I explain Andy hovering in the air? How could I explain the angel holding Andy up, waiting for me to rescue him? How could I explain a two-story drop onto pavement below? How could I explain the cars rushing by directly beneath Andy? How could I explain that the angel knew what a mom didn't and rushed in to save Andy? The law of gravity applies to everyone, no matter who you are. The law of gravity was not suspended just for Andy—rather someone or something suspended him. How could I explain this?

There is no explanation. Since that time, I have struggled through many difficult events in my life, wishing to receive that same kind of miraculous, divine help—and yet, not appearing to receive any help at all. It's tempting to feel lonely or abandoned at those times. And yet, I still have my son and I remind myself the one angelic encounter I had was the difference between life and death. So heat waves shimmering on a hot summer day are a comfort now, not an annoyance, because I know a new truth: We never know what form our angel will take or when it will show up.

~Sharon Cairns Mann

Chapter
5

Touched by an Angel

My Guardian Angel

And She Walks With Me

Sometimes the strength of motherhood is greater than natural laws.
~Barbara Kingsolver

D id I believe psychics could communicate with those who had passed into "the great beyond"? I wasn't sure but I certainly did hope so. In fact, I so wanted to hear from my mother after her passing that I sought the services of a self-proclaimed psychic named Michelle.

Initially, I felt hopeful since Psychic Michelle had come highly recommended by an acquaintance who claimed to have received an amazing message from her dad through Michelle. Yet visiting in the home of this lovely lady now had me feeling more skeptical than anything else. I had to admit that what the woman sitting across the table was telling me didn't make a lot of sense.

After some friendly chitchat, Michelle had begun our session simply enough.

"You do a lot of walking, don't you?" she asked.

That was true. I did prefer to walk to errands in my neighborhood instead driving. I found the activity a relaxing respite from the demands of my day. And as such, walking became my exercise for both mind and body. I nodded, yes.

"Sometimes you walk late at night, too," Michelle continued. "Really late."

I nodded again.

Michelle doodled on the yellow pad in front of her as she continued to deliver her message. "Your mother is worried about you being so fearless. She's telling me that she walks with you to keep you safe."

That came as news to me. I always thought I walked alone. "Uh, really?"

"Yes. Don't you hear her footsteps?"

"Actually, no."

Michelle looked up from her yellow pad and straight into my eyes. "Don't you feel her presence? A cool breeze perhaps?"

I shook my head, no.

"Well, she's there," Michelle stated with confidence. "Check for signs of your mother next time you're walking."

The highly recommended psychic then tossed a few more tidbits my way. To further confirm her abilities, she gave me the names of some other family members, both living and deceased, with what seemed to be a generic fact about each. Then, from her kitchen, I heard a timer bell ring. End of session.

"Well, that was disappointing," I thought as I drove home that May afternoon. I had expected a different type of message than the one I received. I had hoped to hear about what a devoted daughter I had been or maybe a "thank you" for taking such good care of my mother during her many years of illness. But that she walked with me? Now, that just sounded like baloney, plain and simple.

Still, holding on to one remaining shred of hope, I listened carefully that night for the sound of my mother's heels hitting the pavement next to mine. Silence. I looked for her shadow, sniffed for her perfume, and braced myself for the breeze of her spirit passing next to me. None of my senses cooperated. Furthermore, I had the same sense I had each night when I walked in the dark—feeling completely and utterly alone.

Weeks passed and summer arrived, bringing with it my favorite walking conditions: clear, star-filled skies and the lingering warmth of balmy nights. I had already taken my evening constitutional when I realized I had neglected to mail an important letter. I checked the clock—almost midnight. No matter, I thought, the mailbox is just a quick four blocks away on the well-lit corner behind the library. I'd be there and back in a flash. I grabbed the envelope, my house keys and my cell phone and was on my way.

Feeling particularly brave, I decided to cross through the library parking lot instead of staying on the sidewalk. Though the lot was dark, it was still, with no one else in sight. Yet I wasn't halfway through my shortcut when I realized how mistaken I'd been. From behind a nearby hedge I heard the low rumble of male voices. Then I heard the crack of a bottle against the pavement. I quickened my step and snapped open my cell phone. A tall young man stepped toward me, broken bottle in hand. Ha, I thought, as light glinted off the bottle's sharp edge, a lot of good a cell phone will do me now.

The young man stepped into my path. "Hi there," he slurred.

I answered, "Hi," prepared to barrel past him.

"Where ya goin'?" he asked, raising the bottle.

I didn't answer, but kept on walking. My back was straight and rigid, yet inside my guts had turned to mush. I continued walking anyhow, keeping my steps determined and forceful.

Now the young man and I were just inches from each other. I could see a rip in his T-shirt and smell the beer on his breath. This is it, I thought. I pushed my luck too far this time. Yet just as I was about to plot my next move, the young man dropped the bottle to the ground.

"Aw, just forget it," he said. Then he returned to his drunken buddies as they waited behind the hedgerow.

I quick-stepped through the lot and from somewhere past the bushes, I heard one of his pals snicker. "Ha ha, man, what's wrong with you? You afraid of her?"

Needless to say, I made it home that night in record time despite my shaking legs. Once I climbed up my steps and locked the front door behind me, I relayed the details of my close call to my husband Bill.

He could only shake his head. "Someone must have been looking out for you tonight."

Yes, someone had been looking out for me that night. And I knew exactly who that someone was.

~Monica A. Andermann

The Angel
Held My Head

You're not safe because of the absence of danger,
but because of the protection of God.
~Author Unknown

was supposed to be in the car with my father. We were running late to pick up my mom from her job at the hospital and I didn't want to go. I had other plans in my head — a grand adventure that involved heading down the street to my best friend's house. I begged my dad to let me stay home with my brother. Finally, he gave in.

I went in through the front door, snuck out the back, grabbed my tricycle, and hit the street. A moment later, I heard a strange noise behind me. I turned to look over my shoulder and panicked as I saw my father's car backing out of the driveway towards me. I was too low to the ground for him to see me, and it was too late for me to move out of the way. As the car backed on top of me and I started to fall to the road, I saw a bright light descend from the sky. Seconds before my head hit the ground, I felt hands cradle it. I don't remember much after that point, just different people surrounding me at different moments.

I was told later that my twelve-year-old brother and a family friend lifted the car, a heavy station wagon, off me while my father pulled me out from underneath. After being lifted out, I looked at everyone around me and noticed how frightened they all looked. I was unable to speak but desperately wanted to tell them, "It's okay! Don't be scared. The angel saved me. I'm going to be okay!" Later, after being flown to the children's hospital, my mother met me as I was wheeled inside. I remember her wide-eyed face, full of tears, and yet I felt oddly at peace. She rushed over to me as tears continued to stream down her face. I looked at her as she held my hand and said, "Don't worry Mommy, the angel held my head."

The injuries I received that day were rather extensive. The car tire rolled over my leg at the knee and tore it open from side to side. It required hours of surgery and more than a hundred stitches to close. I had abrasions and bruises all over my body, except for one place; my head was completely uninjured. The doctors told my parents they were in complete disbelief. I should have had a concussion or fractured my skull, but they couldn't find even a scratch on my head.

Many times in my life I have encountered stumbling blocks and begun to doubt my faith in God. Every time, I have thought back to that day when the angel held my head. Many memories from that time in my life are faint, but that one is distinct and vivid—the warmth and comfort I felt during a time when I should have been afraid.

~Kitrina Brian

Sara's Angel

Make yourself familiar with the angels, and behold them frequently in spirit;
for, without being seen, they are present with you.
~St. Francis of Sales

My heart pounded as the nurse pushed the needle into my infant daughter Sara's delicate skin. I cringed as she let out a piercing cry.

"You'll need to keep a close eye on her for a reaction," said the nurse. I bit my lip and nodded. While I understood the importance of immunizations, I was leery about this one—her first DPT. Years earlier my son had experienced a frightening reaction to the DPT shot, screaming inconsolably for several hours. Since immunization allergies are often genetic, I feared Sara would have the same experience.

I let out a deep breath as Sara quickly relaxed and dozed against my chest. I paid my bill and carried her to the car. Strapping her into her car seat, I smiled at her sweet, contented expression. It looked like we dodged the bullet this time.

Halfway home, I heard a quiet moan from the back seat and glanced in the rearview mirror. While Sara's rear-facing car seat made it hard for me to see her clearly, I could still tell she was squirming. Suddenly, she let out a high-pitched wail. My stomach fluttered and my chest tightened.

Maybe she's just hungry or wet, I thought. The wailing soon turned into shrieking. This was not hunger or a wet diaper. I knew this cry. She was reacting to the DPT shot. I sighed—we were in for a long haul.

Sitting on my bed and holding my screaming daughter, I called the doctor's office. They agreed that Sara was likely having a reaction to the shot. I was told the crying might go on for a while, but that she should be fine and I should call back immediately if new symptoms arose. They would mark in her chart that she couldn't have the pertussis vaccine again.

Sara's shrieking went on and on. It didn't matter what position she was in, she still screamed. It was an awful, gut-wrenching sound. Her breath came in short gasps and she became hot and clammy. I tried to put her pacifier in her mouth but she wouldn't take it. Slumping with her in a rocking chair, I tried to soothe her with a bottle but she wouldn't take that either. All I could do was hold her and try to console her with words she probably couldn't even hear. I cried with her, our tears mingling. My aching arms begged for relief, but I was terrified to put her down for even a moment. I felt completely helpless.

Finally, after what seemed like an eternity, Sara began to settle down. As her breathing slowly returned to normal and her screaming turned to quiet whimpering, I placed her gently on her back in the middle of my bed and collapsed beside her. Eventually, she stopped crying altogether and fell sound asleep. We were both exhausted.

I stroked her hair and grateful tears spilled from my eyes. "Poor Sara-bear," I said, using my nickname for her. "What a rough day you've had." Her cheeks were flushed and tear-streaked, and her nose congested from crying so hard. But the crisis was finally over and I could relax. As the sun set, the room slowly darkened, I closed my eyes and let fatigue overtake me.

Within minutes, my eyes popped open. The bottles! I forgot to make the bottles! Each afternoon, I would prepare Sara's bottles for the next day. With all the commotion going on, I'd forgotten. I looked at my daughter. She slept deeply, her face serene and her lips moving in a sweet, sucking motion. Yawning, I kissed her forehead and reluctantly went to the kitchen.

I lined up seven bottles on the counter and dropped a plastic liner into each one. As I opened a can of formula, I thought I heard a soft voice say, "Sara." Thinking my husband was home from work early, I quickly turned to greet him but no one was there.

"That's strange," I said. I leaned against the counter for a moment, listening, but heard no sound except the gentle hum of the refrigerator. I shrugged and returned to my task, thinking I must be more tired than I thought.

Suddenly, I sensed a firm, seemingly audible command. "Check Sara!" I immediately stopped what I was doing and bolted to my bedroom. I gasped and rushed to Sara's side. Her face and lips were pale blue, her bright, blue eyes wide open. The peaceful look she'd had minutes before had turned fearful, and her small fists clenched and flailed in the air. Her mouth was open but she wasn't breathing. Hands shaking, I immediately turned her over, and vomit poured out of her mouth.

"Breathe, Sara!" I cried. "Please!" After what seemed like minutes but was probably only a few seconds, Sara whimpered, coughed and let out a high-pitched wail. This time, I didn't cringe when I heard it but sobbed with relief. I held her tightly as she calmed down and I felt her rhythmic breathing.

I looked towards the ceiling. "Thank you," I whispered.

I try not to think about what might have happened that day if I hadn't received the mysterious order to check on Sara at that exact moment. I will never know for sure if I audibly heard that command or if it was somehow planted in my mind. But I believe with all my heart that I know who gave that order—her guardian angel.

~Annette McDermott

Protective Wings

A guardian angel walks with us, sent from up above,
their loving wings surround us and enfold us with love.
~Author Unknown

t wasn't until a few months ago, when I wrote a story about an angelic intervention, that I realized I have had such a presence watching over me all my life. As my story unfolded on my computer screen, a rush of recollection came with it—memories that I'd always brushed away as the product of an overactive child's imagination. Yet, in retrospect, I see now that I was always enfolded in protective wings. Over the years, a beautiful blue-eyed lady has always appeared to me when I needed her the most. Then she'd disappear, sometimes for almost a decade, before reappearing again.

I was six or seven the first time I saw her; although I suspect she hovered over me from birth. That day was a warm spring one. I was walking up and down the alley behind our home looking for treasures in the melting snow. Sometimes I would find pennies or nickels that someone had dropped, or discarded soda bottles that I would sell. The proceeds would enable me to buy a small bag of candy that I could savor, sometimes over the course of a week.

Back then, my brothers and I often roamed within a five-block radius of our home. We knew each and every neighbor, and never worried about danger since we could run into any house and ask for help. In fact, I often used that lane as a shortcut to school. It was a safer world then, free from the predators that seem to lurk everywhere today—or so we thought.

That afternoon I was excited to find not just a dime, but right near it, a quarter! It was a fortune to me. I was ecstatic and clutched it to my chest as I raced home.

Distracted with thoughts of all the treats I could buy, I hardly noticed the car slowly approaching. It wasn't until it came to a stop beside me that I halted in my tracks. I was still grinning about my lucky find, and the driver smiled back. Friendly and unafraid, I waved at him and he leaned over to open the passenger door.

"Hi, sweetheart. What have you got there?" he asked, motioning to my tightly clenched fist.

I opened my palm to show him the still muddy coins and he squinted.

"Come closer," he urged. "I can't see."

Without thinking, I approached the vehicle. When he patted the seat next to him, I slid in without hesitation and extended my hand.

"Lucky girl!" he said in that exaggerated, condescending tone some adults have when speaking to children. "What are you going to do with it?"

"I'm going to buy candy!" I announced with excitement. "Lots and lots of candy!"

"Well, now," he chuckled, reaching into his pocket. He began to jingle coins the same playful way my father did when he was about to give me a few spare pennies. "Let's see if we can find something more to add to your piggy bank," he continued. He produced a handful of silver coins and began digging through them, palming four more quarters and putting the rest of his change back. He thrust the money towards me, but just out of my reach.

"It's getting chilly, sweetheart. Why don't you close your door?" he suggested huskily.

It was then that I noticed his other hand stroking himself in what my mother referred to as a private "bathing suit area." I remembered how she told me that a lady should never touch herself there or let anyone else touch her. His breathing became heavier and I grew nervous.

"Close the door!" he repeated in a breathless tone. This time it sounded like an order.

I was frightened. Always taught to obey my elders, I reached for the handle to do as he said, even though it felt wrong.

"Get out!" I heard another voice insist. "Get out and run!"

I whipped my head up to see a young woman with penetrating azure eyes standing outside looking at me. Although her features were clear, the rest of her was bathed in an illuminating light, almost as if the rays of the sun were peeking out from behind her. Yet the brightness wasn't blinding as it radiated from her shimmering body.

Hypnotized, I felt the man's hand clamp onto my shoulder. The woman's face hardened with anger. I heard him gasp and shout in terror as she shoved an arm past me to slap his fingers away. He bellowed as if burned.

"Run," she urged again, propelling me into action.

I scurried across the seat and fell to my knees at her feet, noticing they were bare. My forgotten money spilled to the ground in my haste to get away. I wanted to retrieve it, but the woman barred my access with her ankle.

"Home!" Go home!" she commanded.

I picked myself up and tore up the lane towards my house, my short legs pumping against the heaviness that comes with fear. Behind me, I heard the man scream again, and I turned to see the same light that had silhouetted the lady emanate from his windows for a moment, then dissipate. He started his car and it roared down the narrow alley, splattering water everywhere. When he got to the bottom of the hill, he turned left and disappeared.

I looked around for the woman, but she was gone. The alley was empty. From where I stood, I could see the glint of silver on the ground. It was my money. Even though I no longer felt threatened, I didn't go back to get it, no matter how big a windfall it was to me. The lady had told me to go home. Even at my young age, I understood that she had saved me from something awful and I felt compelled to obey her.

I never told my parents what happened that day. Part of me was afraid I'd be punished for getting into the car, while another was sure no one would believe me about the woman. In any event, I remained quiet. By bedtime, even I wondered if I'd imagined it all—until I slid my hand under my pillow and felt something cool and smooth. My hand closed around it, and in the moonlight that streamed through my bedroom window, I saw the quarter I'd found, dropped and abandoned earlier that day. Next to it was the dime.

A week later, I overheard my parents whispering about a bad man that had been caught hurting children in his car and I shivered. I wanted to speak, but couldn't. A sense of safety washed over me and I felt warm again. Although the memory of that day faded as I grew, at that moment I knew in my heart that I truly did have a guardian angel that had interceded on my behalf.

~Marya Morin

Always Watching Over Me

We all have a guardian angel, sent down from above.
To keep us safe from harm and surround us with their love.
~Author Unknown

During the two years I was a kindergartner, I lived with my maternal grandmother. At that time, my mother, who'd had me when she was a student at university, was finishing her degree after a long illness.

Because she could not be with me, she told me that I had a guardian angel who was always present, always watching over me. I imagined him looking like a man with cropped hair and filled completely with yellow, bright light. Always a few steps ahead of me, never out of reach. Only I could see him.

On my way home, I would often have long conversations with him, changing my route so I'd be able to talk to him longer without anyone interfering. He always listened patiently, gently nodding his head at whatever I was saying. His presence made me feel secure. Sometimes, when I was concentrating or playing with other children, I would forget that he was there. But he never left my side, whether I was aware of him or not.

When my vivid imagination took over and transformed my short walk to kindergarten into an adventurous voyage, he would watch me with an amused glimmer in his eyes. He'd stand by calmly while gnomes hiding in the shrubbery lining the sidewalks jumped out and tried to untie my shoelaces. He'd wink at the butterflies dancing around my head, turning into tiny fairies who whispered stories in my ear and tickled me under my chin. And there were the cats and squirrels who loved him and begged him to pet them while reporting the latest gossip about teachers and students. Then they would go on fighting with each other over who had the bushier tail.

There was only one place on my way to and from kindergarten where I had to snap out of my reverie: the crosswalk. It did not have a traffic light. We had been taught early on that it was important to look left and right before crossing the road at that spot.

One sunny afternoon on my way home, I reached the crosswalk, eager to go play with my neighbors. I was alone, having been held back by one of my teachers. The other children had already gone home, and the streets and sidewalks were empty. Well, almost. To my left, a lone minivan approached, but it still seemed far away. I confidently stepped into the crosswalk and started traversing the road.

In the middle of it, the sound of the minivan's engine caught my attention. Turning my head, I saw the van was much closer than I had thought. It was driving straight towards me without slowing down, only a few feet away. Puzzled, I looked at the driver to check if he had not seen me. A burly man with a cold expression on his face, he held my gaze. In my terror, I froze. I did not understand why the driver would not slow down when he had clearly noticed me in his way. He made no motion to swerve around me.

Suddenly, two strong hands gripped my upper arms and yanked me back. Flying through the air, my feet did not even touch the ground. In the blink of an eye, I found myself back on the sidewalk, standing securely as if I had been waiting there all along. No one was near me. My mind whirred.

The minivan rushed by me and over the spot where I had paused just a heartbeat ago, seven feet from where I stood now. It did not stop. The driver did not even look back to check whether I was okay. Uncomprehendingly, I watched him disappear around a bend in the distance. Cold shivers crept over my skin.

Still, no child or adult was to be seen anywhere. Nobody had witnessed what had happened. The sun blazed down on the asphalt, unchanged. I stood motionless at the edge of the road, staring into the distance.

And then, warmth came over me. Slowly, it seeped through every muscle and every bone, filling my body completely, until the shock had melted away. Bright, yellow light flooded through me and made the air around me shimmer.

My stupor vanished, replaced by a calm sense of clarity. With the kind of faith and certitude you only find in small children, I knew this had been the work of my guardian angel. For once, I could not see him, but I felt his presence. I felt his love reach out for me.

Gradually, the warmth and light faded away. I smiled and gave a silent "thank you" to my guardian angel.

My mother had been right: He was always watching over me.

~Gina Gutzwiller

My Grandfather's Gift

Physical strength can never permanently withstand
the impact of spiritual force.
~Franklin D. Roosevelt

The painful pattern began when I was only eight years old. Men leave me. My father, an only child, died at the age of thirty-nine after battling cancer for months. My mother's family lived on the other side of the ocean; her father had already passed away. I was left with only one man to love me: my paternal grandfather, Isaac.

He was a small man, mostly bald, with a beatific smile. His signature way of greeting his grandchildren was to wrap his arms around us and inhale deeply. Every time he saw me, he tried to breathe me in. As a kid, I didn't really appreciate this strange ritual. But as an adult, I began to understand. I only visited my grandfather every couple of weeks. He was memorizing me, using all of his senses to keep me near to him during our time apart.

When I was twenty-two, my grandfather passed away from a stroke just days before my winter break from college. My mother broke the news to me over the telephone. All I could say was, "No." No, I would not accept this devastating news, even as the tears poured down my cheeks. No, I refused to accept his loss. My boyfriend and I had recently split up, and now the only man left in my life had also deserted me.

It was a little before Christmas when I drove from Maryland to

New York for the funeral. As his closest living relative, I was charged with identifying the body. The shriveled, drawn face on the corpse looked nothing like my gramps; Isaac had had a soft, gentle face with dancing brown eyes.

A few short weeks later, I returned to the off-campus house where I lived for the start of the spring semester. That very night, I was awakened around midnight. The door to my bedroom opened with a soft creak. I sat straight up in bed and asked, "Who's there?"

A large man I had never seen before stepped into my bedroom. He dove onto my bed, punching me repeatedly in the face and head. I attempted to scream for help. Like the stuff of nightmares, my scream only came out as a high-pitched squeak, no louder than a mouse. No one heard me. No one came to my rescue, although several of my housemates were home at the time.

I fought hard, with everything I had. But it was useless. Soon blood was pouring from my nose. I was no match for this man's size and strength. When he wrapped his hands around my throat and cut off my air supply, blackness closed in around me. Just as I began to lose consciousness, he suddenly let go.

I realized this man planned to rape me, and it seemed he preferred me alive. Once he demonstrated the ease with which he could kill me, I gave up the physical fight. Articles of my clothing were removed, piece by piece. Now he was in no hurry. But my own mind raced ahead. I had no doubt whatsoever that after he raped me, he would kill me. I had to stop him, but I had no idea how.

At that moment, a voice spoke quietly in my ear. It was my grandfather's deep, reassuring voice, filled with kindness and love. My grandfather, who had suffered beatings at the hands of the Cossacks, had lived through pogroms in the *shtetls* of the Russian Empire, had escaped across Europe with a single suitcase, delivered the words I needed. His voice whispered to me, telling me exactly what to say to the man who was hurting me. "Tell him you wish to be his friend," my grandfather urged me. "Tell him if he stops now, you will have respect for him."

And like a miracle, the words worked. My attacker stopped. He allowed me to put my clothes back on. He allowed me to get a tissue to clean the blood from my face. Then he sat next to me on the edge of my bed and talked for almost two hours. He let me turn on a light so I was able to see his face clearly. He told me his name, where he lived, where he worked, where he had recently been incarcerated. He told me he had seen me through my window on his way to work earlier that day. And although he had smoked PCP at the end of his shift, he remembered which house I lived in as he made his way back home. I simply listened. Like a friend.

Eventually, after I gave him my phone number, he got up to leave. I walked him to the door, said goodbye, locked the door behind him, and called the police. The officers insisted on summoning an ambulance and transporting me to the hospital, although I felt perfectly fine. Waiting on a gurney in a hospital corridor in the middle of the night, I finally caught a glimpse of myself in a mirror. I was unrecognizable. I had a black eye, a large lump on my forehead, a bloody nose, two split and swollen lips, a cauliflower ear, and a ruptured eardrum.

My physical injuries healed fairly quickly. The post-traumatic stress disorder was another story. There are still nights, even three decades later, where I wake up in a panic, sweating, sometimes screaming, my heart pounding, imagining a stranger in the room with me. But in these moments of terror, I am able to find comfort. I remember how my grandfather whispered his miraculous words into my ear. And I know he is up there still, his dancing dark eyes watching over me. Thanks to him, I survived. Thanks to him, I lived to meet my beloved husband. Thanks to him, we were able to create our two amazing daughters. My grandfather's gift made all this possible.

~Liz Rolland

My Two Guardian Angels

Angels are principally the guardians of our spirits. Their function is not to do our work for us, but to help us do it ourselves, by God's grace.

~Eileen Elias Freeman

Growing up, my parents told me often that I had a guardian angel. The only proof needed? My harrowing birth.

"It's a miracle that you're alive," my mom would say.

In 1987, I was born three months prematurely and weighed a terrifying two pounds, six ounces. The small hospital where I was born did not have the equipment or facilities to adequately care for me, so within hours of my birth I was flown to a bigger hospital 170 miles away. I remained in the NICU for weeks. At first my tiny body needed a respirator and feeding tubes, but gradually my strength increased. My lungs developed, I gained weight, and finally my parents were able to take me home. As the years passed, I grew into a healthy, happy little girl.

"You are so special," my dad would say. "You must have an angel up there taking careful notice of you."

But who was my guardian angel?

My grandma Auden believed my angel was her mother, who had passed away nearly three decades before. She and her mother were extremely close, and when she died Auden sunk into a deep depression. She cursed God. She had two babies to take care of but could barely summon the energy to get out of bed. Then, one night she came downstairs and saw her mother sitting at the piano, smiling and serene, her fingers dancing across the keys. Her mother had always loved to play the piano, and Auden was immediately filled with joy. From that moment on, her faith in God never wavered. While she missed her mother, she felt at peace. Her mother's spirit was still with her, guiding her and keeping her safe. And when I was born, Auden prayed to God and to her mother to keep me safe, too.

Then suddenly, when I was in kindergarten, my beloved Auden passed away from a heart attack. She was only sixty—she had been so vibrant and full of life, and her death rocked our family. I missed her terribly. I began writing to her in my journal, keeping her updated on the details of my life. If I had a problem or felt alone, I asked for her help. Sometimes she visited me in my dreams and we would hug and talk. And sometimes, during waking hours, I would sense an extra warmth in the room and I would feel her presence there with us—particularly when I visited my Gramps, who never remarried and still slept with her sweater under his pillow.

The years passed. I graduated high school, then college, and then I was accepted to a master's degree program in Creative Writing. I moved halfway across the country, from my California hometown to the middle of Indiana—and ironically, I felt Auden's presence even more acutely. She had grown up in a small Indiana town, and she and my Gramps had met, married and spent many years in the Midwest. I began feeling her presence with me, not as the grandmother I had known, but as the young woman she had once been.

During my second year of grad school, I fell in love with Thomas. He was kind and thoughtful, and our relationship progressed quickly. At Christmas, we got engaged. Gramps gave me Auden's engagement ring, which he had carried around in his wallet all these years. "I know she would want you to have it," he said. I was so moved, so overwhelmed, that I burst into tears. Looking at her sparkling diamond on my left hand made me feel closer to her than ever.

But as the holiday season gave way to the new year, I began to feel unsettled. Thomas seemed to have anger issues and I never knew when he would have an outburst. One time when we were driving, he got so angry that he slammed the steering wheel with his palm and the car swerved violently across the road. Another time he got angry and threw his shoe against the wall so hard it left a mark. He never hit me. And he would always calm down the next day and apologize.

One night in March, I felt unbearably alone. Thomas was upset about something, fuming and stomping around the living room, indifferent to my attempts to calm him down. So I slipped away into the bedroom and curled up under the covers. I loved Thomas, but I didn't recognize the man I had fallen in love with in that man raging in the other room. I couldn't imagine living like this for the rest of my life, anxiety eating up my insides. But I also couldn't imagine my life without Thomas. We shared many wonderful memories, and we had promised to love each other always. I had accepted Thomas's proposal; I had accepted Auden's ring. I closed my hand around it so the diamond dug into my palm.

I didn't want to disappoint Thomas or my family or Thomas's family or our many shared friends. Moreover, I couldn't bear to let down Gramps and Auden—they had entrusted me to carry on their love story with this gorgeous ring they had picked out together more than a half-century earlier.

Suddenly, my loneliness dissipated and I felt like I was being cradled by a warm, calming presence. A voice whispered in my ear, "You could never let us down. You deserve so much more than this. This is not okay, and it's not going to get better."

I started crying. Auden was with me, my guardian angel. I told her that I loved her and missed her so much, and that I knew she was right. Marrying Thomas, who my gut kept warning me against, would not honor Auden and Gramps—it would dishonor them and their beautiful relationship.

The next day, I broke off my engagement. It was the hardest thing I have ever done, but I believe it was also the best decision I have ever made. My life opened up again. My anxiety melted away and I could breathe deeply.

I kept wearing Auden's engagement ring for a few more months, until I graduated and moved back to California. Whenever I felt scared or missed Thomas or worried about the future, I looked down at that small sparkling diamond—beautiful, yet strong—and it gave me courage. Apart from my premature birth, that was the darkest period of my life. But every day, I felt Auden with me, telling me and retelling me that I deserved a truly amazing love, filled with gentle kindness, with no room for doubt or fear.

I gave the ring back to my Gramps for safekeeping until I find the real person I am meant to marry. I have faith that he is out there and I will find him. After all, I have two guardian angels looking out for me.

~Dallas Woodburn

The Purest Gift
of Love

*There is no surprise more magical than the surprise of being loved. It is God's
finger on man's shoulder.*
~Charles Morgan

A few days before Valentine's Day, my father blacked out while at home. My mother called an ambulance to transport him to the hospital, where they promptly admitted him. Since I lived so far away, Mom and I agreed that she would phone every morning with updates and I would call her in the evening to see how her day went.

When she called the day before Valentine's Day, she sounded downhearted. "Is something wrong?" I inquired.

She took a deep breath then softly said, "Your dad's dying." I felt dizzy as I tried to grasp the meaning of her words. Originally, the doctors had predicted Dad would leave the hospital in a few days, not die in it.

"Can't they do anything?" I asked. "I thought they said he would be discharged soon."

"That's before they discovered that his heart is failing. Life support is all they can offer him now, and you know how we feel about quality of life," Mom said. And of course, I agreed.

Mom explained that as Dad's condition had worsened, he had drifted in and out of consciousness all morning. Tomorrow they would transport him to hospice care where he would be made comfortable for the next few days or weeks, depending on how long he lasted. She promised to keep me apprised of the situation.

During the afternoon, my father remained unconscious as his condition deteriorated. However when I made my usual checkup call that evening, my mother said that Dad had miraculously made a comeback. Unfortunately we remembered the dreaded last comeback, as my family called it, for we had witnessed it many times before. Right before certain loved ones had died, they had become lucid.

Of course, Mom recognized this phenomenon and had summoned the family for this blessed moment so that farewells could be said. I asked to speak to Dad and promised to make it quick since he had visitors.

Thankfully, Dad recognized my voice. He told me he loved me; I told him I loved him and we said goodbye. That was it. As soon as I hung up I regretted the abrupt goodbye. I had so many things I wanted to say and it hurt to know I had lost that chance forever.

Later that evening when we talked, I had mixed emotions as Mom reminisced about the family's last visit. Dad had solved math problems, recited poems, told jokes and even sang his old college song. After the family departed, my dad, once again, lost consciousness.

Even though I was thrilled that the rest of my family had such a wonderful visit, my own last words with Dad were disheartening. I reminded myself that many people never even get to say goodbye to their loved ones. However, all the reasoning in the world didn't make up for the unspoken words I wished I had said and the deep regret that now consumed me.

On Valentine's Day, they transferred my dad to the hospice center. Though he never regained consciousness, Mom believed he had squeezed her hand to acknowledge her presence. As evening approached, the staff encouraged her to head home for a bit to shower and eat. They knew she had remained at the hospital throughout Dad's stay and reminded her that she needed her strength for the days ahead. She called to tell me she would be leaving in a little while and then she'd be back.

As soon as I hung up the phone I felt agitated. Like an echoing loop in my head, I heard the words over again, "Say goodbye to your dad; he can hear you."

Back and forth I paced, as the words raced through my head. Finally I flopped on the couch to rest. All at once I felt unbearably hot as the phrase started to repeat in my mind louder, sounding more urgent.

This kind of verbal call to action had happened to me before. I knew I had been given a precious second chance by my guardian angel.

I stood up and closed my eyes. "Dad, Dad, I know you can hear me," I said, and without a doubt, I knew he could.

As I spoke to my dad, I felt his spirit there with me along with my guardian angel as both souls enveloped me with a warm, tingling sensation that filled me with pure bliss. It's difficult to describe, but I felt as if they had protectively wrapped me in the purest love I could ever imagine. I expressed everything that I had yearned to tell my father before he left. As soon as I finished, I understood that the moment had come for him to move on. Even though I found it difficult, I told him he could go and that I would be okay. His presence dimmed as he slipped away.

"Oh Dad, I'm going to miss you so much," I blubbered. As the tingling ceased, a sense of calm washed over me, bringing me comfort and peace. I wiped my tears and waited for my mother's call.

A few minutes later the phone rang. "I'm sorry, I'm calling..." Mom choked up, unable to speak.

"It's okay, Mom. I know; Dad's gone."

It comforts me to know my guardian angel watches over me not only in times of danger, but also in times of need. Sometimes it provides much-needed guidance, courage, or a kick in the bottom to keep myself moving. How fitting that on Valentine's Day my angel blessed me with the purest gift of love, in the form of a second chance to talk to my dad and thus find peace in his passing.

~Jill Burns

A Voice in the Night

Angels are speaking to all of us... some of us are only listening better.
~Author Unknown

t was nearly 1:00 a.m. and my eyes felt sandy and heavy. I was walking through my apartment, doing last-minute mundane tasks before allowing myself to go to bed. As a single mother working two jobs, sleep was precious, and every day I counted the hours until the next time I could sink into my mattress and pull the covers over my head.

I had started my day as usual at 6:00 a.m., trying to get myself ready for work and my two girls ready to go to school and to the babysitter. Twelve hours later, I was rushing to get to my second job, having picked up both girls, fed them a quick dinner, and driven them to the next babysitter. When I finally got off at 10:00 p.m., I knew that sleep was still a few hours away. I needed to pick up the girls, get them home, listen to them tell me about their days, get them into their pajamas, and tell them a story, all while trying to avoid rushing them. They were so happy to see me!

When they were finally asleep, as much as I too wanted to close my eyes, I knew my day was far from over. Laundry needed to be done, lunches and bags needed to be packed for the next day, mail needed to be sorted and bills to be paid. A pile of dirty dishes, caked with breakfast residue, glared at me from the counter. A sticky substance on the kitchen floor halted my footsteps, and food wrappers left lying on the couch reminded me that I needed to make sure the girls ate at the table in the future. I checked my phone messages and e-mails to see if I needed to address anything important. At last, my growling tummy reminded me that I hadn't eaten since lunch. I made myself a quick snack, brushed my teeth, made sure the apartment door was locked, shut off all the lights, then collapsed into bed without even changing my clothes.

I was nearly asleep when I heard a voice. I jumped, thinking that I had been dreaming. Then I heard it again.

"Go make sure the door is locked."

I settled back into bed, comforted that I distinctly remembered checking the door. Then again: "Go make sure the door is locked."

I was beat. I was comfortable. I was positive that I had already locked the door. I nestled into my pillow.

"Get up. Go make sure the door is locked. Now."

There was urgency in the voice this time and by now I was questioning whether I had indeed locked the door. As I stood and reached my arm forward to turn on my bedroom light, the voice came again.

"Leave the light off."

I questioned the wisdom of leaving the light off. What if I tripped over some forgotten toy? What if I ran into a wall that wasn't where I thought it should be?

"Do not turn on the light."

By now I was getting irritated by the commands of "the voice," but in an effort to obey as quickly as possible so I could get back to bed, I decided to get it over with. I felt my way through the darkened living room and dining room and stepped into the kitchen to check the door.

Instead, what I saw made me gasp.

A bright flame flickered from one of the burners on my gas stove, vivid blue against the black of night. In my fatigued state before going to bed, I had forgotten to turn off the burner after my snack. I hurried to turn on a light, then quickly shut off the burner.

I slumped against the kitchen wall in both humility and awe. What if, in my stubbornness, I had refused to get out of bed? What if I had failed to heed the voice's admonition to leave the lights off?

Would I have stumbled into the bright kitchen, walked right past the glowing flame again, checked the door, and then ridiculed myself for being paranoid? More importantly, would my girls and I, along with the others in the apartment building, have survived that night?

Then, and even now, I thank the angel whose voice in the night saved my family from a fiery fate.

~Randi O'Keefe

Touched
by an
Angel

Divine Messengers

Bad Patch

Angels have no philosophy but love.
~Terri Guillemets

The spaghetti had extra Parmesan just the way I liked it. My mother's smiling face leaned in as she handed me the steaming plate. Her cooking had been an attempt to mend my broken heart

"I have extra Parmesan if you need it." Her voice trailed off as she headed back to the kitchen. She added the next words casually. "He wasn't right for you, you know. Your man is out there somewhere."

The hot tears welled in my eyes. The wounds were still fresh and the sting of my disappointment still burned.

The sound of running water almost drowned out yet another overused expression that I was tired of hearing. "You just gotta get right back in that saddle. You're in a bit of a bad patch. That's all."

Bad patch? My entire twenties had been a bad patch in terms of love. It was overrun with the weeds of awkward blind dates and soured relationships. Either I was running from love, or more recently, it seemed it was running from me.

My life was complete in every other area. I had a fulfilling career. My strong friendships and family ties had bolstered me as I sailed the rough seas of my relationships. But now I was one week shy of my thirty-first birthday. My inability to find love and create my own family hurt. I felt like a failure: a lonely failure.

The physical pain that accompanies heartache is sharp. It cuts into your heart and constricts your throat. Tears bring temporary relief. But, the pain needs to be ridden out. Sleep helps, too. So, I decided to spend the night in my mother's guest bedroom that evening. I turned in early, eager for sleep.

I was in a very deep sleep when I felt the blankets pulled up over me. A warm pair of hands lovingly soothed the bedding over me, untangling it and shifting it up over my shoulders. I could feel the deep concern as this person leaned over me, peering into my face.

My eyes were heavy but I managed to open them slightly. It was just enough to see a woman standing over me. I closed my eyes quickly due to the brilliant light that filled the room. My eyelids fluttered as I squinted in an attempt to get a better glimpse. The woman was wearing a white dress and the moonlight shimmered upon her in such a way that she seemed to cast her own light. Her light hair flowed around her face, but I couldn't feel the breeze rippling against her. My eyes closed again just as she leaned in closer to my face. At this point my dream state must have taken over because her warm hands seemed to melt into my body as she smoothed the blankets over me.

"Oh, Michele… you are loved." Her words were full of deep compassion as she whispered them into my ear.

I padded into my mother's kitchen the next morning. My mother had her head in the refrigerator, obviously eager to cook up yet another remedy for my broken heart.

"I must have really worried you last night," I said as I grabbed a coffee mug. "You haven't tucked me in like that since I was a kid."

"Tucked you in?" She emerged from behind the open door of the refrigerator, hands full of eggs and butter.

"Yeah, didn't you come in the guest room last night? And, where did you get that pretty white nightie…." My eyes affixed to her red flannel nightgown. "And, your hair was…" I looked at her graying hair that was up in curlers, a bit confused.

"I didn't come into your room. I turned in early and slept like a ton of bricks." She patted my head as she headed for the stove. "I always sleep better when you're home, hon."

"Well, someone came in. Maybe you don't remember. Maybe you just came in to check the light?"

She cracked an egg. "Weird dreams again?"

My heart was lighter that day. That woman's hands had simply shooed away the darkness that had been eating away at my heart. I knew I had seen the lovely woman. I had felt the blankets move around me and I certainly felt the hands as they moved over me. More importantly, I had sensed her soothing comfort. Whoever she was, this woman had cared enough to show her love and compassion for me. She had also ignited hope.

After that day I approached dating differently. I was a woman who had an angel around her, an angel that loved me fiercely.

Within a year, I had met the love of my life. I had gotten back in that saddle, as my mother had suggested, and bravely went on yet another first date. I knew he was the one immediately, as did he. It was a whirlwind relationship and we were married a year later. Today, we have been married ten years and we have two wonderful young daughters. I realize now that all of those dead ends to love were just God's way of putting me on ice. I was being saved for a rare love that only a few are lucky enough to find. And, I will never forget the woman who had paid me a midnight visit. I believe she serves as a reminder that everyone has that kind of love watching over them every single day.

~Michele Boom

Night Fall

Prayer is the medium of miracles; in whatever way works for you,
pray right now.
~Marianne Williamson

sat straight up and listened intently. I heard only my two little ones' peaceful breathing and the gentle tick of a clock beside me. An almost tangible presence of someone or something had woken me with an insistent message: "You need to pray. Now!"

"Lord, I have no idea who is in need of prayer at this moment, but You do. Please, be with them. Protect them from danger. Send Your angels to intervene."

As my brain fog began to lift, I thought of my paratrooper husband. He'd been out of town, planning and executing a military training exercise. But he should have jumped and safely landed long before now. The division's entire night operation should have ended hours ago.

"Pray for your husband!" I heard.

I fell to my knees, sensing imminent danger for the man I so loved. "Dear Lord, please don't let Scott die. Certainly, You have other plans for him, for our family. Whatever his need, please protect him; protect those with him. Please, Lord, surround them with Your heavenly hosts."

After several minutes of prayer, I felt the most beautiful peace—truly a peace that surpassed understanding. The intense urging subsided. The sense of crisis passed. I glanced at the clock: 3:10 a.m.

I climbed back into bed. And with peace still cradling me, I was actually able to roll over and get a few hours sleep before my little ones awoke.

No sooner had I opened my eyes that next morning than the phone rang. It was my husband.

"Scott, are you okay? Did everything go all right with your jump?"

"We had some fog. But I had a great jump, one of my softest landings ever."

"Really? Everybody else's jumps go okay?"

"Yeah, all good. But something strange happened after everyone jumped. Major Townsend and I had to take the rental car to the edge of the drop zone and wait for the heavy equipment to land."

"Oh?" I knew "heavy equipment" meant the tanks, the Humvees and the pallets that the unit also had to practice dropping by parachute.

"Yeah, it was dark and hard to see. Major T and I were waiting outside the car when all of a sudden the wind shifted. We heard the rustle of chutes and a split second later saw the silhouette of a huge tank falling straight toward us! We jumped in the car and floored the gas. But that heavy drop hovered right over our car. It didn't seem like we would get out of there before the tank landed on us. Yet somehow it floated past us and landed just yards away."

I felt like my heart jumped into my throat, but the peace I felt the night before quickly returned.

"Scott, thank God you're safe. I figured something happened. I was woken from a deep sleep with a message to pray for you. You don't happen to know what time that was when you were trying to outrun the tank?"

"Wow—yeah, I do. Just about 3:00 a.m."

~Kathleen Swartz McQuaig

Danger Over the Mountain

We all have an angel who offers us protection... they're always beside us, for when we need direction.

~Author Unknown

With blue skies and endless fields of wildflowers in sight, it was a perfect day for a hike up the Grand Tetons in Wyoming. We chose an advanced hiking trail that promised to take us to a mountain peak and down the other side. The sign at the bottom of the mountain estimated an eight-hour round trip hike going up one side and down the other. By the look of the dotted line outlining the trail, it seemed the bulk of the hike was on the one side of the mountain. Once we made it to the top, it would literally be all downhill from there.

Our little group consisted of my mom, dad, twelve-year-old sister, and me, seventeen at the time. As novice hikers, we were excited about the challenge. Except for my mother, we were all avid cross-country runners, so the distance didn't intimidate us.

Off we went. Beauty surrounded us. Summer had brought with it numerous wildlife sightings. Groundhogs scurried alongside the path. Birds chirped overhead. Gorgeous green fields stretched around us. Time passed quickly as we chatted and sang songs as we hiked. Periodically, we stopped for a snack and chatted with people we met along the way. As we ascended past different lookout spots, most hikers turned around and went back, claiming they didn't have time for the full loop. We pressed on.

As we turned a corner, a surprise awaited us. Snow! It was the middle of August. Wearing T-shirts and shorts with our hiking boots, we had forgotten to take into account that it would be much colder at the top of the mountain. Thankfully, the hours of hiking had us dripping with sweat and oblivious to the cooler weather. Coming from South Georgia, seeing snow in the summer caused us to dance with joy. We only saw it for the rare beauty it presented, never once considering the danger it might pose to us as hikers.

Continuing on, the path got more narrow and rocky. Staying on the path was a must, because stepping on the slippery rocks would be dangerous. The hiking trail map showed of a beautiful pristine mountain lake at the peak. Our conversation turned to this anticipated sight, as our legs grew more tired with the hike. Just a little bit longer, we kept encouraging one another. Soon we would be sitting beside the lake enjoying the lunch we had packed. After a much-needed rest, we would climb over the mountain and then quickly down the other side, ending back in the parking lot. Soon we would be able to proudly proclaim we did the advanced trail, together as a family. Just a little bit longer...

We all gasped at the same moment when we came over the hill and saw the lake. The map was right. This was God's country! The ground leveled. And in the middle of this plateau-like field, was the clearest, cleanest body of water I had ever seen. We ran to the edge, peering straight to the bottom of the calm waters. No one else had ventured to come this far. We felt like we owned the land. As far as the eye could see were other smaller mountain ranges, green grass spotted with snow, massive boulders jutting out, puffy white clouds, and spotless splendor!

The crisp cool air refreshed us. After dipping our hot sweaty feet into the frigid waters, we felt ready to tackle the remainder of the hike. We could see that the trail went over the top of the mountain and continued onward. Out of nowhere, it seemed, a lone hiker appeared on the top of the mountain coming over the peak.

He had an ice pick and a backpack, impressing us, as we assumed he was an experienced hiker. Since it had been a while since we had seen anyone else, we paused to meet the stranger as he stopped to rest on a smooth rock near us. We chatted about the gorgeous day and the glorious lake. Then we moved on. Calling out to us, we returned to hear his last words. He cautioned us that the other side was much steeper and very slippery. Without ice picks, he advised, we would likely slip and fall. He begged us to turn around and go back the way we came. Then, he got up and proceeded on the trail.

As we considered his advice, we groaned. To go back the way we came would mean we might not get back before dark. With all the majestic sights we had seen on the way up, we were curious to see the other side of the mountain too. My sister and I urged my parents to forget about his advice. "Come on," we pleaded. "Let's go. We can do it!"

My parents huddled, discussing the pros and cons of finishing the trail or turning around. Finally, my father announced we would turn around and go back. Grudgingly and with much complaining, my sister and I gave a heavy sigh and followed.

Shortly after heading back down the trail, we ran into some hikers on their way up. We asked them if they had seen the hiker who was warning people not to proceed over the mountain. They shook their heads. The were certain they had seen no one for at least an hour. But that couldn't be, we exclaimed. The path was so narrow. He wasn't that far ahead of us. There was no way they could have missed him. He had no other option to get down the mountain but to stay on that path carved out between the ice-covered rocks.

We kept asking hikers as we descended if anyone had seen him. Again and again, no one had spotted a man matching such a description. Weird. The next day, as we ate breakfast in our hotel, getting ready for another adventure, my father opened the local newspaper. He groaned. Two experienced hikers had died the previous day. They had continued over the top of the mountain, slipped and fallen hundreds of feet down the icy, jagged mountainside to their death.

Reality hit—that could have been us. Had we not run into that hiker, we would have surely met our Maker. To this day, we know in our hearts that for whatever reason God chose to spare our family. We thank Him for sending an angel, dressed as a hiker, to warn us that danger lurked right around the corner.

~Ashley Thaba

When God
Came Close

When my spirit was overwhelmed within me, then You knew my path.
~Psalm 142:3

The new position looked too good to pass up, and the move it would require to the beautiful Maine coast didn't sound too hard to take either. The only question left was, was it the right thing to do?

It was the late summer of 1999. After thirteen years of serving in the same church a short distance from both the Green Mountains of Vermont and the White Mountains of New Hampshire, we started to feel like it might be time for a change. Dale, my pastor husband, was feeling burned out from pastoring a congregation that was growing too large for one pastor but lacked the finances to hire additional staff. Our children were about to enter the sixth and third grades—if we were planning to move any time in the near future, this would be the best time to do it.

So when a feeler came for an interview with a church on the Maine coast, the timing seemed perfect. We made the necessary arrangements and made a mini-vacation out of the trip. We fell in love with the area, the pulpit committee fell in love with Dale, and the kids actually thought they wouldn't mind attending the little country school we visited. They even began to relish the thought of having such a big yard and barn to play in, along with the possibility of new pets! When the chair of the pulpit committee called a few days later to announce that they would like Dale to be their next pastor, we felt pretty sure our answer would be yes.

Only one thing was missing: reassurance from God that this truly was a new call upon our lives. We decided to take a few days to pray, think, and talk about it before we gave the church in Maine our excited "Yes!"

We visited Dale's mom for a long weekend. Dale and I took advantage of the Sunday off and the free childcare to attend a worship service in Dale's old home church. Both of us prayed for God to please give us a sign so we'd know for certain what we should do.

I'm not sure what I was expecting from God during that morning's worship service, but it certainly didn't happen. The sermon was dry; the music was uninspiring. As the service ended, both Dale and I stood up to leave feeling disappointed in the whole business.

As we stood next to our pew gathering up our things to leave, a bearded man I'd never met before walked up to us. "Oh Dale, it's you! I didn't recognize you from the back of your head." It was a man Dale hadn't seen or spoken to in over fifteen years. "I was standing, praying at the back of the church," he continued, "when I saw a shepherd's crook appear over your heard, so I knew you were a pastor. God gave me a message for you. He said to tell you that the renewal and revival He wants you to be involved in is not at the coast but in the mountains. And God says He knows you're tired and He's going to send a Peter or a Paul to help you. That's it—I don't know what it means, but that's what He wanted me to tell you." And then the man walked off.

And Dale and I dropped back onto our pew and I started to cry. Not because I didn't like the words that I had just heard, but because God had come so close in the words of this person who had no way of knowing our situation.

In that instant our choice was clear. We were to stay in the mountains and not move to the coast. We went home and called the little church in Maine to tell them that we would not be coming. In less than a year, God sent a student intern to help Dale out—and believe it or not his name was actually Peter. And we stayed in that church near the mountains for another twelve years—until God made it very clear to us that it was indeed time to go. But that is a story for another day!

~Laurie Carnright Edwards

Message from Michael

*God not only sends special angels into our lives, but sometimes He even
sends them back again if we forget to take notes the first time!*
~Eileen Elias Freeman, The Angels' Little Instruction Book

A few years ago, I received a surprising gift. It was a book
written by a woman who communicated with angels. It
was sent to me by a friend—a marine turned cop turned
prosecutor in one of the nation's largest cities. The prosecutor and I worked together on the board of a real estate association.
We had never shared a conversation about angels.

The book was an easy, enjoyable read. When I finished reading it,
I felt the need to send it to my daughter who lived in New York City.

On a rainy Thursday afternoon, shortly after my daughter received
the book and had read it, I was at an appointment with my acupuncturist. My left knee was the problem. It was inflamed and nothing
seemed to help alleviate the discomfort. X-rays showed no muscular
or skeletal issues.

My acupuncturist used a specialized protocol to help relieve her
patients' intolerances due to food, environmental and emotional causes.
She treated me for an allergy to grain/gluten. At the end of our visit,
she told me that I should get my thyroid checked and drink more
water. I thought it curious that she would give me that advice, as we

had not discussed anything to do with my thyroid or hydration. Her words to me seemed almost an afterthought.

I said I would try to drink more and that I would look into getting my thyroid checked. It's always been hard for me to hydrate through the day. I am not often thirsty, and I have to consciously work at remembering to drink. I also didn't have a doctor to call on at the time. I might have let her counsel slide if not for a phone call a few minutes later.

As I was about to leave the office, I gave my acupuncturist the prayer from Archangel Michael that appeared in the book I had just read. My acupuncturist is a friend and a very spiritual person. She was grateful for the handwritten prayer.

No sooner had I climbed into my car to drive home than my cell phone rang. I was still in the office building's parking lot, the car not yet started. I answered the phone when I saw it was my daughter calling from Manhattan.

"Mom, I am having the weirdest day!" she exclaimed.

"How so?" I asked.

"A friend and I decided to have a cultural day. We were at the Metropolitan Museum of Art when my friend said her feet hurt so much she had to leave at that very moment. I said, 'Right now?' She told me she couldn't stay an extra minute. And because her feet hurt, we decided to take a cab. I had some errands to run, so she let me off between 61st and 62nd Streets at Broadway. It felt like I no sooner got out of the cab than this woman came out of nowhere and was in my face. She said she had information for me. I told her I didn't have any money for her," my daughter explained.

"What did she want? Did she look crazy?" I questioned.

"No, she was just regular looking. She looked like she could be a mom from New Jersey. She looked Native American and she was wearing a Cartier watch."

"Did she want money?" I asked.

"She said, it was alright that I didn't have money for her. She said she had a message for me from the Archangel Michael."

Complete silence filled the space between my daughter and me.

"Mom, are you there?" my daughter asked.

"Yes, I'm here. I'm listening," I replied.

"She said the Archangel Michael told her to tell me to get my thyroid checked and to drink more water. I said, 'My thyroid? Are you sure? I don't feel like my thyroid is a problem.' She said it could be me or someone close to me.

"Mom! Are you laughing? Why are you laughing? I'm serious," my daughter said in frustration.

"I know you're serious," I said gathering my composure. "I'm laughing because I just left my acupuncturist. She just told me to have my thyroid checked and to drink more water. Also I gave her the prayer from the Archangel Michael from that book I sent you."

"Oh," she quietly replied.

My daughter had her conversation with the stranger in Manhattan at the same time I had my conversation with my acupuncturist.

We marveled over the synchronicity of this event, this miracle that occurred over a distance of 270 miles.

In getting my thyroid checked, I discovered that my body was having a problem processing cheese and grain. Those items created mucous in my system that was affecting my left knee. When I eliminated those items from my diet, the heat and swelling in my knee disappeared. As for my thyroid—it indeed was sluggish. Supplements to my daily regime helped it to healthy functioning.

Thank you, Archangel Michael!

—Lorraine Bruno Arsenault

Meeting Jimmy

Grandchildren are the dots that connect the lines
from generation to generation.
~Lois Wyse

n 2007, while I sat in a session at a writers' conference, the speaker, author and psychic Victoria Laurie made a comment about deadlines: "It's not like you can tell your editor that your Uncle Jack died and you need an extension." Everyone in the room laughed; I felt a chill run down my spine.

After the session, I found Victoria in the hall and approached her. We said hello to each other, and I began. "It's really strange. I did have an Uncle Jack who died, and I used his death to gain a much needed extension on a book deadline." Victoria smiled at me. I continued: "Worst of all, I didn't go to the funeral, but used that time to finish my book."

"He was *your* uncle. I wondered where that comment came from," she said. Victoria went on to do a brief psychic reading and answered my nagging question about how my uncle felt about me using him like that and not attending his funeral. He found it funny, by the way, and was glad to be of service. He had said to us many times throughout his life, "Come visit me while I'm alive, not after I'm dead."

Victoria had said she wouldn't be giving any psychic readings during her weekend at the writers' event. She was there as an author and faculty member, not as a psychic. I felt honored to have received my mini reading with my uncle.

At the conclusion of the conference events a few days later, many of us who attended agreed to meet at the hotel bar for a farewell drink. As I approached our small group, which was spread out at tables in the bar, I saw that Victoria had "save me" eyes. I asked her and another woman if I could join them. Victoria seemed pleased, the other woman unhappy. Turns out, the woman was trying to finagle a reading out of Victoria. My joining them ended that conversation.

After a few minutes, and without comment, Victoria shifted seats at our table and sat directly across from me. She said: "Your family is incredibly loud."

I laughed. "You have no idea how loud my family can be." I thought of all the family get-togethers that were always a raucous mix of laughter and fights.

"No, your family on the other side," Victoria said. "They're not giving me any choice but to share the messages they have for you." She proceeded to do a forty-five-minute reading that centered around my paternal grandparents, primarily my grandfather, someone I'd always wanted to meet.

Do you know the party game where you're asked: "If you could have any three people to dinner, living or dead, who would they be?" My first choice was always my grandfather. The other two might change, but my grandfather was always first. I was born in February 1966, and he died in December of that same year. I was the only grandchild in our family with no memory of the man. I'd always felt some draw to know or understand him.

I'd spent a lot of my life wondering about my grandfather and asking about him. No one offered much information. My own father hadn't been close to his father and he rarely talked about him. Grandpa died many years before my grandmother, but whenever anyone brought him up around her, she'd get teary-eyed, so we all avoided talking about him around her. The bits and pieces I managed to pick up and put together over the years didn't really fit together well. And yet, I felt this drive to know him that I could never explain.

At the end of the psychic reading Victoria said, "Now I know why I had to come to this conference. I rarely attend conferences, but something urged me to be here for this one. Obviously, it was to connect you with your grandfather." Chills ran down my spine again.

When the reading was over, I looked around. The woman I'd "saved" Victoria from was nowhere to be seen. For a second time that weekend, I had been honored with a reading from Victoria Laurie. I was so pleased she had come to the conference, too. I bought her another drink and offered to pay her reading fee. She accepted the drink, but refused payment.

When I got home from the conference, I called my father's sisters. I shared what I had learned from the psychic author. My aunts, surprised I knew so little of him, in turn told me many more stories about my grandfather. I'd always thought of him as James, but it turns out he wasn't so formal and went by Jimmy. As other stories came out, I discovered that I had taken on many of his traits over my own lifetime, down to the clothes I liked to wear and the foods and beverages I preferred. Like him, I spent years as a heavy smoker (a habit I've since kicked!). In the process of trying to know him, I'd become a musician, as he had been. Unlike him, I turned the hobby into a career for about ten years and got to travel the world, something he always wanted to do. He worked in the train yards his whole life, but never traveled more than 100 miles from his home.

Among the many things Victoria shared with me that Saturday night was the fact that my grandfather now spent a lot of time looking over my shoulder, especially when I write. He likes when I write humor pieces the most. And, he is incredibly proud of me. At this moment, like the moment when Victoria shared the sentiment, a wonderful flood of love and emotion rushes over me accompanied by light tingles throughout my body. The difference today is that I know that rush of feeling is an energetic hug from my beloved and long-departed grandfather, Jimmy.

~Gregory A. Kompes

My Bookstore Angel

He shall call upon me, and I will answer him: I will be with him in trouble;
I will deliver him, and honour him.
~Psalm 91:15

had just gotten out of the hospital a couple of days earlier and wasn't walking well, so when a steady drizzle began, I stopped at a secondhand bookshop. Quickly perusing a shelf, I picked up a hardcover book and dropped into a rocking chair, the large plate-glass window right behind me. I felt weak and tired.

In a minute, a man came out from behind the cash register and approached me. He was short and dressed conventionally in black slacks and a plaid shirt.

"How are you doing?" he asked cheerfully.

"I've had better days," I answered. "I was just in the hospital and want to try to walk every day and build up my strength."

He nodded as if he understood. "What's that you're reading?"

"Oh, I found a Jane Austen novel—*Pride and Prejudice*." I realized I should buy something for the privilege of sitting here and looked for the price of the book—$7.50. With looming medical expenses, I didn't know if I could afford that.

The clerk smiled in response and walked to the shelves, where he began examining the books. A couple of minutes later, he returned, a slender volume in his hand. "I have exactly the book for you," he said with a great deal of enthusiasm.

He handed the book to me, exchanging it for the novel already in my hand at the same time. Strangely, at that very instant, the sun came out.

He had given me a book of poetry—and I don't enjoy poetry very much. Still, I saw its price was under $2 and decided to buy it to thank the store for the moment of rest and the refuge from the rain.

"Great," I said, and paid the clerk.

Later, at home, I looked at a couple of the pages. Really, nothing moved me, but I'd saved a few dollars. When I picked up the book to put it in one of my bookshelves, a printed page fell out. What was this?

It was a copy of the 91st Psalm.

I had tried to pray in the face of my illness. Exhausted, I'd prayed as much as I could during my hospital stay, and I'd prayed in similar terms since I'd gotten home. I wanted to be well again, if God would consent to it. If God, in fact, would step in and heal me with His power.

I read out loud:

He that dwelleth in the secret place of the Most High
Shall abide under the shadow of the Almighty.
I will say of the Lord, He is my refuge and my fortress:
My God; in him will I trust.

I liked the elegance of the words, and I liked the sentiment very much.

I had read the psalm before, but I didn't know it that well. I put the book of poetry away, took the page to my "comfort" chair and carefully read through each line of the psalm.

I had prayed, as I said, but I didn't really know how to pray. This reading of the psalm seemed right. I decided I would say the 91st Psalm out loud to myself every day, three times a day.

When I got up from my chair, I felt a little less exhausted. And I remembered how I'd come by this piece of paper—it had been hidden in a book that the bookstore clerk had said was "exactly the one" for me.

I wondered if he'd known what I'd find, but I doubted it. I figured it was some great coincidence. Or maybe something arranged by God, who had heard my earlier prayers after all.

I began to say the psalm before every meal and then before I went to bed as well.

As the days went by, I said the psalm so often that I had memorized the words, and the words began to change something within me. I didn't heal all at once, but I started to have hope that I would get well and gained a little more energy.

Although I often still felt afraid, I now had periods when I felt a trust in Him.

On a beautiful fall day, I felt inspired to return to that bookstore store where I'd been given the gift of such encouragement, maybe even transformation. On this occasion, I wasn't too tired to walk there and beyond, so I stopped in the store when I returned from buying a few groceries. A middle-aged woman stood at the cash register behind the desk and we greeted one another.

"I was hoping to find the gentleman who sold me a slim volume of poems," I said. "He gave me something I've enjoyed more than I thought possible."

"Gentleman?" she said, seeming puzzled.

"Yes, the clerk, a man." I gave her a bright smile of assurance.

"I'm sorry, but no one else works here except for me. I'm glad to hear though that you liked the book." She still seemed a little thrown by my statement but obviously wanted to be polite.

"Maybe he was here before your time—a couple of months ago..."

"No," she said. "This store is mine, and I'm the only one who works here except for my daughter on Saturdays."

That, obviously, was impossible.

"He's kind of short and not overweight but not too slender." I remembered the clerk very well and I couldn't understand how the woman didn't know who I was talking about. "Maybe a friend of yours came in one day to do you a favor."

"No," she said. "We've never had a man working in here even as a favor. Could you be thinking of some other bookstore?"

She and I looked at one another, both of us knowing that this was the only secondhand bookstore in our neighborhood.

We couldn't come to any resolution, so I left.

Because thou hast made the LORD, which is my refuge, even the
Most High, thy habitation;
There shall no evil befall thee, neither shall any plague come nigh
thy dwelling.
For he shall give his angels charge over thee, to keep thee in all
thy ways.

That night, I had a dream. In it, I saw the man who'd given me the book as clear as day. He was smiling. "I knew the book would help you," he said. And I understood that God had sent a helper to answer my prayers.

I'm still, today, continuing to heal, with lots of help both from medical professionals and from alternative healers. I know, at least, that I'm on the right road. And from having little faith before I found my psalm, I have transformed to one who has a certain knowledge.

~Gail Hayden

Maybe, Under Some Circumstances

The angels are the dispensers and administrators of the divine beneficence toward us; they regard our safety, undertake our defense, direct our ways, and exercise a constant solicitude that no evil befall us.
~John Calvin

will call my encounter a she. And you, if you wish, may call her an angel.

An angel? A ghost? A spirit? Or the residual energy that can connect us with another after the self is gone? I truly don't know. It's hard to determine absolutes in a story like this.

What I am sure of, however, is that she was a definite presence, that I was her emissary, and that she sent through me an indelible message that spared me the unexplainable, unnamable grief of losing a child.

She had no wings and no halo, no quivering air mass and no sound of bugles. Nothing of the stereotype—just a gentle, urgent presence that lifted me from my troubled vigil and sent me on one of the most contained, most important missions of my life.

For the first decade of my three children's lives, I was a single mom five days a week. My husband came home on Friday evenings and left again on Sunday after dinner.

Our home was large and old, a late-1800s masterpiece we were restoring as time and finances allowed. It was four stories and had a huge cement and stone cellar. The second level had hardwood doors, floors and trim in each of the large, spacious rooms as well as floor-to-ceiling windows throughout. The bedrooms, similarly large and spacious, and with floor-to-ceiling windows, were on the third floor. That floor also had a bathroom with an exterior door that strangely opened onto a porch along the front of the house. The fourth level was a full walk-up attic space where we were planning to create a loft.

It was magnificence awaiting restoration, but it was old and it groaned and shivered with its age. It was a very vocal house and I was not the bravest of young women. So during the night, as the creaks and whispers seemed to portend skulking intruders and all manner of beings with nasty intent, I tried to sit vigil with a book on my lap.

One night, I had fallen into a cramped, uncomfortable sleep on the couch. This was not something that I had done before. When fatigue won out, I always climbed the winding staircase, checked on my three little ones, and then, my heart and mind clenched in foreboding, slipped into a shallow sleep.

This night, however, as I lay asleep on the couch, I felt a gentle, persistent pressure—curing my normal nightly agitation and wrapping me in a state of perfect calm and silence such as I had never before felt. I lay hushed and unmoving, holding to the perfection of the moment. I was consumed.

And then, gently creeping under my awareness, I saw my name.
Robyn…
Robyn…
I rolled onto my elbow and my book slipped to the floor.
Robyn…
I could feel her message and I could see her message, but still there was no sound. There was only the perfect calm and silence.

"You will need a cold, wet cloth. Put it on the little one's head. Call for an ambulance. Strip him and wrap him in a fresh sheet and his blanket. Call Mary to stay with the others. You will have to follow the ambulance in your car."

I moved with an absolute certainty. I wet a cloth and, upstairs, I found Declan thrashing and rasping. His breath came in short puffs of agony; his little face glistened from an effort almost beyond his endurance and from the intense heat of his body.

I called 911 from my room, wrapped him in a fresh sheet and then telephoned my neighbour Mary. She answered immediately. "It's Robyn," I said. "Declan needs to go the hospital."

"I'll be right there," she said. "I got up a bit ago. I wasn't able to sleep."

I stood at the door with my son in his sheet and a light blanket, the cool, wet cloth draped across his head. There was no panic—just a calm, understood urgency. Mary arrived, as did the ambulance.

"I'll follow in the car," I said to my neighbour. I couldn't tell her how I knew that the rules prohibited me from riding in the ambulance.

In the hospital, I waited until dawn. "We were very lucky. Much longer and he wouldn't have made it. Convulsions…" The doctor shook his head. "Very lucky," he repeated.

Declan stayed in hospital for the next two days and then was released on a Friday. His father, Martin, who had driven home to be with us, collected him.

"Who's the Blue Lady?" he asked me.

"The Blue Lady?"

"Yes, Declan said that she swept the hotness off him with her broom. And she wrote him a letter."

"A letter? What about?"

"His name. He said that it was his whole name, Declan Liesen Gerland. But he's three. He can't read yet. Can he?"

I paused. "Maybe," I said. "Maybe. Under some circumstances. Maybe, just under some circumstances."

~Robyn Gerland

Spiderman

Angels are not merely forms of extraterrestrial intelligence.
They are forms of extra-cosmic intelligence.
~Mortimer J. Adler

t was official: none of the warm birthday wishes I'd received from friends and family had stuck. I was twenty hours into what was quite possibly the worst birthday I'd ever had.

My closest friends were 3,000 miles away, and my local ones had erratic schedules and weren't great about making plans. As a result, there would be no celebration. A few of them forgot the day altogether, which hurt more than I wanted to admit.

My workday had been fraught with stress and disappointment. The tomatoes in my deli sandwich at lunch had been spoiled. I'd had to brave the crowded rush hour supermarket for some groceries. The local mass transit had been fouled up for both the morning and evening commutes. In fact, that morning I had to spend money on a cab to get to work because my bus never showed up. After work, it had taken me three hours to go seven miles because the scheduled buses had never appeared. To boot, as I'd waited at one bus stop, someone had shouted horrible things at me from a passing car. For the grand finale, during the last leg of my journey, I had to deal with the passive-aggressive bus driver who never stopped at the curb. Instead, she always glared at the people waiting, zoomed past us, and stopped all the way down the block, so we all had to run to board the bus. It happened every single night, so it wasn't a mistake.

The message was loud and clear: a happy birthday wasn't happening this year. I wasn't even going to get a moderately pleasant birthday. I'd given up on it. It was late, I was exhausted, and all I wanted to do was go home, have some ice cream, and go to sleep.

After I got off the bus, I put my things down on a bench for a moment to grab my house keys and readjust my bags of groceries. As I tended to my belongings, a middle-aged man walking up the block stopped dead in his tracks and stared at me.

Oh great, I thought. The day's been awful enough, but I suppose street harassment will be the cherry on top, won't it? I didn't live in the sort of place where people approached you on the street with a friendly greeting; they usually had more sinister motives. As a result, I always refrained from talking to strangers and I was suspicious of them by default. I tried not to look at the man and busied myself with my groceries. He didn't move.

"Be careful," he said. Even though I had headphones on, I could hear him loud and clear. "There's a spider. Black widow."

Unlike a lot of people, I'm not afraid of spiders at all. In fact, I won't let anyone squish a spider in my presence. I'll always scoop it up and carry it outside. But the words "black widow" were enough to make me jump, and something in the man's tone of voice told me that he wasn't joking. "What? Where?" I asked, and recoiled.

"Right there. Look!" He came closer and pointed under the bench, where, sure enough, a bulbous, threatening arachnid sat in the middle of its web. There was no mistaking it. This particular black widow also happened to be right under my groceries on the bench, and, more ominously, very close to my leg. I knew that widows never hurt humans unless they felt threatened, but I also realized that I was on the brink of inadvertently provoking this one. If I moved even a little closer, I would disturb the web, and that would warrant a bite. "Be careful," the man said, and walked away.

I kept one eye on the spider, backed away and gave my backpack and grocery bags a few shakes to ensure that I hadn't inadvertently picked up an unwanted companion. As I crossed the street, I realized how odd the situation had been. The man had been walking in the opposite direction and it was dark; there was no way he could have spotted the spider or its web from that vantage point. And yet, he'd known it was there, and he'd known it was dangerous. How? Maybe it didn't matter how; it just mattered that he had.

I felt better as I continued my walk home. My angels never forgot me, bad birthday or not. Saving me from a black widow bite had been their present to me.

~Denise Reich

The Messenger

An angel can illuminate the thought and mind of man by
strengthening the power of vision.
~St. Thomas Aquinas

was the advertising manager for Harveys, an independently owned chain of department stores in Nashville, Tennessee. Although I received a decent salary and benefits, it was a middle management position with lots of responsibility and little authority. Frustrated and burned out, I clung to my illusions of safety, security and survival. My marriage was not in great shape, either.

In early June, my husband and I left on a vacation. As we pulled out of our driveway, my inner voice softly announced, "You're going to meet someone."

The days passed quickly. We left Fort Myers, Florida and headed for Jacksonville. The trip had been pleasant but uneventful. Again my inner voice said, "You're going to meet someone." Frustrated, I chose to ignore it because there was only one more stop, a brief visit with one of my favorite people — my Uncle Bob. He was working on a temporary job assignment in the small, sleepy southern township of Jesup, Georgia. How could I possibly meet anyone of importance on this trip?

We arrived in Jesup around noon, and Uncle Bob suggested lunch at a place called Suzie's. Located on a quiet, graveled side street, it was a down-home kind of place with country cooking and hearty meals served family style.

The aroma of fried chicken welcomed us and we found three vacant ladder-backed chairs at the end of a long table. On my left sat an elderly couple who appeared to be in their eighties. They were busy filling their plates, but the woman eagerly passed bowls to us as she chattered away. She seemed grateful for the company and wanted to talk. For the past three weeks her husband had been in the hospital and lunch at Suzie's was their first outing in months. She talked; I listened. Her husband interjected a few words, but mostly he ate in silence. What choice did he have?

I glanced across the table at Uncle Bob and shrugged, disappointed at finding myself trapped in a non-stop monologue by this stranger who claimed my full attention.

When the meal was finished, my husband and Uncle Bob pushed back their chairs from the table. At the same time, the couple rose. A man of few words during the meal, her husband walked around the table and introduced himself to the three of us.

As the rest of my party started toward the cash register, I remained seated, searching for my purse under the table. When I sat up, the stranger was bending down by my chair. He looked me right in the eyes. "Be good to yourself," he said softly.

"I try to be," I said, smiling up at him, somewhat confused.

"I'm serious, little lady; be good to yourself," he repeated.

A chill ran up my spine. I turned to look for his wife, but she had disappeared. We were alone.

The man walked around to the other side of my chair so that his back was to most of the room. Then, he leaned down until his mouth was close to my ear.

"I don't want you to worry," the stranger said with studied calmness, "no matter what happens. Don't be anxious or get depressed. And don't be concerned about money." He let that sink in and continued. "Just remember, there's no trouble you can get into that God can't get you out of. Just let go of it, and let God handle it. He will take care of you."

Again, he paused as if for emphasis. "Remember, no matter what happens, you're in good hands."

With that he turned and walked quickly away.

For a moment, I sat stunned and immobile with a chill spreading from the top of my head to the soles of my feet, knowing in my heart, I had met a messenger from God. I looked around for him, but the man had disappeared. His message didn't make sense to me at the moment because I wasn't particularly concerned about money. Apparently he knew something that I didn't.

When I arrived home the next day, I called the office to see how things were going. To my dismay, I found the company I worked for had been sold.

By August, at the age of forty-two—for the first time in my life since I began working at the age of fifteen—I was unemployed. If that weren't enough, that major event was followed by a close encounter with a hurricane, a serious illness, a divorce and major concerns about money.

During all these difficulties, I kept hearing the stranger's words, remembering the promise, knowing God doesn't create the challenging situations in our lives, but He does provide the strength and Grace to get us through them, and most importantly, to learn from them.

Over the last several years, along with millions of other people, I've learned there is no such thing as security in the outer world. Any of us can lose our job, our mate, our home, the peaceful nature of our existence, our wealth and even our health. Yet, our hearts, minds and spirits can store up an unlimited abundance that no place, person or thing can take from us—strength of spirit, faith, and love, our own inner peace, awareness and wisdom.

The message was not just for me, it is for everyone—for now, for always, in all ways—"You are in good hands."

It's something you can take to the bank.

~Karen Trotter Elley

A Penny from Heaven

Put a penny in your shoe, you'll have good luck all day through.
~Old childhood chant

"It will take a miracle to get me through this day," I muttered, dragging myself from my bed. Fumbling through the bathroom cabinet drawer, I located a thermometer and put it in my mouth. Oh, no. A shade over 101 degrees. I stared at my flushed face in the mirror, and fought back an urge to burst into tears.

No doubt about it, I was doomed! At thirty-nine, I'd received a tentative acceptance to UCLA's graduate school of social work. Whether I'd actually be admitted might hinge on my scores on the Graduate Record Examination. This day was the last possible opportunity for me to take it. I'd have to drive to Westwood, thirty miles north on crowded freeways. The previous day my doctor had diagnosed a kidney infection and prescribed antibiotics.

"Get plenty of rest," she'd cautioned. "Don't stress yourself."

Great advice, I thought, struggling into jeans and sweatshirt and slipping on a pair of loafers. I promised myself I'd try to remain calm.

As I chugged up the I-405N, I realized I'd have to pull over somewhere along the way. One of the symptoms of my ailment required frequent pit stops.

Oh, no, I fretted. How would I ever make it through a four-hour-long examination?

At that moment I realized that my husband had left for work without handing me my lucky penny. From the time we'd met at a community college twenty years earlier, this had been our little ritual. Before every test, every job interview, every negotiation, from buying a used car to leasing an apartment, Bob would hand me a penny. And I'd put it in my shoe for good luck.

We'd always believed that it was double luck, too, if the penny had been found. When I was around five, Grandma had told me that if I found a penny it meant that somebody in heaven was thinking of me and wishing me well. So we kept a jar of found coins in the kitchen cupboard, ready for any challenging occasion. It would seem strange, indeed, to take this test without a penny in my loafer. Especially since I'd been sick and had no chance to study or review. It had been fifteen years since I'd taken this exam, and I'd heard there had been major changes. I'd have to rely on dumb luck and plain old faith that I could do it.

A few miles before the Wilshire Boulevard exit, I pulled off the freeway and searched for a service station.

Last chance, I thought. I hurried inside, used the restroom and then scampered back toward the entry.

Wait, I thought. I better get some juice.

"Drink liquids frequently," my doctor had said. "You don't want to become dehydrated."

I hurried back to the refrigerated drinks section. As I reached inside for a small container of orange juice, a chill enveloped me, head to toe. Unlike the chills that had accompanied my fever, this one didn't make me shiver, even though I could see my forearms were covered with goosebumps. I felt suddenly elated, as if I could levitate and simply float back out to my car.

Oh, good Lord, now I'm delusional, I decided, shrugging. Then somebody tapped my shoulder. I'd heard nobody approach, but surprisingly I wasn't startled. I turned slowly.

"Miss?" A young man dressed in white slacks and a medieval-looking gold-embroidered tunic stood beside me. Though he looked as if he were headed to a joust at the Renaissance Faire, he didn't seem threatening or combative. Instead, he wore an expression of kind concern.

He gazed into my eyes for a moment, and then glanced toward my feet. "Look down there," he whispered. "I think you'll find something you'll need."

Before I could reply, he swung around and headed out the door.

I looked at the floor and spied a single copper penny. I picked it up, shoved it in my right loafer, plunked down some money for my juice and headed back to the parking lot. I wanted to thank the oddly-dressed young man. My benefactor was, to my dismay, nowhere to be found.

Somehow I managed to get through the examination without any need for a sudden run to the bathroom.

That night, when Bob came home, he grabbed me and gave me a big hug.

"I'm so sorry," he murmured. "I forgot to give you your penny this morning before I left for work. And you feeling so miserable too."

"I feel better," I replied. My fever actually had broken by the time I'd arrived home, I explained, and then I launched into an account of the day's events.

"Dressed like a medieval jouster?" Bob's eyes crinkled at the corners.

"Well, it's the seventies and people wear anything they want these days," I said. "A few months ago you escorted me to a party in your Nehru jacket and love beads." I giggled, remembering how dashing he'd looked as I removed my shoe.

"Look, here's my lucky penny." I handed it over to Bob, who peered at it for a moment.

"Do you know what this is?" He raised an eyebrow, studying the coin more closely.

"Sure, a penny."

"Not just any penny," he replied. "It's a 1925 wheat penny. What's more, it looks in near perfect condition. It's worth quite a lot… maybe enough to buy your books if you get admitted."

Talk about double luck! Sure enough, when I got my test results, I'd passed the GRE with high scores, and I got admitted to UCLA, a dream of mine since girlhood. Bob and I did sell the penny for enough to cover the cost of my first term's books. At long last, I began taking the courses that lead to an MSW, and my subsequent career as a psychiatric social worker and health specialist.

In June 2006 the UCLA Alumni Association honored me with its Community Service Award, for my work with the Peace Corps and other volunteer programs. In my acceptance speech at the ceremony that sunny Sunday afternoon in Westwood, I didn't mention a single word about that penny or how I became convinced that the young man at the service station that day must have been divinely directed.

I thought I knew better. This sophisticated and savvy university audience wouldn't hold with superstition.

I'm not particularly superstitious myself, and I do understand about post hoc fallacies. Because a rooster always crows before sunrise doesn't mean that his crowing causes day to break. So because I'd stuffed a found penny in my shoe, doesn't really mean that's why I passed the GRE, sick as I was. Or does it?

Now I wonder if perhaps I should have told my story. There's always the chance that if I'd told it as it really happened, just as I have here, that somebody else might come to believe, as I still do, that I'd been given a penny from heaven.

And that the "somebody" who'd been thinking about me in heaven that day surely had been an angel.

~Terri Elders

Touched by an Angel

Miraculous Healing

61

Angels and Nurses Both Wear White

You should never feel alone, there's always someone to turn to—
it is the guardian angel, who is watching over you.
~Author Unknown

Some years ago, I slipped in the shower and hurt my back, or so I thought. I managed to go to work, but as the day progressed so did my pain. Thankfully it was Friday. I went straight home from work and developed a fever, along with muscle stiffness. Throughout that night my fever went as high as 105 degrees.

I was going through a divorce and miles away from anyone who would make me soup, get me medicine, or hold my hand. By Sunday I knew I had something far more serious than the flu. I could barely move and my fever was raging. I called a co worker whose brother was a chiropractor for advice. Luckily, he had a friend over who was a medical doctor. This friend asked me only one question: "Can you touch your chin to your chest?" When I replied no, he immediately told me to get to the hospital. He would call ahead and meet me there. Having no idea what he suspected and dizzy from the fever, I slowly and carefully drove across town to the hospital.

I was given the royal treatment when I arrived, as if everyone knew what the doctor suspected. Everyone but me. After a few tests and one extremely painful spinal tap, they suspected meningitis. Signs reading

"RESPIRATORY ISOLATION" were taped to my door. Then the doctor came in, asking who to call and who was my next of kin.

I had no one. No family in Florida and my own parents were 1,200 miles away in Massachusetts. Sometime in the middle of the night they moved me to a private room where I placed the call that all parents dread. In the dead of night, on a quiet street in Massachusetts, their phone rang and before I could say a word, they knew something was terribly wrong. My mother, a registered nurse, knew exactly what I was saying. I was, in fact, dying.

As I lay there, completely alone, with only the sights and sounds of the Florida highway outside my window for company, I began to cry. Hot tears streamed down my face. I wasn't afraid of dying; I was afraid that my mother and I would never see each other again. With pain shooting up and down my body and my fever spiking at 107 degrees, I felt like this was the end. "Please put my hat on," I whispered to the nurse. She carefully put my baseball hat on my pounding and sweaty head, and sat down next to me. "I don't want to die with my hair like this." I smiled. She nodded and smiled back at me.

She carefully replaced the warm compresses on my forearms that had been put there to keep the "streaking" down in my veins. My arms looked like roadmaps from the IV solution, and the warm compresses were supposed to keep the pain down.

"Think about your toes," she said. I was too tired to ask why or argue, so I lay there thinking about my toes. After several minutes she said, "Now, think about your ankles." As instructed, I thought about my ankles. After a few more minutes, she instructed me in the most patient, quiet voice I had ever heard to then think about my shins. She continued asking me to think about every body part one by one. By the time we reached my head, I felt more relaxed and even a tiny bit better. Through the window I could see the sun rising. I closed my eyes and took in a deep breath. This would be my last sunrise, I said to myself.

When I opened my eyes, I saw a priest hovering over me. "Oh great," I said. "I did die."

"No, no, no," he reassured me. "You are very much alive. I noticed your chart said Catholic, so I wanted to stop by and say hello."

The nurse was gone, and I wanted to thank her for staying up all night with me. "Can you tell her I said thank you?" I asked the priest.

"Who?" he asked, puzzled. He said he would, and left for a moment. When he returned, he patiently explained that the night nurse had not been in. No one, he claimed, had been in and no one fit the description of the lady I described.

I stayed in the hospital for three more days. I was eventually released, still with a fever, but on the mend. I never saw her again, this woman in white who held my hand, wiped my brow, and helped me deal with the pain that comes from a high fever and from missing my mother. I never got to thank her.

Some years ago, I slipped in the shower and hurt my back, or so I thought. What I didn't know was that my guardian angel was nearby and she would help me heal.

~Christine A. Brooks

62

Watched Over

Remember, Angels are both God's messengers and God's message, witness to eternity in time, to the presence of the divine amidst the ordinary. Every moment of every day is riddled by their traces.
~F. Forrester Church

awoke suddenly and sat bolt upright in bed, then immediately curled into a fetal position. Never before had I felt anything as excruciating. I writhed in pain as I tried to find a position that provided just a moment of comfort, just a second of relief from the stabbing sensation in my right side. Worse than the seventeen hours of labor I had endured twelve years earlier, worse than the migraine that throbbed incessantly for three days several months before, worse than slicing my finger with the knife while chopping carrots a few weeks ago. This was a twelve out of ten. I was in tears, hardly able to breathe.

As I rolled from one side to the other, and rocked back and forth, my medical mind went through the differential diagnosis. Was it appendicitis? A ruptured ovarian cyst? Diverticulitis? An impacted stool stuck in my bowel? I couldn't think clearly as the torture persisted, and eventually I stopped trying to figure it out. The pain seemed to move, from my flank to my right lower quadrant, from my belly to deep inside my groin. It wouldn't stop. I pulled myself out of bed and, doubled over, made it into the bathroom. Perhaps if I evacuated, the pain would cease. I hugged myself tight, hoping for relief, and sat there until I had a bowel movement. But still, the pain was intense.

Puffy-faced and red-eyed, I looked into the mirror. "What is happening?" I asked myself. "Why won't this stop?" Unable to tolerate the misery a minute longer, I called my ex-husband and asked him to take me to the hospital. Within minutes, Peter, filled with concern and confusion, was at my side, helping me into the car and rushing me to the Emergency Room. On the ER gurney, the nurse fired questions at me. "When did it start? Can you describe it? Does anything make it better? Do you have any allergies? Any medical problems I need to be aware of?" And on and on. Feeling as if I were in a trance, numbed by the pain, I tried to gain some lucidity and answer her questions.

Within minutes, the doctor was at my side telling me he suspected a kidney stone. They started an intravenous line and administered morphine. I felt a rush to my head and vomited! Peter, thankfully, was quick with the bin. I continued to pray for mercy and begged for the pain to stop, and eventually, in a fentanyl haze, it did. Feeling a momentary respite, I was whisked of to the CT scanner and the diagnosis was confirmed — right ureteral kidney stone.

The next twenty-four hours were some of the worst of my life as we waited for the stone to pass. Between episodes of intense physical suffering, I was drugged to the point of slumber. Due to the continuous administration of IV fluids, I made multiple trips to the bathroom and had to pee into a pan in search of the elusive stone, which never came. This sequence repeated several times throughout the next morning and afternoon until, without any expectation of my prayers being answered, the pain just stopped. For the entire evening, I smiled. I ate dinner. I talked jovially with the nursing staff. And then, Hank arrived! I had only met Hank three weeks before, but in that short time this fervently Christian man, a radio announcer at the community Christian radio station, had become a genuinely caring friend and my co-host on a new show.

With his cherubic grin and cheerful voice, he brought a bright shining light into my otherwise dark and dreary day. He shared with me that everyone at the station had been praying for my speedy recovery, and they were just managing to hold down the fort without me. The warmth in his voice consoled me, and for the next pain-free hour, I felt comforted and at peace. After his departure, I slept soundly until 2:15 a.m., when again, without warning and with shocking rapidity, the pain returned. Again the tears, again the nurses administering fentanyl, again the feeling of hopelessness and futility, for no matter how I moved, how I tried to escape, the pain stayed with me. It hurt so much.

When I awoke the next morning and the pain had once again subsided, I noticed, through glassy eyes, a peculiar faint white mark on my left forearm. It was not there before and I wondered if I'd scratched myself in my sleep. But it was not a scratch. It was new, but not fresh. In fact, it looked more like a scar that had always been there, like a birthmark, a part of me. I examined the mark more closely, licked my fingers and attempted to wipe it from my skin, but it was a permanent brand—two lines intersected in the shape of a cross. Slightly disoriented from my drug intoxication, I stared at it, perplexed, fascinated, and slightly freaked out, but not frightened. It made sense to me. For only the week before, a woman I'd only just met gave me a beautifully painted watercolor depicting the crucifixion of Christ with an intensely dark sky, soldiers and distraught bystanders looking upon his thorn-laden bleeding head, witnesses to the pain and suffering He endured for us. The message was clear... I was being watched over.

While the stone never spontaneously passed and I required a cystoscopy to retrieve it, the remainder of my hospital stay was uneventful, and, more importantly, pain-free.

The day after my discharge, as I enjoyed the company of a few new friends at an outdoor beach barbecue, I glanced up to the clear blue sky strewn with the most delicate wisps of clouds. Without trying to understand or analyze, I simply absorbed, with grace and thankfulness, the vision of a cross in the sky above me, identical in shape to the one now permanently adorning my arm. I asked the others in my company if they saw it too. They acknowledged that it was not my imagination—there was, indeed, a cross in the sky. For me, this made sense.

Things always seemed to happen in threes in my life. I believe things happen for a reason. I believe we are not alone during our suffering. I believe I am always and eternally, watched over...

I am a physician and a singer-songwriter, and I wrote these lyrics about the angels who are by our sides in the song "Watched Over" on my new album, *Faith*:

You never know who you'll meet on the street
What kind of message they might want you to see,
But somehow I feel I'm watched over.
You never know where or when it might be
Or who the messenger will turn out to be,
But I know that I am watched over.

~Dr. Shari Hall

Nurse Katherine

Nurses are angels in comfortable shoes.
~Author Unknown

She approached me as I entered the hospital's wide vestibule. I didn't recognize her face, but dressed in her starched white uniform, she looked every inch a nurse. She smiled. "Don't worry," she said. "Your dad will be just fine."

"Thank you... Katherine," I answered as I checked her nametag, noting both her first and last names. The friendly woman smiled again and gave me a warm pat on the shoulder. Then I watched as she turned to exit the building. Funny, I mused, after all these weeks I thought I knew all of Dad's nurses by sight.

Nurse Katherine's words had been kind. Still, as I made my way to Dad's room in the intensive care unit, I didn't feel particularly encouraged. The team of professionals that had been attending to my dad during the long weeks he had been in the hospital hadn't drawn a very hopeful picture of his recovery. In fact, only the day before, one of his doctors told me candidly that the likelihood of Dad being weaned from life support successfully this second time around was highly unlikely. "I'm very sorry," he added, then nodded and left the room.

It had been a tough road. Well into his eighties, Dad had already survived two emergency surgeries and the myriad complications that entailed. I looked at him now, as he lay prone in his hospital bed, pale and unresponsive. Hopeless was indeed the only word that came to mind.

Still, day after day, I kept vigil at Dad's bedside, often in prayer. My cousins were on board too, visiting, lighting candles in church, and offering novenas. My dad was their last surviving uncle. I wasn't the only one holding on; none of us wanted to let go of our patriarch, the final link to the older generation of our family.

The days passed and Dad remained in what I called his holding pattern, relying on life support. If it were not for his surgeon's adamant refusal to admit defeat, I suspect I would have been encouraged to disconnect the machinery to which my father's life clung.

But then one day Dad's attending physician approached me as I sat in my usual seat next to his bed. "I've just reviewed your father's new blood work and X-rays. It looks like he's turned a corner," he said. "It will still be touch and go for a while, but I think he's going to make it."

In the days that followed, Dad indeed continued to make progress, amazing the medical staff. At first he awakened, quickly becoming able to respond to simple questions by nodding his head. Shortly after, he was scheduled for a trial period off the respirator and had breathing treatments in preparation.

Then one day I arrived in the intensive care unit to find Dad's bed empty. Frantic, I ran to the nurse's station. "Can you tell me what happened to the patient in bed D?" I asked, breathless.

"I just came on duty," the nurse answered. "Let me check."

My heart pounded as she clicked the keys on her computer. After what seemed like an eternity, she turned to me. "That patient has been downgraded to a regular room in the surgery unit—number 103. Take the elevator to the first floor and make a right at the corner."

Too anxious to wait for the elevator, I sprinted down the stairs, then rounded the corner at breakneck speed—right into Nurse Katherine.

"See," she said, smiling, "I told you your dad would be just fine. Here, let me show you to his room."

Nurse Katherine and I entered the room and she greeted Dad

with a quick "hello." Just as quickly, she turned to leave. "I'll let you two visit now."

Dad shook his head. "That nurse took such good care of me in the other unit. I could tell she really cared."

My father's remark surprised me. I didn't know that he remembered anything from his time in the ICU since he had been unresponsive most the time. However, I had heard reports of even comatose patients being aware of what was going on around them while they appeared unconscious. Still, I questioned him because I had never seen Katherine on the unit myself. "Dad, are you sure this nurse cared for you?"

Dad clucked his tongue in annoyance. "Of course I'm sure. Every day she would take my hand in hers and say, 'Don't worry, you're going to be just fine.' I could never make a mistake about something like that."

I was still shaking my head when the hospital's Director of Nursing entered the room. "Hello. I'm stopping by to check in on our prized patient. Did you know that you're the talk of the hospital?" she asked. "The way you are recovering is amazing us."

"Well," I answered, "I'm sure a lot of it has to do with the good care Dad has gotten here. As a matter of fact, he was telling me now how well he was treated by one of your nurses."

"Oh really," the woman said. "Which nurse is that?"

I gave her Nurse Katherine's first and last name.

The Director of Nursing scrunched her eyebrows. "We don't have a nurse here by that name."

"Are you sure?" I asked.

"I've been Director here a long time and I know each member of our nursing staff personally. Maybe she was from a different department?"

"No, I don't think so," I answered. "Her nametag indicated RN and besides, Dad said she took care of him in the ICU."

"That's odd," she said before she left. "I can't explain it."

Dad and I looked at one another. "Odd," he echoed.

And so, perhaps some things simply cannot be explained—like how my dad defied all medical opinion to make a complete recovery, and how a mystery nurse named Katherine knew all along that he would be just fine.

~Monica A. Andermann

A Miracle Named Chloe

Miracles, in the sense of phenomena we cannot explain, surround us on every hand: life itself is the miracle of miracles.
~George Bernard Shaw

My pediatrician's voice was somber. I knew something was wrong by the way he avoided my eyes, keeping his gaze down on her chart on his desk. "Chloe's sweat chloride test results indicate that she has cystic fibrosis," he said, tapping the papers with his pen. "She will need to go to Atlanta to Egleston Hospital to their Cystic Fibrosis Unit to confirm."

As an R.N., I knew exactly what cystic fibrosis was. My mind immediately went back to one of my first patients after nursing school. Grayson was a thin man in his early thirties. He was special because he had survived a long time with CF, even though he deliberately went ten years without treatment. He wanted to live life on his own terms, and he did — going without treatment was his choice. But when I met him, he was back in treatment.

"Here is your medication," I said to him, smiling as I stood by his bed. He nodded curtly, and motioned for me to leave the paper cup of pills on his bedside table. I shook my head, new to nursing and going by the book. "I can't leave them here," I told him. "I have to watch you take them." Grayson sat straight up in bed and glared at me. "Leave the pills. I'll take them when I'm good and ready."

Flustered, I stood there for another minute before shaking my head again and walking out, pills in hand. I went straight to my charge nurse and related what had happened, expecting her to go back to the room with me to demand that he take them under our supervision. To my surprise, she burst into laughter. "Grayson has been coming here for years, except for when he took his time off," she explained. "We let him break some rules. He will take the pills. He just doesn't like to be told how or when, so we let him. It's okay. Just take the pills back and leave them for him."

I was flabbergasted, but I took the pills back and left them like she said. He grinned sardonically, and I could have sworn I saw a smug triumph in his eyes. From that day forth, however, Grayson and I became friends as well as patient and nurse. When he would leave the hospital, he would ask for me to come in and say goodbye. When he was admitted again and again over the next year and a half he asked for me to be his nurse. Sometimes he would have the nurses call me at home, and I would drive to the hospital at night and talk to him for hours. It wasn't protocol, and I am not sure that I would do that now as a seasoned nurse, but back then I was young. And I worked at a facility that liked to encourage patients to take an active role in their treatment plans, even when that meant unorthodox methods—like letting them decide when to take their meds.

"Mrs. Reames," the pediatrician interrupted my reverie, "we have notified Egleston. You can take Chloe there tomorrow morning." I nodded, my thoughts still in a whirl, and looked down at my beautiful toddler. Blond hair framed her sweet face, and her hazel eyes, identical to my own, looked up at me. She smiled. Chloe was always smiling, except when she was coughing. My heart contracted. I prayed in that instant for a miracle. I knew it would take one. I couldn't help but think of Grayson again, remembering that, in the end, his miracle did not come.

I had left the hospital for a volunteer missionary nursing opportunity in Quezon City, Philippines. Just outside of Manila, QC was a lovely, humid place and I was soon up to my elbows in patients speaking a language different from my own. I mastered a rudimentary version of Tagalog, a local dialect, and found myself giving shots for TB, working with patients who were malnourished, and seeing strange tumors and illnesses for which I felt woefully unprepared. Still, nursing there was vital and alive. I felt I was actually helping people, using my training in a way that validated and motivated me. Lost in the new experience, I was jolted back to reality with a long distance call one evening. Stepping outside of the mission house, surrounded by the albino peacocks that strolled the campus, my heart broke when I heard the voice of my best friend Betsy, a fellow nurse. "Donna, I just wanted to know that Grayson died this week. He asked for you," Betsy said, her own voice choked with tears. I could not believe it.

That night, holding my baby close, I prayed harder than I'd ever prayed before. "Dear God," I whispered, so she wouldn't wake up, "please make a miracle happen for Chloe. Please don't let her have CF. Please."

Early the next morning, my parents picked us up for the two-hour drive to Atlanta. Once there, things moved fast as we got Chloe to the CF Unit and had the test performed. After it was over, we went down to the hospital's cafeteria to have lunch and wait for the results. Standing in line with Chloe in my arms, a young man in scrubs suddenly approached me. He stared at Chloe intently. Uncomfortable, I turned to my father, who asked the man why he was staring at us. The man smiled. Pointing to Chloe, he said, "She has a halo around her head."

My heart sank. I thought he meant that she was going to die, that she would be with angels soon. My father was angry. "Please," he said tersely, "leave us alone."

The young man looked into my eyes. "Whatever was wrong with your baby," he said, "it's gone now. Your daughter is healed." Before we could say anything else, the man disappeared into the crowd of people lining up to buy their meals.

Thirty minutes later, we were called back to the CF Unit. A technician met us with a confused look on his face. "We need to redo her tests," he said, "because the one we did was 14, completely normal. The ones from the other hospital were 52 and 70." When we were called back the second time, the technician was grinning from ear to ear. "Well," he said, "both tests indicate that your child absolutely does not have cystic fibrosis."

I do not know whether Chloe's initial tests were wrong, or whether she was healed of CF that day in the cafeteria, and I don't care. All I know is that my toddler is now a healthy beautiful seventeen-year-old, who dances through our home with the most joyous spirit I have ever seen, and who makes life magical for me, her father, and her two sisters on a daily basis.

To me, her very existence is a miracle.

~Donna Reames Rich

Angel in the Butcher Shop

I've seen and met angels wearing the disguise of
ordinary people living ordinary lives.
~Tracy Chapman

t was a gray-sky, cloudy day when I met an angel. Although it happened nine years ago, the feeling of peace and his comforting words are still fresh in my memory.

That gray day in early March I felt as I had every other day of late. For months, I bore the terrible weight of unrelenting grief after my father's sudden death. There was no place, not even church, where I could find a moment's solace. I prayed constantly, hoping for a little relief, but none came.

On this particular day, I'd done my work as usual. I was in the middle of writing travel stories for a publisher's anthology. This used to leave me with a feeling of exhilaration, but writing about exotic places to entice others to travel to no longer pleased me. Except for the love of my immediate family, nothing seemed to make me feel fulfilled and satisfied with life. Without Dad in my life, I was just existing.

If Dad could die, then anything could happen, I thought as I drove to the grocery store. Nothing and no one was safe. Even love couldn't save anyone — not even me.

I began my usual shopping — lettuce and tomatoes for that night's dinner salad, decaffeinated tea for myself, macaroni and cheese for the kids — but my mind wasn't really on what I was doing. I was like an automaton.

Suddenly I came out of my reverie. In front of me stood a grocery clerk, complete with nametag and red apron. "You look like you need help finding something," he said with a broad and gentle smile. "What is it you need?"

I hesitated before saying anything. His large brown eyes were calm and serene. I'd never seen this guy before and I checked his nametag. "Well, Philip," I said, "I've just been wandering around. I don't really know what I'm looking for."

"We have a special on catfish," he said, still with that same, serene smile. "Follow me and I'll show you where they are." Without another word, he turned; I followed without saying anything.

He stopped by a display of various frozen fish. "Here they all are," he said, turning to me with that smile again. "You can have your pick of just about any kind of catfish they make. They have nuggets and whole filets as well."

As I looked up to see the display, then reached for a package that looked like something my kids would enjoy, Philip said in a low voice, "You know, things will get better for you. You just have to be patient and wait upon the Lord."

I turned toward him, stammering something in surprise — and no one was there.

I looked all around. Shoppers looking over the dairy case and meat counter were all I saw. No clerk was anywhere in sight, and I hadn't heard anyone walk away.

Intrigued, I headed toward the meat department to find Philip and ask him how he knew I was grieving — and what he meant by being patient. I pressed the buzzer on the butcher counter and another clerk came out of the back room.

"May I help you?" he asked.

"I'm looking for Philip."

"Philip?" the man echoed, looking perplexed. "There's no Philip back here."

"He had on a butcher's apron," I insisted. "He looked exotic—maybe Samoan. He had a nametag on. The tag said 'Philip.'"

"Let me ask the others," he said, and went into the back room. After about a minute, he returned. "There's no Philip here," he said. "We've never had anyone named Philip working here. Not at all." He paused and looked into my eyes. "There something you need that we can help you look for?"

I shook my head. Suddenly, inexplicably, I felt like some of the weight of my sorrow lifted. "No," I said to the man. "I guess I was mistaken."

As I walked away, pushing my cart ahead of me, I smiled. I thought I knew who Philip really was. God had sent one of his angels to comfort me. Dad was okay and I would be, too.

I finished the rest of my shopping and checked out, looking around for my angel but knowing I wouldn't see him. When I pushed my cart out of the store, the sun was peeping through the afternoon clouds. For the first time in months, I noticed birds calling. It suddenly looked like a beautiful spring day, and there was a lightness in my step that hadn't been there for a long time.

On a day when I was at my lowest spiritual ebb, God sent a comforting angel to bring words of solace to me. Only instead of wearing wings, he wore a butcher's apron and a nametag.

~T. Jensen Lacey

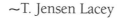

Carry On

Oh, my friend, it's not what they take away from you that counts.
It's what you do with what you have left.
~Hubert Humphrey

trudged through the Maui airport weighed down by despair and an overstuffed carry-on. A man who had played a central role in my life for the last two decades had died. He was my teacher and my mentor. He had opened my mind to a view of life that offered extraordinary possibilities. Through his teaching I had been able to make sense of the world, to understand my place in it. I had a goal and he kept me on course with gentle nudges and occasional hard shoves.

With this man's help, I had changed. No longer the heavy-hearted lost soul, I had become more content, focused and sure. But now his death left me devastated, and worse than the grief was the terror. I was afraid that without his support, reminders and re-directions, I would not maintain my new perspective or fulfill my highest potential.

I made my way to the departure gate and queued up with the rest of the passengers waiting to board. The line was long, and I stood far from the door that opened to the tarmac. A woman shuffled in my direction. She was gaunt and birdlike, all jutting bones and sharp edges.

"Can I cut in front of you?" she said. "I can't stand for very long. I'd like to board as soon as possible."

I stepped back to open a space in front of me and wondered

why she hadn't gone right to the head of the line. Anyone could see she wasn't well. There were dark circles under her eyes and her skin had a greenish tinge. She dragged her carpetbag along the floor as the line inched forward. I offered to carry it for her and she handed me the strap.

There were no seat assignments on the short hop to Oahu. As we boarded the plane, I suggested we sit together so I could stow and later retrieve her bag for her. She slid into a window seat. I hoisted our carry-on bags into the overhead and then sat down next to her. She stared out at the tarmac and I fixed my attention on the flight attendant who was pantomiming safety instructions. When the seatbelt light went out I fumbled in my handbag for my paperback, but before I could open it my newfound travel companion launched into a lengthy monologue. She unraveled the tale of her ten-year struggle with breast cancer, which had metastasized to her bones causing numerous hairline fractures and a broken clavicle. This, she explained, was why she had been dragging the carpetbag.

"Still," she said, "I feel even more well now then I did before the cancer."

The statement puzzled me, but before I could question her she continued. She had heard a doctor speak at a conference. He said that one day, while making his rounds, he had a spiritual awakening. It gave him insight into what it meant to heal on a deeper level. The experience was life changing. He gave up his cure-focused medical practice to engage patients in a process that would help them heal body, mind and spirit. This doctor became her spiritual teacher and guide.

"He didn't cure me," she said. "But he did help me to heal myself."

I was stunned. Why had she told me this story? It was so personal and I was a stranger. And how odd that she too had a teacher with insight into a deeper reality. I knew how very rare and special it was to have a teacher of that kind.

She had grown still, but continued to hold me in her gaze. I sensed a steady calm and steely strength beneath her fractured frame, yet I began to tremble.

"You're grieving and you're despairing," she said at last.

How could she know? I had told her nothing about myself. My skin prickled.

I looked into the dark wells that were her eyes, and seeing compassion there I let myself fall into them. I told her all about my teacher, his death, and my dread that, without his guidance, I would lose my way. The words poured out of me in a torrent until there were no more. I felt like I was drowning.

She studied me in no rush to respond. I concentrated on restoring an even rhythm to my breath.

"It's time for you to listen to your own voice," she said at last. "Your teacher's death freed you so you could continue to grow." She assured me that his teaching was part of me and with it I could find my own way.

Her words were like a life preserver, and grabbing hold I remembered something very important my teacher had told me. "When in doubt," he had said, "ask yourself what I would tell you to do and why." With this technique, he explained, I could always reach inside myself and access the teaching. The memory of his words came as a confirmation of hers. I did have the means to find my own way. I could move forward even now with him gone.

Salty rivulets of relief ran down my cheeks. My heart expanded, grateful for the unexpected encounter with this bearer of healing words.

She closed her eyes and turned her head back toward the window. There was no more talk as the plane continued northwest to Honolulu.

After deplaning, she and I walked together to her connecting gate. She was headed back home to Australia.

"I want to give you this," she said, handing me a cassette tape. "It's a talk my teacher gave."

Thanking her, I bent down to tuck the tape into my carry-on. When I straightened back up I was alone. I searched for her throughout the gate area but she was gone. How was that possible? She moved so slowly dragging her bag, and I had only looked down for a moment.

It was so odd the way she had appeared out of nowhere and then disappeared in the same way. And what was her name, had she even told me? I couldn't remember, but it didn't matter. It was her words I would never forget.

~Lorri Danzig

Healing Touch

The golden moments in the stream of life rush past us and we see nothing but sand; the angels come to visit us, and we only know them when they are gone.

~George Eliot

My twenty-three-year-old son had been diagnosed with Guillain-Barré syndrome (GBS), an autoimmune disease that attacks the nervous system. His entire body was paralyzed. He was only able to shake or nod his head, and he needed breathing and feeding tubes. He was at VCU Medical Center's Neuro ICU and had been in the hospital for forty-five days. I had taken off work to be with him, but I was running out of leave time. I needed to go back to work, but I just couldn't leave him in this condition.

Knowing that this syndrome destroys the myelin sheath around the nerves, but it eventually grows back, I prayed that God would give me a sign that my son was on the mend. I had watched his blood pressure and heart rate go crazy on the monitors and knew this was the most critical time for him.

One day, I went to the hospital's chapel and prayed for God to give me a sign that my son was starting to recover.

When I returned to his room, they had him sitting up in a reclining chair, which they frequently did, just to get him out of bed. I settled down to read my book. A little while later, a lady stuck her head in the room and said she was looking for William. My son's name is William Shane, but we have always called him Shane. I figured she was a social worker or something like that and told her she had the correct room, but we called him Shane.

She came in and introduced herself. She had come from Roanoke Rapids, North Carolina because a mutual friend had asked her to come to pray for William. I told her I didn't think I knew anyone from that area and asked who the friend was. She could not remember the name. I told her all prayers were welcome.

Shane had his hands on the arms of the chair. She placed her hand on top of his, and asked me to put my hand on hers. When I did, she placed her other hand on mine then said a prayer. She told us she would check on him later. I thanked her for coming and she left.

I sat there a while longer until the nurse came in and told me to leave the room while they got Shane back in bed. After wandering the hospital for a bit, I went back to Shane's room and found him asleep in bed. I sat back down, picked up my book and started reading. Then the respiratory therapist came in to check on him.

All of a sudden, she motioned for me to look. She said she saw some evidence that he was breathing on his own, and was going to turn the machine off. I panicked, and she assured me that she could turn it right back on and there was no risk involved. I held my breath while she turned it off. I watched. Sure enough, the monitor showed that my son was actually breathing some on his own. I started crying, and so did she. This did not mean the battle was over, she said, but it did mean that he was on the way back.

When she left the room, I started to put together what had just happened.

I had prayed for a sign that things were improving. Then the lady came to pray for Shane. And she had just walked into our Intensive Care Unit room. Getting into the ICU usually required ringing the bell for a nurse to let you in — after you'd said who you were there to visit — and then a nurse had to check with the family in the room prior to letting the visitor enter.

When I asked the nurse if she had let anyone else into the room, she said there had been no visitors for my son except me that day.

She checked with the other nurses and reported that no one knew anything about a visitor.

From that day on, Shane began to quickly improve. They exchanged his breathing tube for another that allowed him to talk. As we were talking one day, he said, "Mom, I almost died, didn't I?" I told him that he had us all scared for a while. Then, as I told him about the lady who came to pray for him while he was asleep, he interrupted me, saying he remembered that. And he repeated parts of the conversation! Like when I had asked her which church she was from, she had said her church was non-denominational. When he said that, I remembered that she had in fact said that. Then he described the lady perfectly.

I went home that night and told my husband about this conversation. He got a strange look on his face and reminded me that Shane had been on Versed (sometimes called the forgetful drug) and did not remember any of our family visiting during that time.

Shane continued to improve and was moved to rehab shortly thereafter. I have no doubt that God sent an angel in answer to my prayers. And when she laid her hand on his, and then her other hand on mine, we were both touched by an angel.

She never appeared again, but her visit will never be forgotten... by me or by Shane.

~Teresa Keller

A Calming Presence

The magnitude of life is overwhelming.
Angels are here to help us take it peace by peace.
~Levende Waters

My husband passed away six weeks after being diagnosed with cancer. That gave us very little time to prepare for what lay ahead of us. This was particularly true for my son Mark, who had a special bond with his dad. They were very close. They were alike in many respects, but completely different in others. Perhaps that was the key to their wonderfully unique relationship—enough alike to enjoy many of the same activities, yet different enough to complement one another's personality.

As the weeks turned into months, Mark's sadness over his dad's death worsened. He seemed to find little happiness even in the brighter moments of his daily life. Every conversation turned into reminiscences of his favorite times spent with his best buddy. But then these fleeting moments of happiness would reignite his sadness as he realized, once again, that he could never add another event to his storehouse of treasured memories.

Mark was only thirty years old, yet in a real sense, he seemed to feel his life had ended with his dad's death. Those of us who knew him best began to see signs of serious depression as he withdrew more and more into himself.

Fifteen months after my husband's death, Mark was kneeling by his bed praying one night. He was pleading with God to somehow show him that he was not alone on his sorrowful journey and that the rest of his life would not be as painful as his present situation. He felt he could not go on much longer feeling as he did.

He later told me the events that followed his desperate prayer.

"Mom, I had been praying and asking God to please let me know that He was going to help me. I don't know how long I had been praying, but then something really unexplainable happened. I suddenly felt a strange presence beside me, but I knew I was the only one in the house. It wasn't frightening. It was actually peaceful and comforting. It was something I had never felt before, and it was so strong."

Mark continued praying, being intensely aware of everything going on around him—the desperation in his heart and soul, the quietness of the night, and the mystery of what was transpiring around him.

"I didn't open my eyes because I did not want to interrupt what was happening to me. I could not explain it, but I knew it was very special and that it was meant just for me. I was afraid that if I opened my eyes, the presence would be gone. I wanted the situation to last as long as possible."

Mark had made his bed that morning, smoothing out the covers as he had been taught to do. He had knelt to pray near the foot of his bed, leaving the upper portion of the bedclothes untouched.

"As I kept praying, Mom, a deep sense of peace came over me, and I continued feeling that presence beside me. I wanted it to go on forever, but I knew it wouldn't. When I finished praying, I stood up and looked at the bedclothes beside me. I couldn't believe what I saw. Right there beside where I had been kneeling was a depression in the bed like someone had been sitting there. I know what it was, Mom.

"God knew how desperately lonely I was without Dad, and I know He sent an angel to be with me that night so I would know I was not alone. I was not imagining it, Mom. It was real! Can you believe it?"

Yes, I could believe it because I had previously encountered an angel. God, in His infinite wisdom, knew that the people who loved Mark had done all they could to help him. He knew it was time to send an angelic messenger to a desperate young man who was pleading for divine help.

The angel who came to my son's aid that night was able to strengthen him for the journey ahead when we humans had done all we could. I want to find that angel in Heaven some day and express my heartfelt gratitude for the comfort and encouragement my son received that night. From that day forward, until Mark's sudden death from natural causes a few weeks later, he exhibited a renewed sense of courage to face each day. He had felt the angel's presence, and he knew he was not alone.

~Carol Goodman Heizer

I Believe in Miracles

Prayer enlarges the heart until it is capable of containing God's gift of himself.
~Mother Teresa

t began when my husband Richard was helping our seven-year-old son Steven remove his hockey equipment after a Saturday morning hockey game. Suddenly Steven cringed and cried, "Dad, you hurt my neck!" We had no idea the impact those five words would have on the rest of our lives.

Richard, being a physician, checked out Steven's neck, and reported, "Okay, he's got a lump about the size of a nickel." He was very troubled.

It was early January 1987, a very busy Saturday following New Year's celebrations with family and friends. Our Christmas tree stood in the corner of our family room with some of our opened presents still lingering under it. Christmas decorations both inside and out were still up, as I liked to wait until Epiphany on January 6th to start putting everything away. That Saturday, we were hosting a large sixtieth family birthday party for my mother at our home in Ancaster, Ontario.

Over the course of the day Richard continued to watch the lump on Steven's neck grow bigger. By early evening the lump was clearly visible, now the size of a small orange.

Doctors prefer not to diagnose their own families, so Richard called our family doctor who ordered a chest X-ray and blood work to be done as soon as possible. That evening we were settling into our normal family routine when the phone rang. The doctor had just heard from the radiologist, and they wanted Steven to see a specialist the next day to "check things out further." When Richard asked why, he learned the radiologist had found a spot on Steven's lung, and they didn't know what it was.

"How big?" asked Richard.

"Seven centimetres," came the shocking answer.

"You must mean millimetres," Richard insisted. "Seven centimetres is huge! That would be the size of a small grapefruit. This is only a seven-year-old boy! His chest isn't much bigger than that!"

I was upstairs with our three children at this time. Laura, our five-year-old, was showing me a picture she had drawn at school. Ryan, our two-year-old, wanted me to play with him, and Steven was watching TV after a trying day with medical professionals. Sensing something was terribly wrong, I went downstairs to find my husband choking back tears.

Richard relayed the conversation to me, but I could not grasp what I was being told. Realizing I needed help to understand the severity of the situation he said, "This is a really bad thing; to have a tumour in your chest and a lump on the side of your neck means that a cancer has probably already spread."

Steven was only seven—how could he ever survive what was surely coming next?

In an instant I understood, and felt a tingle shoot through my body. I was dizzy and my legs felt weak. I gasped and knew I had to leave the room—I had to try and get away from what I had just heard. I became violently ill, and kept repeating, "This cannot be happening." In one moment, just like that, our lives were turned upside down.

The phone rang again; this time it was our parish priest.

"Richard, this is Father Con," he said. "I'm calling about Steven's upcoming First Communion." Never before had our priest called our home. Ever.

Richard then explained to Father Con what was happening with Steven. "The situation does not look good," he said, and ended the conversation by asking Father Con to pray for our son.

Was the timing of the priest's call a simple coincidence? Or had Father Con, in some way, learned of our situation? We had no way to know that Richard's request was just the beginning of our request for prayers. It was not until many days later that we would realize the powerful part that prayer would play in our lives.

That evening, Richard's brother, another physician, came over immediately to give us support. "Don't forget they could be wrong," he reminded us. "One, or even both of the tumours could be benign, and they may not be related."

Both Richard and his brother knew that if the tumours were related and malignant, it would be a death sentence for Steven. We all agreed we were in desperate need of support, encouragement, and hope and would need to ask for help.

From that moment forward, I made a decision to do everything possible to save my son's life. I had to keep my heart open to the possibility of a miracle, too. I just didn't know how or when. Facing medical facts wasn't going to be easy, but I knew that whatever the medical professionals told me, I was not going to give up hope.

The next day a biopsy was done on the lump in Steven's neck. The pediatric oncologist confirmed that our son had a malignant tumour and would need to be admitted to the hospital right away. The oncologist painted a bleak picture, making us feel we might as well buy the coffin. Since the biopsy had clearly confirmed the neck tumour was cancerous, the doctors were ninety-nine percent certain the chest tumour would be too. This man took away all hope when he told us our son had no chance of survival. "This is a very aggressive form of cancer," he said. We were told then, that our son would be "dead in three months."

This terrible reality was proving to be a bigger challenge than our family could handle alone. We began to pray, and then earnestly asked for the prayers of many others... our families, friends, colleagues, Steven's school, our church, two convents of praying sisters, and anyone, in fact, who offered their help and prayers—because we asked.

There were many moments when we were face to face with medical science focusing on one thing (cancer), but at the same time we began experiencing the feeling that our faith was also playing a huge role. With all those people praying for Steven, unexplained changes—even miraculous changes—began to happen.

The next week the doctors surgically removed the large tumour in Steven's chest, hoping to give him a bit more time. To everyone's amazement, despite the doctors having told us it would be malignant—the tumour turned out to be benign! We were now facing a great deal of discrepancy in the medical diagnosis. But because Steven still had the malignant tumour in his neck, we were told he definitely had cancer and would still need immediate treatment. Considering all these discrepancies and questions, we decided to proceed very cautiously for a few weeks. We continued to pray and watch over our son's condition, but made a decision to delay any further treatment. We consulted with other specialists, and then one pathologist saw something that others did not and gave us some precious hope. And because of her opinion there was enough discrepancy to cautiously bring Steven home from the hospital a few weeks later. Once at home, he continued to get better and stronger. The tumour slowly shrank until it finally disappeared altogether, and eventually there was no trace left of any cancer in his body.

Twenty-seven years later Steven is a healthy adult and a physician himself practicing in the same office as his father. A biopsy had clearly shown the neck tumour to be malignant—so was it a misdiagnosis? Or was it, in fact, a miracle?

We learned through this experience that you must never, ever take away someone's hope. There is always hope, always a chance that things are not as they appear. There are mistakes; there are miracles, and there is the power of prayer. It is so important to hold onto your faith and your hope, and to trust in the power of your own belief in something beyond this world. It was this "something" that profoundly affected our family and showed everyone around us that miracles do happen.

I believe in miracles, and I believe that my family experienced a beautiful miracle that Christmas, one for which I am profoundly, and forever grateful.

~Karen Vincent Zizzo

Touched by an Angel

Answered Prayers

A Hand to Hold

When we put our cares in His hands, He puts His peace in our hearts.
~Author Unknown

"Where are you going?" my commanding officer screamed.

"I wish I knew!" I hurled back over my shoulder, and kept walking away from my duty post in Vietnam. I knew I was risking an Article 15, the military's official reprimand, but I didn't care. Life had bottomed out for me.

Barbed wire surrounded my base camp, so I couldn't go far. But I couldn't concentrate, couldn't think. Vietnam was a dangerous place for a depressed boy. Too many weapons around. Too much alcohol and too many drugs available.

I walked to the gate, stood there thinking about catching a departing deuce-and-a-half to anywhere and going AWOL, but decided against it, and walked back into the camp. With no place else to go, I just headed toward my hootch. That's what we called the shacks we lived in.

A lot of guys fought depression in the war, but my depression was not about what was happening in Vietnam. It was about the mess going on back home.

When I got drafted into the Army, my high school sweetheart and I got engaged. Perhaps it was a silly thing to do, but it was our way of proving our three-year love for each other. I envisioned returning home to my job at the engineering firm, finishing my degree, buying that house with the white picket fence, and having kids! With the love of my life.

My family was loving and loyal. They were faithful members of the same church my fiancée attended, and life was pretty wonderful back home. I lived with the hope that as soon as I got back from the dreaded war, I could pick up where I had left off, and that was good.

Then the letters from home started carrying hints that something was amiss. I couldn't put my finger on it, but it was most certainly there.

"Any mail for me?" I had called out to the mail clerk numerous days in a row, only to get the shake of his head in response. No mail. No love. No word.

Then three letters from three different people came in the same day, and I knew my life would never be the same. One was from my fiancée.

"Let's cool it," she said. "When you get home, we'll see where we stand."

Another was from my mom. "Your cousin died in a car accident taking his fiancée back to her home," she wrote. Then, she added, "Your fiancée is dating a friend."

And the other was from another relative. "In case no one is telling you, your fiancée is dating someone else, and your family has been asked to leave the church. Their presence is embarrassing to the fiancée."

The thing about Vietnam was not just the 8,000 miles that separated us from home. It was the "snail mail," as we called it. It took seven to ten days to get a letter. By the time you wrote a response and they received it, the world could change. You couldn't solve problems with a two-week delay.

I felt so helpless. My parents had been asked to leave the church? Church was their life, their joy! And now they were asked to leave? And my fiancée was done with me? All those promises meant nothing to her? And my cousin was dead? I had nothing to go home to, nothing to hope for.

Back at my hootch, and knowing nothing else to do, I simply fell on my knees and lay across my cot. I wasn't praying. I wasn't sure I liked God at that moment. I just lay face down, cold as stone.

Plywood dividers separated the cots in our hootch, standing about two feet off the floor and up to six feet high. You could stand beside your bed and not be seen by your buddy next door.

Hidden by this wall of privacy, and after a long time of lying emotionless, I did what seemed right at the moment. Still on my knees, I rose from the bed, and with my eyes closed, reached one hand straight up toward heaven. The posture said I was praying, but I never opened my mouth. I didn't know what to say to God.

In that precise moment, one of my buddies must have pulled over a stool and climbed up to look over the divider, because as I stretched up my hand, he reached over the divider and gripped it hard, like a handshake.

I was startled, then embarrassed, then angry. The shock of his touch made me gasp. Then the idea that he was watching me at my lowest moment embarrassed me. I kept my eyes squeezed shut while I counted to ten, trying to think of a way to respond to my buddy.

I was angry that he would reach over my divider and grab my hand when it must've been obvious that I was in some state of silent prayer. My countdown nearing ten, I decided that I would just grin, and say something dumb like, "You nut job! What's the matter with you?" And he would probably grin, and let go of my hand, and then we'd sit and talk about two-timing girls or something.

I was calm now, and ready to face him. Then he squeezed my hand! Incredulous! I felt like a fool, but I squeezed back, and then I opened my eyes to see which friend gripped my hand.

No one was there! I still held the hand. I even squeezed it to see if I was imagining it, and it squeezed back! But no one was there!

And then, in that instant, a voice came: "If you'll just hold onto this hand, and trust, everything back home will work out exactly as it should. Don't let go. Trust me!"

And then it was gone. The hand, I mean. There was nothing but air.

But the air felt electric. I knelt in shock for several minutes. Then I wept. And after a short while, I rose and felt transformed.

I went back to my duty post. "Where did you go?" yelled my commanding officer.

"I had to go find something," I said.

"What?" he asked.

"Hope!" I said, and I smiled. And so did he.

Forty-five years later, I still smile because life worked out perfectly. I never quit holding that hand, even though I've never felt it again.

~Danny Carpenter

Snow Angel

For every mountain there is a miracle.
~Robert H. Schuller

shivered, despite the car heater blasting warm air at me. It wasn't the cold that made that icy feeling go up my spine—I was terrified. The weather on this Central Oregon highway had turned. It wasn't just the dropping temperature, and the snow and sleet coming down. No, this was something altogether different—and much worse. I reached to pull down the car's visor and peered in the mirror at the landscape behind us. I saw nothing but an unbroken wall of white.

It all started with a winter weekend getaway to the big city—Portland, Oregon. But as we packed our luggage to head back home over the Cascade Mountains, the TV news soured our joyful mood. The weatherman warned of a large winter storm looming. Pileups had already begun on the heavily travelled highway cresting Mt. Hood. What would have been our first choice was no longer an option.

My husband, a retired Teamster, sat at the small motel table, a map spread before him as he plotted our course. Safety trumped speed. Sipping his coffee, he turned to me, deep lines etched on his forehead. My stomach tightened as his index finger traced out the route he'd chosen. The wide open grasslands.

"We'll go the long way around. I'll circle us past Mt. Hood and alongside the Columbia River. Then we'll drive south from The Dalles.

We'll do better in the lower elevation, and avoid all the collisions we'd see up by the summit."

"If you're sure. I trust your judgment."

"The usual way home is too dangerous. Black ice forms on shady curves and the pass is full of them. I don't want to pull somebody out of the creek again. Could be our turn this time."

"You're right." Too many times we'd watched helplessly as motorists spun out of control. The vehicles veered across the yellow lines or off the road completely, as wild and erratic as a pinball. "Even if it takes longer, it'll be worth it." I wished I could believe the reassuring words we were saying to each other.

We piled the bags into the car and it was time to go—no sense in stalling.

Moving with the traffic along the river-hugging interstate, I reached for my husband's hand and gave it a quick squeeze. "This isn't so bad." I breathed a sigh of relief.

Minutes later, my husband flicked the turn signal as we left I-84. No more safety in numbers.

The two-lane highway we'd drive, like most in our state, had neither guardrails nor streetlamps. A sprinkling of tiny communities would provide the only break in an otherwise lonely ride.

Snow fell steadily now, creating a sensation of traveling through space as each flake flashed star-like past the windshield. One or two other vehicles joined our slow procession through the vast empty fields, the landscape already resembling marshmallow frosting. As we descended several hundred feet into the narrow gorge created by the Deschutes River, we noticed the other drivers turn off.

We continued, bridging the river at the tiny hamlet of Maupin. Tracing switchbacks up the winding roadway, we reached the crest. I bit my lip. What greeted us was a barren wasteland, devoid of any signs of life. No charming farmhouses dotted the hillsides; no oncoming traffic reassured us that the route ahead was passable.

The wind gusted now, hard and fast, its wails sounding through our station wagon like a runaway train. For a short distance, snow fencing bordered the asphalt. But it was soon rendered useless by the blizzard's heightening fury. And then even the posts disappeared.

In an instant, visibility dropped to but a few yards. We couldn't distinguish the lanes from open land. We were trapped, moving blindly in a full-blown whiteout.

My heart raced and I glanced at my husband.

Both hands white-knuckling the steering wheel, he stared dead ahead. He wouldn't let on—he always protected me, even from my own fears—but I knew. We were in trouble.

"Should we slow down?" I spoke the words quietly, hesitant to pierce his concentration.

"We're only going fifteen miles per hour as it is. Any slower, and a car approaching from behind won't have time to brake before hitting us."

"Maybe we should pull over and wait this out." My voice shook.

"No, honey, we can't stop. There's nothing out here. We don't know how long this is going to keep up, and we'd freeze. But I can't see the road anymore." He tore his gaze from the blanket of white for a fraction of a second. "I don't know what to do. If we can just make it to the junction, there'll be other travelers. We won't be alone."

I stared at the ice forming along the edges of the windshield, as a wall of snow seemed to swallow our car.

"God help us." I heard desperation in my spouse's words, and saw tears welling in his eyes.

"Yes, please, send help," I echoed his plea.

David gasped. "Heidi, do you see…? Can it be?"

I squinted, straining to where he pointed. And there they were. I blinked, wanting to believe my eyes, but afraid I might be seeing things.

Just in front of us, not twenty yards ahead, a set of taillights shone, bright as beacons. We were safe! We'd follow these folks!

We sped up, opting to get as close as possible. Slowing as we approached a hairpin turn, we worried we might lose them. We rounded the corner in time to see the brake lights. The vehicle had stopped, waiting for us to catch up. As we neared, they moved forward to lead the way. Perpetually just out of reach, we tagged along like puppies on a leash. At last, we came within sight of the junction. Nothing but a half mile of unbroken asphalt with no driveways, no intersections and no obstructions.

David heaved a deep breath. "We made it. If not for them…" He tipped his head toward the heroes that had delivered us—but they were gone. They'd vanished into the landscape without a trace.

"Where'd the car go?" His brow furrowed as he scanned the area. "I don't get it. It was right in front of us a second ago. What happened?"

"You saw the car? What kind was it?" I'd never been able to focus on more than the super-bright lights.

My husband's lips pursed. "I didn't actually see one. Just those beams that showed up out of nowhere and left without an exit." He let loose a nervous laugh. "Do you think? Nah—never mind."

I reached out my hand to touch his shoulder. "I don't just think it, I'm certain. God sent someone to watch over us." My heart warmed, suddenly aware that would always be the case. All because when we were blinded and didn't know which way to go, a snow angel guided us home.

~Heidi Gaul

72

The Night an Angel Boarded the Train

God's promises are like the stars; the darker the night the brighter they shine.
~David Nicholas

We'd gone to bed worried about our daughter. Only weeks out of college, she had driven cross-country to work in Washington, D.C., and to live alone. This move would put her closer to our home in Pennsylvania but not nearly as close as we'd hoped, and certainly not close enough for us to be there at a moment's notice. Worse, I never turned on the TV or read a major paper without learning of a frightening story about muggings, murders, and rape. But did my daughter understand what precautions she needed to take as a single woman boarding a late-night bus and then the train? And what about the dimly lit neighborhood she had selected? Not only were there few streetlights in the first place, but many had been shattered by vandals.

"I wish you hadn't moved to that place," I'd told her more than once. Yes, her vintage apartment was charming, with its colonial brick, plantation shutters, and the park-like setting, complete with an ambling creek. Tonight, however, I again felt afraid for my daughter. I had shared my fears with my husband for more than an hour—until he just couldn't discuss it any longer and, after a long day at work, fell asleep. I, on the other hand, continued to toss, fret, and pray.

"I'm worried about my daughter," I whispered, hoping God heard. "She'll be closing the store where she works, walking alone from the mall, and waiting for I don't know how long on a dark corner to board the last bus." She would then transfer to the Washington Metro. Then, when she finally arrived at her stop, she would cross a street hidden in the shadows of vacant buildings and offices closed for the evening. From there, she would travel three blocks, down broken steps sandwiched between darkened buildings identical to her own. Other young professionals lived nearby, of course, but this late and with most occupants sleeping and nearly every porch and indoor light off?

I tried not to think of the worst that could happen. But Lisa would be darting through a tunnel to shorten the distance, which meant she would be visible to no one—except for some troubling stranger—and what, I wondered, would he be doing at this hour?

"God," I breathed again, trying without success to dispel my feelings of panic, "please take care of my daughter."

Repeatedly reshaping my pillow, I'd only just closed my eyes when I heard what seemed to be a whisper: "Pray for an angel for Lisa." I bolted upright! Because right on the heels of the first message I hadn't yet processed completely, a second whisper followed: "Pray she does not go through the tunnel."

A tremble ran through my body. Pray for an angel, and do not go through the tunnel? "Scotty!" I cried, shaking my husband awake. "Scotty!" I pleaded. He needed to hear what I had to tell him. "We need to pray for Lisa," I cried. We were to pray for an angel, I explained, and Lisa was not to go through that tunnel.

Reaching for my hand, my husband said, "She'll be okay, babe. She'll be okay." Then we bowed our heads. Even though I couldn't stop shaking, I recalled aloud God's promises and His love, and told Him we believed Him when he said angels encamped around those who feared him.

We'd only just said our "Amen" when Scotty fell back to sleep—and I listened, my body rigid, to a pendulum marking time in another room.

I was still awake when, only minutes after midnight, the phone rang. Lifting the receiver, I heard my daughter's winded, "Mom!" I envisioned her running as I heard a second, "Mom!" Followed by, "There was an angel on my train!"

My heart raced and I found it impossible to utter a single word.

"There was no one else waiting to get on at my stop, Mom," my daughter said. "He was already on the train... only it was the beginning of the line, so I should have been alone!" When she first saw him, she'd been frightened, because where could this person have come from? "But then he looked directly at me, and he had the most beautiful eyes." I heard my daughter grow calm. "I'd never seen eyes like his before, Mom, and then he started speaking, but it didn't seem like he could hear." He must be deaf, she thought at first. "But he wasn't just a man, Mom," Lisa said. "I'm serious, he wasn't!"

I wanted to say something intelligent or, at the very least, ask the questions reeling inside my own head. But I still could not find my voice, and now Lisa was saying the man — "Angel," she repeated — told her he knew her life had been difficult. He was right; it had been. But all of it was going to become good, he said, so she wasn't to be afraid.

"Lisa..." I began, trying not to cry but wondering how such a miraculous thing could have happened.

"And, Mom?" My daughter still hadn't completely caught her breath, but now she was also near tears and nervously laughing. "When I got off the train?" She paused. "You know where," she said.

I certainly did; it gave me the chills just to think.

"Well, I started toward the tunnel..." Lisa paused again to catch her breath. "Something kept saying, 'Don't go through the tunnel. Don't go through the tunnel.'"

Don't go through the tunnel? And an angel had boarded my daughter's train? My mouth feeling full of cotton, I told her what I had heard and then about our prayers. I added that we loved her very much. When we were both too exhausted to say another word, I replaced the receiver and shook my head in amazement. Pray for an angel? And don't go through the tunnel? Had God actually done this, and had an angel really said that? Or had it simply been an incredible coincidence?

Not until several days had passed did I receive what, for me, was my answer. Only then did I wholly understand God had, in fact, sent an angel for my daughter.

My husband had driven to D.C. to attend a national meeting and had purchased a local newspaper for me. On a middle page, I read the story of a rapist who'd been eluding the police for months, but had finally been arrested.

Just a stone's throw from the tunnel, and only yards from our daughter's apartment.

~Nancy Hoag

73

Just Ask

Spiritual force is greater than material force — thoughts rule the world.
~Ralph Waldo Emerson

On a warm summer's afternoon I loaded my eight-year-old twins into my father's car and headed out in search of a new home. Three weeks prior we had left our home on the West Coast and travelled east in search of a better life. Since then we had been living with my parents, who had graciously offered to take us in until I could get back on my feet. The time had now come to make our move.

I had an idea of where I hoped we would live. It was a quiet part of town, close to my parents' home. Even though I was certain the monthly rent for that area would be out of my comfort range, I'd come to the conclusion that I owed this to myself and to my children, and made the decision that I would make it work. A famous quote flashed through my mind, "Be bold and mighty forces will come to your aid." I knew I could do this.

There was an air of anticipation in the car as we cruised through the streets canopied by lush leafy trees. Children bounced through sprinklers as mothers kept a watchful eye, chatting over the fence with friendly neighbours. A kindly looking gentleman mowed his lawn while a happy couple strolled past hand in hand. At one point we stopped to buy a glass of lemonade from a young entrepreneur who had eagerly plopped himself behind a card table on the edge of the curb. It was reminiscent of the neighbourhood in which I had grown up. And it was exactly the place where I would feel comfortable raising my children.

Despite the obvious distractions, we kept alert for any sign of a home available for lease. I'm not sure what I had been expecting that afternoon as we headed out on this journey, but in my mind's eye I imagined a red "For Rent" sign perched in a front window or stapled to a corner telephone pole.

We continued through the area for a good while with no luck. Every home seemed to be occupied. No "For Rent" signs to be found. My heart sank as we reached the final street of the lovely neighbourhood I had hoped we might call home. I decided it was time to ask for some help. I pulled the car over and turned to my children, who had patiently accompanied me on this mission.

I must confess that I am not a devotee of organized religion, though I have always had a strong awareness of a higher power guiding my way through life. I have strived to open my children's minds to knowing this same higher power. To listen to their intuition, to recognize right from wrong and to always follow those feelings. So sending out a prayer was not a foreign concept to them.

I suggested to the kids that we ask the Universe for some help. I asked them to say a silent prayer, being sure to send out a thank you to their grandparents for inviting us to stay with them, and if it be the will of the Universe, to please help us find a special place where we could be happy. After a few moments of quiet reflection I flashed my kids an energized smile and said, "Let's go find our new home."

The remaining street in the neighbourhood was much quieter than the rest, as it took a dogleg right and ended in a cul-de-sac. At the bend in the road I caught the eye of a man curiously watching us creep up the street, pointing at houses as we passed. I felt uneasy with the way he was watching us, as if he thought we were up to no good. The feeling stayed with me as I made the turn to head back. On our return trip down the street I was happy to see that he was no longer in his driveway. Just a protective homeowner, I guessed.

Moments later I looked into my rearview mirror to see the man from the driveway racing toward us in his car. What was he up to? Did he think we were casing his neighbourhood? As he pulled alongside us, he honked his horn and through his open window asked me to pull over. I could tell by his demeanour that he was not angry or upset, but friendly and receptive. I pulled over and stopped behind him.

He leaped from his sedan and sprinted back to our car. "Am I glad I caught you. I saw you driving slowly up the street. Are you looking for your lost dog?" he asked, gesturing toward his vehicle. Peering out at us through the rear window was a happy mutt, panting in the heat, tongue hanging out the side of his mouth, and tail wagging excitedly. "He wandered up my driveway shortly before you drove past. I could tell he was someone's pet because he was so friendly and fearless. But he didn't have a collar. I was sure he must be yours since you were clearly searching for something."

I explained that no, we were not looking for a lost dog but for a house to rent. I felt compelled to explain our situation and confided that we had recently moved back to the area from the West and were searching for a new place to live. This seemed to amuse him. With a roguish smile he extended his hand to me and introduced himself. He said he was a local real estate agent and a home in the area he had been renting had just become vacant that morning. If I was interested, we were welcome to drive over and take a look at it.

I was interested, and inquired about the address. The house wasn't in this exact area, but a short drive north to Lakeshore Road. My heart sank. I kindly thanked him, then reluctantly declined his offer. If this neighbourhood was a stretch for me financially, the one he spoke of was out of my league by leaps and bounds. Lakeshore Road was one of the most desirable areas of our picturesque lakeside town, where old growth tree-lined drives ran between perfectly manicured lawns up to the most opulent waterfront homes. I reminded him that I didn't have gainful employment at this point, and was certain that I couldn't afford what he would possibly expect for rent on a home in such a prestigious area.

By the look on his face, I think we both felt deflated. But after a moment he seemed to have a recollection. He asked how much I had been paying for rent before and seemed content with the amount I told him. He shook my hand again, gave me the exact address of the house and handed me his business card. "Go out and take a look. If you're interested, give me a call and you can have it for what you were paying. It was a good thing this dog wandered up my driveway today or we might never have met."

We spent the next couple of years in that fantastic home. And our family grew shortly thereafter with the addition of a wonderful man and his two terrific kids. It was the perfect home for the six of us to bond and grow. I think back on that period of our lives with a great sense of peace. Sun-filled summer days at the beach, falling asleep at night to the waves washing onto the shoreline, and a backyard rink in the winter that kept all of the kids, big and small, happy for hours on end.

I can still picture that friendly, fearless pup without whom this story would not have happened. From the man's description, he wandered up his driveway at the exact moment we had appealed to the Universe for help. Some may say it was a coincidence. But when I look back on everything that transpired, I know in my heart that mighty forces did come to our aid that day. When you are ready, the Universe will provide for you. You only need to ask.

~Susie Brunton

Breath of the Heavenly

Angels are never too distant to hear you.
~Author Unknown

The doctor's words terrified me, and I clutched my baby girl tighter to my chest. No, Lord. No. Please, not again.

Growing up, I'd always wanted to be a mom. While other girls dreamed of careers or exotic travels, I'd dreamed of motherhood. So when I married my husband Terry, it wasn't long before we started trying to have a family.

We were overjoyed when we found out we were pregnant with our first baby. Everything I'd ever dreamt about was finally coming true! But soon after the positive result, I miscarried.

We were devastated. The doctor told us we were young and should try again, so we did. Another attempt ended in a miscarriage. I managed to carry a little girl named Shannon full-term. But minutes after being born, doctors whisked her away to perform open-heart surgery. She died almost instantly. Thirteen months later, a little boy named Christopher followed.

Four babies lost within four years.

There are no words for such tremendous loss. Terry and I waded through the pain, clinging to hope on some days, to each other on others.

Our hearts had finally started to mend once we'd adopted our three girls.

Now the doctor was telling me that the youngest, Rachel, had respiratory syncytial virus, or RSV, a dangerous respiratory illness that would have to be monitored closely. I listened numbly as he told me about the oxygen tent and nebulizer I'd need to pick up for her. It was treatable, but it could also be deadly. Especially in infants.

When we made it home that night, I couldn't even think about sleeping. How could I when I knew my little girl would be laboring for every breath she took? The oxygen tent wouldn't fit into our bedroom, so Terry set it up in our daughter Lizzie's room instead. I was petrified to not have Rachel in the same room as me, but what could I do? She needed help breathing, and I couldn't help with that. The oxygen tent could.

Laying Rachel down in her crib that night, I told Lizzie to call if she or Rachel needed anything. I lingered over goodnight kisses much longer than necessary, then reluctantly stepped out and closed the door behind me.

Terry fell asleep instantly, but I couldn't even close my eyes without starting awake, thinking I heard Rachel crying. Twice I got out of bed to check on her only to find her sleeping peacefully.

Standing at their doorway for the third time, listening to her ragged breathing and the hiss of the oxygen tent, I finally let the tears fall. I hated seeing my baby like this. As I walked back down the dark hallway to my room, I prayed. This was bringing back a lot of unwelcome memories. The grief was still so fresh.

I fell asleep praying.

Sometime after midnight I jerked awake. When had I fallen asleep? Was everything okay? Was Rachel okay?

I threw the covers aside and sped across the hall. I forced myself to calm down before I opened their door. The hinges squeaked open as I caught Lizzie sitting straight up in her bed.

I was just about to ask what she was doing up when she spoke, her tone soft and reverent. "Mommy, it's okay. There are angels in here!"

I stared at her in shock, wondering if she'd just woken up from a dream. But she didn't sound sleepy at all. In fact, she sounded wide awake.

Finally, my mouth moved. "What do you see, Lizzie? Where are they?"

I followed Lizzie's finger to first one side of Rachel's crib. Then the other.

Peace overwhelmed me, and I knew Lizzie was talking about more than just a dream. I realized God was here and I could rest easy because He would take care of my baby. I went back to bed and fell into one of the deepest sleeps I have ever experienced.

The next morning, I grilled Lizzie as she colored pictures of the angels she'd seen. I asked her what they looked like.

"Well, they had big feet," Lizzie said.

"Big feet?"

She nodded. "And big wings."

"Did they say anything to you?"

She shook her head.

"Then why did they come?"

She chose another color from her crayon box. "To take care of Rachel."

"How do you know?"

She shrugged.

"Why did you tell Mommy it was going to be okay?" How did she know how worried I was?

Lizzie tilted her picture toward her. "Because the angels wanted me to tell you."

Tears came to my eyes, this time for another reason entirely. Thank you, God. He'd heard my plea. He'd sent two of his angels just to watch every rise and fall of my baby's chest.

All I'd dared ask for was a healthy baby, and He'd shared a glimpse of the holy with me. A breath of the heavenly.

Many years later, Lizzie described the angels she saw that night as being like a shadow in reverse. They didn't have any details or features, but were simply white-hot forms with big wings and big feet. She can't remember how she woke up that night, only being startled to see two figures next to her sister's crib, and then feeling peace and love like she's never felt since.

As for Rachel, she's now a healthy and outgoing eighteen-year-old. It's hard to imagine her ever struggling for breath. But there are those of us who know better.

~Robin Veldboom

Lifted by Love

Faith is not without worry or care, but faith is fear that has said a prayer.
~Author Unknown

The weird feeling hit me like a fist to the midsection. I grabbed the top rails of the fifteen-foot ladder I was standing on to paint the exterior of the house. I shut my eyes and regained my balance before I closed the paint can and descended. Step by step, I inched my way down and staggered into the house. Then I began my litany of what might be wrong.

The noonday sun was too hot. I must have been hungry. Was I sick? After I washed my face, I fell across the bed to rest. As soon as my head hit the pillow, I knew. Pray! I needed to pray for Stephanie. Our daughter was on a rafting trip with her church youth group. But what could go wrong? She was a lifeguard. She was strong. Besides the Guadalupe River ran slowly through the city of New Braunfels.

The knot in my stomach twisted again and I quickly slipped to my knees.

"God, help my daughter. I have no idea what's wrong, but I know You are looking over her. Please send angels to guard her. Lift her up to receive your blessing. Help her please, Father God! Help my daughter!"

Feeling better, I stood and did some house cleaning. It was Friday and my husband would be home early. I decided to stay off the ladder for the rest of the weekend. By Sunday, the incident was all but forgotten.

Sunday, Stephanie came bounding in the door after church. Sunburned, tired and hungry, she dropped her bags, rummaged through the refrigerator and came to sit beside me as I folded clothes. She sat close, her skin radiating heat.

"Wow!" I said. "You better get something on that burn."

"You know me," she answered leaning toward me. "It will turn to a tan in a few days." I leaned in toward her and enjoyed the rare moment of my teenager actually wanting to stay close to me.

"Mom," she continued. "I almost died."

"What?" I asked, thinking I didn't hear her correctly. "How?"

"I fell off my raft at one of the little falls. It was stupid because the water wasn't very deep and it wasn't white water or anything."

"Did you have a cramp or something?"

"No, the raft was on top of me — so I dove under a ways. Then I couldn't get up. No matter how hard I kicked, I didn't go anywhere. It was like something kept pulling me back. Then everything turned dark and I knew I was going to die."

"How did you get up?" I asked.

"I don't know." Stephanie's blue eyes sparkled with emotion. "Something just lifted me."

My stomach wrenched. "When did that happen?"

"Friday. It was right before lunch." Her voice faded. "It scared me."

"I knew!" I said. "I really knew." Then I told her about the gut-wrenching feeling I had on the ladder and how I went inside and prayed.

The words to the old song "Love Lifted Me" swirled through my head as we talked.

"That explains why I felt like something pulled me up," Stephanie said as she hugged me. "An angel lifted me."

~Peggy Purser Freeman

The Power of Prayer

Before, by yourself, you couldn't. Now, you've turned to our Lady,
and with her, how easy!
~Saint Josemaria Escrivá

Although spiritual, I wasn't much of a churchgoer. So when a saint appeared to me in a dream one night, I was more than a little surprised. She told me that she was known as Our Lady of Mount Carmel. I knew little about her, yet there she was, looking like an angel with her billowing scapular and telling me firmly to go and buy a statue of her form.

I awoke with a start and raced to my computer. I had so many questions. Who was this saint and why had she come to me? As I began to read the information, my jaw dropped.

An Internet search revealed the history of Our Lady of Mount Carmel, how she had initially appeared hundreds of years ago, and that her celebration day was the sixteenth of July. Hesitantly, I checked the newspaper my husband had left on the desk. I got goose bumps. It was July 16th. I immediately went out to buy myself a small statue of the saint.

A year later I saw my three-year-old daughter, Isabella, having some trouble breathing. We were in the yard and Isabella was chasing her grandfather joyously, a huge smile across her cherubic face. It didn't seem to bother her that she was panting hard, she was having so much fun, but I was concerned.

"Does her breathing seem normal to you?" I asked my mom.

"She can't seem to get enough air in," was her response. "I think you better have her checked."

Isabella had just recovered from a string of small illnesses, but they all should have been resolved by then. I was worried. That night I watched her sleep and I noticed that she was snoring. Then she stopped breathing. I shook her gently until she began to breathe. I had barely let out a sigh of relief when she stopped breathing again. I counted the seconds: one, two... ten, eleven... finally she gasped and breathed again.

"I'd better stay with her a while," I told my husband Lu uneasily.

But Isabella's breathing didn't improve. I spent the night beside her bed, concerned and helpless.

After many evenings repeating the awful pattern, I took her to the doctor.

"We should wait a few days and see if the medicine helps," he said.

More seemingly endless nights and another trip to the doctor resolved nothing.

Night after night I sat beside Isabella's bed watching her struggle for air in her sleep. During the day her condition would improve, so countless trips to the hospital and medical clinics were futile. I started to feel desperate, and the lack of sleep was affecting my own sanity.

"Please, God," I prayed, as I dressed for bed. "I need help!"

Then I spotted her. The tiny statue high atop my armoire—Our Lady of Mount Carmel. She was hidden from view, and I had forgotten her.

"Please," I begged. "Help our daughter breathe. You know what it means to watch your child suffer; only you can help us now."

I held the object tight as tears streamed down my face.

The next day our doctor ordered an X-ray, confirming that Isabella had abnormally large tonsils and adenoids. "They seem to have enlarged out of nowhere! I'll refer you to see a specialist, but," he warned, "it may take a few weeks of waiting."

He explained that in slumber, Isabella's muscles relaxed the throat, making her condition much worse.

I tossed and turned in bed that night while Lu took a shift watching Isabella. My angel came to me again. "Within one week, your child will have surgery," she said in the dream, "and all will be well."

It seemed impossible; we had been warned of the wait list. But that morning, the phone rang. It was the doctor's secretary, and she could arrange us an appointment with the specialist for the following morning if we were willing to go at 8:00 a.m. "YES!" I cried.

I was thrilled, but terrified — would this new doctor tell me that my child's condition could be fixed? Nightfall brought the now familiar dread.

The next morning was dreary and grey as we headed to see the specialist, a notable surgeon. As he held Isabella down to look inside her mouth, her tears broke my heart. I struggled to be strong and suppressed my own urge to cry.

"She needs to be operated on as soon as possible," he stated bluntly. "But right now, I'm booking October; I doubt I can do it sooner."

"October?" I gasped, looking from him to my husband in horror. "That's five months away!"

I didn't know how I could endure another five nights, never mind five months, of the torturous worry. I was delirious with lack of sleep. The tears now streamed endlessly down my face as we drove home in the pouring rain.

"I guess my dream was wrong," I said, sniffling to Lu. It had already been two days since the supposed premonition. I was beginning to doubt that I'd even seen Our Lady of Mount Carmel.

Nightfall came, and I took up camp beside my daughter's bed. As I lay on the floor staring at the ceiling, I talked to my angel.

"Mary," I called her by name, "you know what it is like to be a mother in pain. Please use your power to help Isabella."

Driven by an urge I couldn't explain, I leapt to my feet and raced to get my statue. With trembling hands, I placed the small object on the table by Isabella's bed. "I leave this to you."

The next morning marked the fifth day since I had received the nocturnal message.

I jumped when the phone rang. It was the surgeon's office.

"Hello, Mrs. Diodati, I have good news for you. We've scheduled Isabella for surgery the day after tomorrow."

My heart leapt with joy! My angel had come through for Isabella.

Isabella was operated on exactly one week from the night I had seen the blessed saint in my dream. As promised, all went smoothly. My daughter immediately was breathing better and without obstruction.

I found out later that Isabella had only been left with a small percentage of space to breathe, and how terribly critical her situation had been. She was given a gift, a miracle, by my loving angel's divine intervention. Our Lady of Mount Carmel placed her hands on my child, on my family, and I will never doubt again!

~Sylvia Diodati

Wilderness Angel

You'll meet more angels on a winding path than on a straight one.
~Terri Guillemets

I was lost in a remote section of wilderness just north of Anchorage, Alaska in the dead of winter. This was years before the wonders of the smartphone or GPS. The only reference I had to go by was a crude map I'd hastily scribbled on a paper napkin as the Newcomers Luncheon hostess, whom I'd never met, gave me directions over the phone.

"My home is easy to find," the woman had said. "You shouldn't have any trouble at all."

But somehow, and to this day I still don't know how it happened, I'd taken several wrong turns and ended up on a deserted stretch of road miles from any sort of civilization. No gas stations. No corner grocery stores. And eventually, not even a clearly defined stretch of road.

I tried not to panic, but that was rather difficult when I saw nothing but wilderness through my icy windshield. I thought about retracing my route, but the narrow road made it difficult to turn around. Finally, though, as I inched my car forward, my tires crunching the thick layer of snow beneath them, I realized that if I went any farther I might end up stuck in a snowdrift. I was dressed warmly and wore gloves and snow boots, but still, the prospect of abandoning my car and walking scared me. It was already afternoon and the temperature had only warmed up to thirty-four degrees. It was bound to plummet as the day went on.

"Help, Lord," I prayed aloud as I eased my car to a halt and shut down the motor. What should I do? If I tried to make it out on foot, I might end up even more lost than I already was. Also, I had to consider the very real threat of bears and other hungry wildlife lurking outside the shelter of my car. I sat still, trying hard not to cry, considering my options and praying for a miracle.

After a few moments I looked into my rearview mirror. A brown, compact automobile of a make I couldn't identify was inching its way slowly toward me. A government car, maybe? Flooded with relief, I swiped my teary eyes and scrambled out of the car. "Thank you, Lord," I cried as I waved my arms, signaling for the brown car to stop.

"What's the problem?" a young man of about thirty dressed in a business suit and overcoat yelled as he exited his car and walked toward me. "Are you stuck?"

"No," I said. "Just lost. I must have taken a wrong turn." I laughed a little, but it was a nervous laugh. "Do you know where I am?"

"Where do you want to be?" he asked, and I told him.

"Wow. You really did take a few wrong turns," he said. "You've gone about two miles in the opposite direction. You need to turn around, take a left when you get to the fork, and just follow that road back out to the main highway. The highway will take you straight into town. You won't be able to continue much farther on this road anyway, I'm sorry to say. It dead-ends a few hundred yards up ahead, but there's a turnout right around the next bend that will allow you to get pointed in the right direction."

I was so relieved and thankful for his help I wanted to collapse at his feet. "Left at the fork; main highway; straight into town," I stammered. "I can't thank you enough."

The man smiled, and at that moment I sensed a wave of such warmth and peace that every shred of anxiety I'd felt was gone.

"You're welcome," he said, heading back toward his car. "Glad I could help."

I watched him for a second, then climbed back into my own car and cranked the motor. But then something strange happened. As I looked into my rearview mirror, I saw nothing but the back end of the road and a few miles of snowy wilderness. The young man and his brown, nondescript car had vanished—just like that! It couldn't have been more than thirty seconds or so since I'd seen him. So, where had he gone?

I sat there, stunned. Then I clambered out of my car again to get a better look—to heck with any lurking hungry bears. He couldn't have turned around and disappeared that quickly. Impossible!

But the man was nowhere in sight. He and his car had vanished. Slowly, I walked the few yards back to where he'd stopped to help me. Searching the ground, I couldn't find a second set of tire tracks in the snow, only my own. How could that be?

Beginning to shiver, it occurred to me that something truly extraordinary had just happened. Why, if the road I was on only led to a dead end, had the young man been traveling down it himself? Why was his car so unremarkable? I didn't even remember it sporting license plates or any other emblem that would identify its make.

Then, suddenly, I knew. I knew beyond the shadow of a doubt who that man was. I'd prayed for help and God had answered. Oh, how He'd answered! Down to the roots of my being, I understood that the young man in the nondescript brown car had been an angel.

It's been years now since I'd lost my way on that dead-end road in the wilderness, but the memory of meeting an angel there has never faded. I'd not only made it back to the highway that day, I'd made it to the luncheon, albeit a little late. But I made up for my tardiness by having an awe-inspiring story to tell everyone there.

I've been telling it ever since.

~Paula L. Silici

78

A Mighty Hand

For I cried to him and he answered me! He freed me from all my fears.
~Psalm 34:4

n late fall of 1989 my marriage derailed. I packed up Patty, our six-year-old daughter, and moved to an apartment. My husband, Jake, stayed in our home, the house he'd built as a surprise for me only four years earlier.

We'd endured a crazy miserable winter. We started divorce proceedings, but Jake and I continued to see each other. By May we decided to try to put our marriage back on track. Our family reunited, but we faced another challenge. Jake had sold our home and signed the contract on another.

The sale proved especially hard on Patty. She'd spent the winter thinking of ways to help me. Early mornings I'd go into her room to wake her, but she'd bounce into my arms and say, "Surprise Mommy. I'm already dressed." Throughout the horrible separation she never complained but continued to shower love on both her daddy and me. Now we were moving out of the small apartment, but she still couldn't go home. It was gone.

She chose to replace her heartbreak with joy. "The house doesn't matter so much. We're us again!"

Armed with her insight and fresh hope, we went to see the new house. Jake ushered us through the front door. Patty ran off to explore while I stood dumbstruck in the split-level's entryway.

Overhead, where an elegant chandelier should have welcomed

visitors, a single bulb dangled like an interrogation light. Dingy gold-flecked wallpaper covered the stairwell walls like fungus. It crept into the middle of the living room where it abutted a country-scene wallpaper. A chair rail had been installed in half the room, coming to an abrupt stop midway through it.

The tour went downhill from there. The strange paint colors, the jungle scene mural in the master bedroom, and the missing fixtures still didn't prepare me for the lower level. Hundreds of BB-gun holes pierced the animal print wallpaper in the dungeon-like "finished" basement.

Jake went to check on Patty and I slipped into the garish bathroom to hide my tears. I remembered the care we had put into building our beautiful former home. From counters to flooring, we'd made every choice with love. In comparison, this house's demented design seemed to reflect the mess we'd made of our marriage.

But standing there in the grimy bathroom, I had a revelation. Patty and I had given our lives to the Lord that winter, and we'd asked God to restore our family. He'd answered our prayers, yet here I was sniveling about a house. I dried my tears and purposed to be grateful.

There was much to be thankful for. We had wonderful neighbors, and Patty became great friends with the girls nearby. Jake and I pieced our lives back together as we pieced together our peculiar new home. Most of the time we laughed our way through our ridiculous remodeling situations. Like the day we pulled down a damaged wall and a mound of used underwear tumbled out from between the studs.

In spite of my best intentions, sometimes melancholy crept in. I wished the cracks in our marriage could be mended as easily as the cracks in the walls. What we had lost weighted on me. The downgraded house seemed a symbol of our depreciated marriage.

One morning I picked up the Bible and read verse after verse about God's restorative power. I knew He could restore us, but I needed to make a change. I told myself, "You can either pray or you can cry. Make a choice." I decided to stop whining and, instead, ask God for help.

I also asked the Lord daily to put His angels around us to keep us safe while we repaired our marriage and our home. Jake excelled as a handyman, but he hated painting. So early in our marriage I'd taken over the task. This house desperately needed an exterior paint job, and I planned to start on my day off. Jake didn't want me on the ladder without him nearby.

"What if you get hurt?" he asked.

"Relax," I said, "I'm careful."

"No you're not," he insisted. "Once you climb a ladder you always stretch too far."

I let it drop, but as soon as he left for work I dragged out the paint and extension ladder. I made great progress. In one morning I'd painted half of the east side of the house before I hit a snag.

Directly under the roof peak, the eave sat inches out of reach, tantalizingly close. I felt sure the paintbrush could reach it if I only stretched a bit more. Jake's warning rang in my mind, but I silenced it. After all, I'd been painting for years. I knew what I was doing.

At the top of the ladder, about twenty feet off the ground, I stood on tiptoe to reach the last unpainted inch of eave.

And felt the ladder tip backwards.

A thousand thoughts flashed through my mind in an instant as I fell back: glimpses of silent movies where the bumbling character rides the careening ladder to the ground; images of my broken body crumpled on the weedy lawn. And of course I thought about Jake's warning: "Once you climb a ladder you always stretch too far."

I dropped the paintbrush and grabbed for the ladder, but it was too late. It continued its backward arc with me clinging to it. There was no avoiding it. I was going to crash to the ground.

Toppling backward, tipped at a forty-five-degree angle, I cried out, "Jesus!"

Immediately, what felt like an enormous hand stopped my fall. It covered my back from waist to shoulder blades. For a moment I hung there, supported by the huge hand. Then it pushed me, still clinging to the ladder, gently back against the house.

I leaned my head against the wood siding while the hand held me secure. Once my trembling eased, the hand disappeared. I climbed down the rungs and noticed the fence behind me. I began shaking again, this time in awe.

If I'd fallen from that position on the ladder, the trajectory would have impaled me on the fence post below. I stood there whispering, "Thank you Jesus," over and over. A Bible verse I'd read the day before came to mind: "For the Angel of the Lord guards and rescues all who reverence him." Psalm 34:7

God heard my prayers, and He answered my desperate cry.

When Jake came home I showed him the ladder and shared what happened. He stared at it for a minute, then grabbed me and held on tight. We agreed that the God who held me steady could stabilize our marriage too.

We put ourselves into His mighty hands that day. And now over twenty years later He still holds us, bound together in love.

~Jeanie Jacobson

79

The Gift of Music

Music is the mediator between the spiritual and the sensual life.
~Ludwig van Beethoven

n the summer our young family loved spending Sundays at the swimming pool in a nearby mountain park. One afternoon in July, I heard my name paged to come to the office for a phone call. Immediately I was apprehensive because calls were not allowed unless it was an emergency. My brother-in-law was on the phone and told me that we had to come home because my brother had died in a tragic accident.

In disbelief, my husband and I packed up everything and drove home. It didn't seem possible that Danny was gone. I had just talked with him the night before. We were three years apart and growing up we loved playing music, singing, and dancing. When he was eight years old our mother bought him a youth guitar and he asked me, "How do I learn to play this?"

"Maybe you should try practicing 'Twinkle, Twinkle, Little Star' since it is a song for kids," I suggested.

"That's a good idea," he said and ran to his room.

About fifteen minutes later he came back and played and sang the song. Looking at him in wonder, I asked him, "How did you learn that song so fast?"

After thinking about it, he explained, "I practiced like you told me to."

Laughing out loud, I told him, "Go practice 'Mary Had A Little Lamb.'"

Again he was back in about fifteen minutes playing and singing the entire song. This time I joyfully told him, "I think you have the gift of knowing how to play a musical instrument by ear."

Over the years he brought so much joy and music to our lives. In recent years he had kept his musical equipment in my large family room because he lived in an apartment. In addition to the guitar, he also owned and played a set of drums and harmonicas. Sometimes he would even play my piano or keyboard while we sang gospel, country, and popular songs. I admired him because his musical talents were outstanding and seemed effortless, whereas I had to practice quite a bit just to sound good. When Danny and his girlfriend, Laura, planned their wedding, they asked me to play the organ music at their ceremony. It had been an honor. Now he was gone.

The day after my brother's funeral, I was standing in the kitchen looking out the window crying. Suddenly a red robin landed on the brick windowsill and looked up at me. Blinking its eyes, the robin stared and stared at me, seeming genuinely concerned. I was amazed that it didn't fly away when I wiped my eyes, and I thought that maybe it was my brother or my guardian angel coming to console me. When it eventually flew away, so did the music.

Life went on, but it was painful. For the first time in my life, I wasn't interested in singing in the church choir or playing the piano. When our washing machine broke down and needed to be replaced I decided to sell the piano. After all, I reasoned, no one played it and the cash would come in handy. When the new owner rolled it out the door on a piano cart, I ignored the slight twinge in my heart.

As our children grew up and turned into teenagers, their father and I had sadly grown apart and amicably divorced. Together, my kids and I kept the faith and worked our way through those hard times. It was about five years later, the day after Thanksgiving; I sat and thought about my life. Even though I was only aware of a few times that my guardian angel had positively made her presence known, I decided to call out to her. Sitting at the kitchen table I bowed my head and prayed that I might find someone special to date and maybe spend the rest of my life with. When I finished my prayer and looked up I couldn't believe my eyes. In front of the kitchen counter and the silverware drawer was a foggy blurred image of a husky man about 5'10" standing with his back to me. My spirits soared because I knew my guardian angel was letting me know that I would meet someone special.

A week before Christmas, some friends invited me to go to a Saturday night oldies dance that a local radio station was hosting. I hadn't been dancing in years, so I was excited, but also afraid that I wouldn't be asked to dance. To my surprise there were many people in their forties attending and a couple of guys did ask me to dance. One was a fantastic dancer. After a fast dance, three couples stopped us and asked how long my husband and I had been dancing together. We laughed and confessed that this was the first time. At the end of the evening, when Gene asked for my phone number, I gave it to him. He called the following Tuesday evening and asked me to a movie on Friday night. After the movie we picked up some ice cream and headed to my house.

As I filled the coffee pot and turned it on, Gene got out the dessert bowls. Then he asked, "What drawer is your silverware in?"

Looking over towards him, I froze. He was standing with his back to me in front of the counter and the silverware drawer. The outline of his body was an exact match to the foggy blurred image that I had seen a month ago. When I didn't answer right away, he turned around and asked, "Are you okay?"

Recovering fast and smiling, I assured him that I was. Later as I put the cups, bowls, and silverware in the dishwasher, Gene went into the family room and all of a sudden I heard "Angels We Have Heard on High."

He was playing my keyboard and singing. As I went over to him, he asked me, "Why are you crying?"

Unaware that tears were streaming down my face, I simply replied, "The music is back."

I explained how I had pushed music out of my life after the death of my brother, but now I was ready to welcome it back. He brought over his guitar that weekend and told me he had the gift of playing it and his other instruments by ear. It was stunning how his talents resembled those of my brother. We started practicing songs, and not long after we began playing and singing duets in church.

The following June we played and sang to each other "The Wedding Pledge" and "You're My Best Friend" at our wedding. Once again music was a big part of my life and my family and friends loved it. Moving into our new home was like déjà vu as my husband set up his guitar, set of drums, harmonicas, and piano in the family room. Bowing my head I whispered, "Thank you, thank you, I could not ask for more."

~Brenda Cathcart-Kloke

Chapter
9

Touched by an Angel

Divine Intervention

Thank You Lord

The feeling remains that God is on the journey, too.
~Teresa of Avila

I was quite well known as an actress in the 1960s and 70s and this story took place in 1966. I was on my way from London to Italy, where I was to shoot a movie almost entirely on location in a small fishing village called Lerici. This is now an "in" holiday spot for the smart and trendy.

I was booked to fly to Rome from Heathrow and given a send off by friends and the press. Although it had been months since I had met Dr. Mary Young, the clairvoyant and friend of Natalie Wood, she had told me some amazing things, some of which I had been thinking about a lot.

She made me promise that when I got what, at that time, I referred to as "buzzes," I was to act on them.

In the car on the way to the airport, I had some sort of moment. A psychic flash? Perhaps. Or my Guardian Angel Daniel warning me of something? Either way, I heard or felt this voice telling me "Do not get on this plane!" Three times I heard it. This was something I felt compelled to act on.

I told the driver I wouldn't be getting on the plane, so he didn't need to hurry. Well, I guess he thought I was just some movie star acting crazy. Perhaps he thought I was on drugs, who knows. But he ignored me.

The events of the next hours still leave me awestruck.

On arrival at the airport I told the press guy I would get the next plane. Of course he threw a fit. But I didn't care; I stuck to my guns. I refused to get on the plane, even said I would scream if they tried to carry me on.

This was before cell phones and texts. In fact just to make a landline call could take up to seven hours with delays. So we had no way of warning the director and cast waiting for me in Rome that I was going to be on the next plane.

The PR people booked me a seat on the next flight and it took off an hour later. The first inkling I had that anything was seriously wrong was when we began to circle the airport instead of starting our descent into Rome. When we did at last land, I could see out the window. There were large pieces of debris and the emergency services in action everywhere. The earlier plane had crashed on landing, with a large loss of life.

The shock of what could have happened if I had ignored that warning made my knees wobble.

I cannot describe how I felt at that moment except that I kept saying under my breath, "Thank you Jesus, oh, thank you Jesus."

My name was still on the earlier flight's passenger list, and more than a few of the ground crew did a double take when they saw me walking towards them in the terminal. Someone was already on the phone to London, talking about recasting the role. The press guy, who had the awful task of writing my obituary, glanced up as I was walking towards him, saw me and passed out cold on the concourse. Bless him, he was a large guy and I swear the whole terminal shook.

The director and other actors pressed me to say why I didn't get the plane I was originally booked on. But in those days if I had said what really had happened, either no one would have believed me or they would have belittled what had happened, or even ordered a little white van to carry me away. So, for years I kept quiet about the voice or feeling warning me not to get the plane. It was too important. I kept thanking Jesus, because I knew what He had done for me. I just wish that all the other passengers could have been saved, too.

Although I have been blessed and open to more happenings in

my life since then, this one always leaves me breathless when I think about it.

~Suzanna Leigh

81

Angel on the Footbridge

God is our refuge and strength, a very present help in trouble.
~Psalm 46:1

was trapped in a secluded area of a large park. The two assailants were only a few feet behind me. I knew my fate: either rape or death, or both. How had I arrived at this particular dangerous situation? Simply by being at the wrong place at the wrong time. I'd had extensive abdominal surgery a little more than a week before. And as anyone who's had abdominal surgery can surely attest, you suffer intense gas pains. The best cure—long walks.

I loved walking the Franklin Delano Roosevelt Park located in South Philadelphia near the Naval Base. Living close by, I would often walk from my home near 10th and Oregon to the park, completing a walk around the entire length before heading back home. So, off I went that day, hoping the gas pain would ease.

As I had entered the park, I had noticed the circus was in town. I'd forgotten all about it and hoped to get a glimpse of the elephants inside the circus tents on my way back. It was a nice day; spring weather was on the way. I headed down the trail that leads mothers with strollers, joggers and bicyclists through the beautiful park, which is part of the larger Fairmount Park System.

After walking for about thirty minutes, I came to the more secluded section of the park. No one was around; it was quite early in the day.

Then a young, scruffy-looking man exited from the nearby bushes and walk past me. I got a good look at him and kept turning around to make sure he wasn't following me. As I walked further past the tennis courts and toward the I-95 overpass, another man, this one heavier but just as scruffy, came out of the bushes to my right. I was in trouble.

Both men started following me. As I increased my speed, they did too. No one was around to hear me call for help. I had no cell phone at that time, and I could not run because I was still healing from my surgery. I prayed for my life.

I had come to a little stone footbridge when I noticed an old man walking his dog on the bridge. Still praying to God to protect me, I went straight to the man. Would he be able to help me or would the two men in close pursuit also hurt him? As I reached the elderly man, I opened my mouth to ask for help, but my tongue stuck to the roof of my mouth.

This was no man who stood before me. It was a ghost. Standing on the footbridge was my late father-in-law. He had passed away two years before. Yet, there he stood with one of the family dogs that had passed away a few years earlier.

"Dad," I said, my heart thumping. But at first he did not reply. My assailants had stopped cold at the foot of the bridge, watching me and the ghost. Yes, they saw him too. "Stay here," were the only words uttered from the apparition before me. I stayed put.

While the ghost studied the two men and they him, I realized the apparition protecting me was not my father-in-law. I was standing before an angel who had taken on my father-in-law's appearance so I would not be frightened. I felt my fear leave as I watched, stunned, as the two assailants backed away slowly from the angel. They were afraid. The fear was evident in their eyes. They turned and quickly walked away from the bridge, the angel, and me.

I may have been in shock, because I did not move. I stood awaiting further instructions from my rescuer. His eyes were still on the men, who by now had disappeared over the hill. How do you thank an angel? I was about to touch his arm, get his attention, and thank him, but a voice in my head warned, "Don't touch." I dropped my arm. Just then a park maintenance truck came over the hill, headed our way.

"Follow that and go home," the apparition commanded.

Still in shock, I asked no questions. When the truck passed, I was about to follow, but wanted to say thank you to the angel. He was gone. Just like that, as if I dreamt the whole thing. I wanted to cry. Not because my life had been spared, but because I never got to say goodbye or thank you. I never told anyone this story except for my sisters and my daughter, but I felt the time was right to share this outside my family.

It had been twenty years since I returned to the park. But this past March, I went back with two of my grandsons to participate in a Zombie Run for charity. I went to that little footbridge after the race. Even though I saw no angel that day, I know that God hears us when we call to him and he replies in ways that amaze.

~Marie Gilbert

82

The Flickering Headlight

He spake well who said that graves are the footprints of angels.
~Henry Wadsworth Longfellow

lived on the Greek island of Corfu one summer at the height of tourist season. I enjoyed the diverse, international crowd, but I occasionally felt the need to seek solitude. I would usually rent a motorcycle and head into the interior of the island in search of isolated trails and sleepy villages. One such day, I rode for hours along dirt roads flanked by bright yellow wildflowers, winding through steep and rugged hills. I had to keep a close watch on the gas gauge as the only gas station was in the town where I had rented the motorcycle. At half a tank, I had no choice but to return home.

As I turned around, I saw an abandoned cemetery so small and overgrown with weeds it was almost unnoticeable. I decided to stretch my legs before beginning the long ride home. I rode to the entrance and cut the engine. As I passed through the creaky wrought iron gate, I noticed how silent the place was. I whistled to reassure myself that I hadn't gone deaf. There was only an hour or two of daylight left. A strong wind blew, stirring the overgrown grass that obscured the scattered tombstones.

In Greece, people aren't usually buried below ground. Instead, bodies of the deceased are laid to rest in aboveground tombs with easily removable lids. Several times I walked by tombs with visible skeletal remains. I found this very disturbing. Where I come from—Los Angeles, California—death is sanitized and brushed away quickly so as not to make anyone uncomfortable.

The head of the tombs have small cabinets that contain a photograph of the deceased. This tugged at my heart more than anything else—to see the faces of the people buried there as they were in life: their warm smiles and the kindness in their eyes. I spent a long time wandering around, kneeling in the grass next to the graves, talking to the people lying there and wondering about their lives.

At the back of the cemetery, a tomb twice as large as any of the others caught my eye. When I looked inside the cabinet, I found out why. It held a photograph of a young couple, arm in arm, smiling widely. The date of their deaths, etched in the stone, were identical. Apparently, they had died together in an accident. Roads on Greek islands are mostly unmarked and can be very dangerous. They had been laid in each other's arms inside the tomb.

I can't begin to relate all the feelings I had while looking at that picture of them together, bursting with youthful energy, their eager smiles full of excitement and anticipation of their lives together. A line from a poem by Andrew Marvell crossed my mind:

The grave is a fine and private place
but none, I think, do there embrace.

I hoped it wasn't true.

A marble cross marking their graves had been broken at the base and fallen on the ground at the head of the tomb. Wildflowers had grown up around it. This wouldn't be worth mentioning except for the fact that they were the only flowers growing anywhere in the cemetery. The contrast of these symbols of springtime next to the tombstone was so striking that I wanted to take a photograph of it. The best angle was from the top of the tomb, but I felt that standing on it would be disrespectful so I took a few shots from other angles. Unsatisfied, I said to the young couple buried there, "Excuse me. I'd just like to stand on your tomb for a few seconds to take a picture of your flowers. I hope you don't mind." I took the photo, then stepped back down and said thank you. Before I left, I brushed the dirt off the lid, pulled the weeds around their grave, then picked up the broken piece of the cross and put it back in place.

I left the cemetery and started the motorcycle. After being immersed in such profound silence, the engine seemed louder than ever. As I rode home, the faces of the people I had seen in the time-yellowed photographs repeated in my mind like a slideshow, especially the photo of the young couple. I prayed for their souls as darkness fell.

Though tainted with sadness, I had found the solitude I was seeking. There was peace in the old cemetery, but it was a dark peace and I was anxious to get back to the resort, and to life.

As it got darker, I reached for the headlight switch and discovered that it didn't work. That meant I would have to ride home through winding, often treacherous dirt roads with only the faint starlight to guide me. At one point, I was riding up a very steep hill, unaware that the road leveled and turned abruptly just beyond the peak. A steep cliff awaited anyone who didn't negotiate the curve correctly. Hungry, cold and in a hurry to get home, I was traveling too fast, oblivious to the danger ahead. But as I reached the top of the hill, the headlight flickered on and off, just for a few seconds, but long enough for me to see the cliff before it was too late. I slammed on the brake and skidded to a stop with only inches to spare. My heart pounding, I looked over the edge into the darkness and heard the rocks my tires had kicked up rattling down the rocky hillside. The headlight then turned off again and stayed off for the rest of the night.

I left Greece a few days later and traveled elsewhere for several months. I didn't develop the film until I returned to California. I took approximately five hundred photographs on that trip, and about ten at the cemetery, but the only photo with an abnormality is the one of the young couple's broken tombstone. A white mist swirls around it as if something, or someone, is rushing upward. The mist has defined edges in several areas, eliminating the possibility of a lens flare or light refraction. I don't like to think that their spirits were hanging around that old cemetery, but maybe they had died so young, with so much life left to live, they had not yet accepted death and were eager to rejoin the living. That might also be the reason the only flowers in the entire cemetery were growing by their grave.

It also occurred to me that the headlight turning on during those crucial seconds as I approached the cliff, which undoubtedly saved my life, was not caused by an electrical glitch. It was caused by the spirits of the young couple, saving me from the same fate that had befallen them. There is no doubt in my mind that they were my guardian angels that night.

~Mark Rickerby

Road Angel

We are never so lost our angels cannot find us.

~Stephanie Powers

admit it; I'm directionally challenged. I lack an internal compass and use landmarks for directions. I'm extremely grateful for high-tech vehicle navigation systems, as well as those maps and diagrams that have the words: "You are here."

To feel confident and not worry about getting lost, I've always made a few trial runs when required to travel to an unfamiliar destination. That's exactly what I did when I was summoned for jury duty at the courthouse in the city. The day before I was to appear, my husband showed me the best route for bypassing busy commuter traffic on the freeway. I had no worries about being late for jury duty the following morning.

Driving to the courthouse via an expressway and surface roads, I arrived early enough to purchase a cup of coffee before reporting to the juror waiting room at 8 a.m. The jury pool consisted of 200 people. Waiting for our numbers to be called was difficult. Many of us nervously fidgeted and squirmed in our chairs, or strolled to the back of the room to see what the three vending machines had to offer. Finally, fifty numbers were called for prospective jurors at 10 a.m. At noon, the rest of us were given an hour lunch break and told to report back to the juror waiting room at 1 p.m.

After lunch, I passed the time by reading a paperback mystery novel I'd tucked in my purse for the occasion. At 3 p.m., my number was called and my group of potential jurors were ushered into the courtroom and seated in the jury box. The judge informed us that jurors were being selected for a robbery trial. Since a large embezzlement of funds had occurred at the company I worked for, the prosecutor wanted me to serve on the jury. Needless to say, the defense attorney disagreed and requested that I be dismissed immediately. The judge complied, thanked me for my service and excused me from jury duty for three years. A feeling of disappointment mixed with relief washed over me when I left the courtroom.

But then I thought about my plans for the evening. In less than three hours, my husband and I would join my best friend and her husband for dinner at our favorite Italian restaurant. It had been a while since we'd caught up on each other's lives.

As I left the parking garage, I turned right onto the surface street behind the courthouse leading to the expressway. To my dismay, I spotted a detour barricade with flashing lights up ahead and a policeman directing me to turn left instead of right. I had no choice but to drive into an area of the city I didn't know. Even though I didn't recognize the street signs, I kept driving and hoping I'd recognize a landmark to get my bearings. But I seemed to be driving in circles. I thought I was home free when I pulled into a gas station to ask for directions. Alas, that was not the case.

"Hey, pretty lady, you gotta pay for that information," a young man taunted after I'd rolled down my window and asked him for directions to the expressway.

Before I could speed away, two cohorts joined him. "Give us your money," they chanted in unison and began to rock my car back and forth. A jolt of sheer terror rushed through me. I trembled uncontrollably as one of the men raised a tire iron to smash the car window to grab my purse from the passenger seat. The car door was locked, but I realized my negligence in having a purse in full view, which had made me a target.

Suddenly, a large white sport utility vehicle with blinding spotlights and headlights appeared and pulled in behind my car. Fortunately, the three hoodlums scattered. I couldn't see his face clearly, but my fear subsided as the SUV driver, wearing a white epaulette uniform, approached my car. "Follow me and you'll find your way home," he said.

For a moment, I sat there dumbstruck and unable to speak. How did he know that I was lost? And how did he happen upon me at exactly the right time? But I came to my senses when he blinked his headlights to signify he was ready to proceed on our journey. For ten minutes I followed him until I could see the familiar expressway sign in the distance. Then the vehicle disappeared as quickly as it had appeared to save me.

I was thankful for being safe and able to find my way home after such a frightening ordeal. Never had spaghetti tasted so good.

~Georgia A. Hubley

My Speech Day Song

> *Every happening, great and small, is a parable whereby God speaks to us,*
> *and the art of life is to get the message.*
> ~Malcolm Muggeridge

A s I boarded the school bus that morning, my heart was pounding and my palms were sweaty. I had begged Mom to let me stay home from school that day, but she knew I wasn't really sick—just scared. But who wouldn't be? After all, it was Speech Day, the scariest day in all of seventh grade.

And if getting up in front of my classmates wasn't bad enough, I also had to worry about the content of my speech. The assignment was to write a speech about someone we admired. Most of my friends had picked actresses and sports stars, even former presidents. I'd chosen Joni Eareckson, a Christian woman who had become a quadriplegic after a diving accident as a teenager. But instead of being angry about her injury, she used it to reach out to other people and help them overcome their own problems. While I truly admired Joni Eareckson for all that she had been through, I worried about what my classmates would think. I really just wanted to fit in with everyone else, and I worried that people might make fun of me for writing my speech about a Christian.

I sat on the school bus that morning, sure I was going to be sick to my stomach. This was the worst day ever. And then the bus driver turned on the radio, something she'd never done before.

To distract myself, I paid careful attention to the song playing. I'd never heard it before, but I kind of liked it. The chorus went, "It's all right, I think we're gonna make it." As I listened to the words, I a peace came over me. My breathing slowed and my stomach calmed. I didn't know why, but the song just made me feel better.

The chorus played again. "It's all right, I think we're gonna make it." While intellectually, I knew the song was probably about a romantic relationship, emotionally, I was convinced that God was speaking to me through that song. As I listened, I focused on the word "we." It reminded me that I wasn't alone. God was with me on that bus, and He would be with me when I read my speech later that day. I really believed that things were going to be all right because God was with me.

A few hours later, I went to my English class, where I would read my speech to the class. I felt nervous again, but not nearly as bad as before. I kept reminding myself of the song's words. "It's all right, I think we're gonna make it." And I knew that God was there with me. When the teacher called my name, I took a deep breath, smiled at my classmates, and started to read my speech.

When I finished, my classmates clapped, just like they did for everyone else. No one teased me about my speech, and the teacher gave me a good grade.

Everything had turned out all right, just like the song said.

That night, I called the leader of my church's youth group and told her about my experience. "I know it was probably just a coincidence," I said, suddenly embarrassed that I was making such a big deal out of a simple song.

But she said, "No, it wasn't. There is no such thing as a coincidence."

"It was just a song," I said again.

"Didn't you say this was the first time the bus driver ever turned on the radio? And how did that particular song just happen to be playing?" she pointed out. "God made those things happen because He knew you needed His comfort."

And I knew that she was right. If God knows every hair on my head, surely He knows when I'm afraid and need to feel His presence.

My seventh grade speech day was a long time ago now, but I've never forgotten that day. It was the first time in my life that God felt real to me. I know it was just a song, but God used it to show me that He really does care about every aspect of my life, no matter how small.

Maybe my speech day song was just an amazing coincidence, but that day, it felt like a miracle.

~Diane Stark

Help Amidst
the Storm

For he will command his angels concerning you to guard you in all your
ways; they will lift you up in their hands so that you will not strike your foot
against a stone.
~Psalm 91:11-12

was fifteen and so excited to take a friend with me on my family vacation. My parents had rented a camp on a lake in upstate New York, only an hour away from where we lived, but I knew it would be a great adventure. I was a dreamer and could always find magnificence in the smallest things. So the idea of spending a whole week on a lake in the woods made for great anticipation.

My parents packed up the car with luggage and groceries. My friend and I, and my brother and his friend hopped in the back seat and off we went. This was the first time we had ever taken a vacation like this, so everyone was looking forward to it. In less than an hour we were driving up a dirt road through the woods and on to our destination. The three-bedroom cottage with a large kitchen and living area was set in the midst of pine trees, picnic tables, and a boat dock.

With no other camps close by, it felt secluded. It was the perfect setting for a fun experience. We stayed up late and told stories around the campfire. We swam and barbecued lots of good food. My friend and I set out early in the mornings to walk and explore the area. We talked about our futures, clothes and boys, like most teenage girls. Every morning when we left for our walk, my mother would say, "Don't get lost, girls. Your father will be making us all lunch at noon."

One morning, the two of us took out the rowboat instead of taking a walk. It was an overcast and humid day. We leisurely rowed for about an hour toward the other side of the lake. Then we heard thunder. Within minutes, the dark skies opened up and bolts of lightning hit the water.

We knew we had to get off the lake, so we rowed back to shore. But then we had no idea where we were. We ran through the woods trying to find our camp. I was barefoot and the ground was rough with twigs, rocks, and pine needles. We had to yell to each other over the noise of the pouring rain and thunder. We didn't see any other camps as we made our way through the dense trees. Everything was wet and loud and frightening. We were blazing our own path, dodging branches and shoots.

My feet were burning and I was well aware that being in the woods near a lake in the middle of a thunderstorm was the worst place to be. In my mind, I heard my mother's words: "Don't get lost, girls." Yet here we were deep in the forest with no one around to help us. I silently prayed for assistance.

I knew that my family had to be frantic wondering where we were. My mother was a worrier and I knew she had probably called the authorities by now. I thought if we could just get to a road and out of the woods, we would be all right. But we couldn't find the road. We just kept moving and hoping the storm would stop. I was never much of an athlete; breathing became more difficult, and my feet felt like they were shredded.

After about twenty minutes, the pain in my feet eased and I could breathe easier. It felt like I was being carried. I still saw lightning and felt the rain, but it got quiet for me. I lost all track of time and place and felt like I was shrouded in a protective embrace. I saw my friend running alongside me, but somehow I knew someone else was with me too—someone who knew the way back to camp, someone who knew I couldn't run anymore. It wasn't my strength or sense of direction that was taking me back to camp. I felt a guiding peace, and an assurance that we were going to be okay.

We never saw a road, or person to help us, but all of a sudden we were in the back yard of our camp. We emerged through a break in the trees as if we had been delivered and placed back into the safety of my family. My mother was clearly relieved to see us, and in fact had called the authorities to help locate us. She got us towels to dry off and sat us down on the sofa. The bottoms of my feet were blistered and bleeding, but I was safe, although a little shaken and mystified.

Something happened in those woods—something extraordinary. I knew I didn't get back to camp safely by my own doing. Later that day, after we had gotten into dry clothes and had something to eat, I said to my friend, "I felt like someone was carrying me and guiding me back to the camp." She looked at me in amazement and said, "I don't understand it either. I wasn't going to say anything, because it seemed so crazy, but I felt the same thing."

The rest of the week was peaceful and beautiful. We all stayed close to the camp, cooking together, sharing stories, and laughing. It was one of my favorite vacations and still stands out in my mind today. I had been anticipating a great week away, but what I got was far more than a fun vacation—I got a helping hand from above.

~Marijo Herndon

Imogene's Girls

I cannot forget my mother. She is my bridge.
~Renita Weems

For years I had been searching for my mother. Oh, I had a mom and a dad who raised me. They took care of me when I had staph infections and chickenpox and measles. They grounded me when I ignored my curfew, and comforted me when my boyfriend dumped me.

But since I was adopted, a huge part of me was still unknown. I had no idea who I looked like or where I got my personality. I wanted to fill in the missing pieces. I also wanted to find my birth mother so I could let her know how grateful I was for the decision she made, because I had been raised in a loving home by wonderful parents.

As a toddler, my family read picture books to me about being a "chosen child." So when I was an adult and my parents shared all the adoption paperwork they had, I was not surprised by their openness. From the court papers they gave me, I discovered the name of my birth mother. It was an unusual name—Imogene Marcelle Gann. After I had called all the women who had the same first and last name and were around the right age—and none of them admitted to giving up a child for adoption—I gave up.

With all my heart, I wanted to find my biological mother… but I wanted it to be easy. I wanted her to just appear.

Unbeknownst to me, my husband Michael was doing some research, which was unlike him, since he usually viewed the Internet as a source of entertainment or a way of getting information on the weather. When he told me he dug into some online files and discovered my birth mother had died decades ago, I was amazed at what he had done for me... and saddened over what he had discovered.

The woman I was looking for had died when I was nine. I never even had the chance to meet her.

Again I thought my journey to fill in the missing pieces was over. I'd never see what the completed puzzle looked like.

Then Michael did something else out of character—he contacted a neighborhood friend who was a genealogy expert. This friend was an expert at navigating electronic bulletin boards and databases. A few days after she accepted the "mission," she sent me an e-mail.

"Sioux—I think this message is for you. I found it on an adoption bulletin board. 'Looking for a baby girl born in Missouri and given up for adoption in the mid or late fifties. Her biological mother was Imogene Gann.'" An e-mail address was included.

Without Jackie's help, we never would have stumbled onto this. I replied to the notice (it was a cousin who posted it) and we arranged to talk later in the evening, after we both had gotten home from work.

I had a long conversation with the newly found cousin that evening, and my sorrow over my birth mother's death turned to joy. I had a half-sister. And her name was Chris.

After the cousin was confident I was not crazy, she felt safe enough to give me my half-sister's e-mail address. I was getting the chance to piece together the puzzle of my past.

In the months that followed, Chris and I had marathon phone sessions—sometimes talking so long our ears went numb. E-mails went back and forth in an attempt to catch up on lost time. What was my favorite Saturday morning cartoon? My best birthday memory? Who was the first celebrity I had a crush on? I had endless questions for Chris, too, since she had lived with our mother for seven years. We were both trying to fill in the holes.

I flew to Oregon to spend Thanksgiving with my sister. When our eyes locked across a crowded airport lobby, we ran into each other's arms and sobbed. It was an instant connection—as if we had known each other decades ago and were now reuniting. And as I held on tightly to Chris, I felt another pair of arms encircling me... I felt the woman who gave birth to me embracing both of her girls.

During my visit we hunched over pictures. I finally got to see what Imogene looked like, and I received a much-treasured gift—a photo album filled with pictures of my birth mother. So that's where I got my high forehead and my smirky smile—from her.

After almost two years of cards and calls and e-mails, Chris and I settled into being sisters. She was coming to St. Louis for Easter. We were getting excited about decorating eggs and eating chocolate bunnies—stuff that we missed out on during our childhood. But then, two weeks before her flight, we got word that someone else had responded to the same Internet notice that had introduced us. It seems that Imogene had given birth to a girl before she had me, and this girl—like me—had been given up for adoption. And she lived only a two-hour drive from me.

Chris and I drove halfway across the state to spend the day with Nancy, our newest (and oldest) sister. More photos were pulled out and compared. We chatted and laughed and cried together. Chris and I shifted a little to make room for her in our sisterhood.

But as glad as we were to piece the puzzle together, I wondered why the notice on the Internet bulletin board had not been removed once I responded. Why had it been left up for Nancy to find? And why had my husband gone against his character to elicit Jackie's help? What were the chances that Jackie might have missed that single notice on that one bulletin board?

In my heart, I know it was not coincidence. I know these weren't just ordinary events. I know these weren't just random happenings that resulted in the three of us finding each other.

No, in my heart, I know that it was our mama making the arrangements. She made sure that everything was aligned so that her girls would be together. We didn't have each other growing up, and we had lost her, but now we could live on as sisters… with her loving embrace encircling all three of us.

~Sioux Roslawski

An Angel in the Laundry Room

Put your ear down close to your soul and listen hard.
~Anne Sexton

The first indication that something was wrong with my four-teen-month-old son, Jeb Daniel, was during bathtime. Most nights, all three children splashed and played tirelessly in our expansive garden tub, a luxury they'd not experienced in our previous home, a small base-housing residence in Jacksonville, Florida.

But that night, Jeb Daniel began to fret while holding onto the edge of the tub and soon started crying, lifting one leg slightly off the tub's floor.

I took him out of the bath, checked his leg for any sign of injury, dried and dressed him for bed, and then cuddled with him in the rocking chair. No fever, nothing out of the ordinary, he just seemed unusually calm and subdued. I read a couple of his favorite books to him and then tucked him into his crib. He fell asleep easily.

Several hours later, I was awakened by his cries. Upon entering his room, I realized he'd just vomited. "Oh, he has a stomach bug," I muttered under my breath.

I changed his pajamas and sheets and then took him to the spare bed in the next room. I wanted to be near him if he got sick again, but I didn't want to wake my husband David, an exhausted naval medical officer working to complete a master's degree in Military Studies at Quantico, Virginia.

Jeb Daniel quickly drifted back to sleep on one pillow; I dozed off on the other.

In a short time, however, he roused, distraught and crying. He kept throwing up and I managed to protect his clothes and blankie with a towel each time. But one time, I didn't move his blankie fast enough. So after Jeb Daniel drifted off, I tossed it in the washing machine and placed an identical one in his small hands. He only accepted these two blankies, no exceptions.

The next time Jeb Daniel woke up, he seemed more fretful and didn't fall back to sleep easily. I carried him with me to the laundry room to move the clothes from the washer to the dryer.

When I bent over to drop his blankie into the dryer, Jeb Daniel, nestled on my hip, cried out as if in pain. I assumed his little tummy hurt, empty now and sore from throwing up so many times.

"The pain is in his lower abdomen; turn on the light and take off his pajamas." I heard the voice, audible and clear. Startled, I looked to see if David had awakened, but I knew it wasn't his voice.

I tiptoed downstairs, laid Jeb Daniel on the floor of the den, turned on the light—I'd been finding my way around with just a nightlight so as not to wake the rest of the family—unsnapped his footie pajamas, and removed his diaper.

My heartbeat quickened. There was a tangerine-sized bulge in Jeb Daniel's belly, just below the diaper line. I stumbled up the stairs with trembling legs and woke my husband.

"We've got to get to the emergency room, now!" I said.

David dressed and held our precious son; I woke four-year-old Jenifer and seven-year-old Jeremy. We'd lived in Stafford for less than a month; I didn't have phone numbers for any of our neighbors, and at three in the morning, I couldn't think of a better solution.

We prayed in the car on the thirty-minute drive to Fort Belvoir Community Hospital. Jeb Daniel rested peacefully in his car seat with only a few occasional tears. I tried to remain calm, but my thoughts and stomach churned with possible outcomes.

The doctor on call gave orders for an intravenous drip feed and then said we'd be going by ambulance to Walter Reed Army Medical Center. The technician assigned to start the IV proceeded swiftly but lackadaisically, assuming that my lifeless toddler would show no resistance to a sharp needle going into the top of his chubby foot.

Jeb Daniel kicked, jerking the needle loose. Blood splattered on both technicians and all over the tiny room. Finally, after they cleaned off the blood, the technician worked with more precision this time and inserted the needle in the fold of Jeb Daniel's little hand.

I carried Jeb Daniel to the waiting ambulance. Paramedics strapped me to the gurney and allowed me to hold a once-again sleeping child. David and the kids followed closely behind.

At Walter Reed, doctors quickly diagnosed Jeb Daniel with a testicular torsion and said that he needed surgery immediately, adding, "Every minute counts when dealing with impaired blood flow."

We nervously waited for surgery preparations. My husband couldn't stop watching the monitor; Jeb Daniel's breathing was so shallow from the medication, and he barely moved on the adult-sized bed.

I cried when they rolled my baby away and silently prayed.

What seemed like days later, the surgeon returned with news that all was well with Jeb Daniel. The torsion was corrected, and my son was resting comfortably in recovery. The doctor commended me for getting Jeb Daniel in before the restricted blood flow caused permanent, irreversible damage.

As I held my beautiful baby boy, I thanked God for Jeb Daniel's guardian angel who met me in the laundry room in the wee hours that morning with explicit instructions for my son, His precious child.

~Julie Lavender

Goatman's Bridge

Although we may not see them and they don't make a sound,
whenever they are needed, our angels are around.
~Author Unknown

My world was falling apart. I was twenty-four and going through a period of bad luck, loss, tragedy and drug abuse. I felt I had no way out. One August day, with a heavy heart, I wrote my goodbyes to my roommate on my mirror with a dry erase marker. I packed a small bag with a picture of my little brother and sister, and a photo of my mother and me, and I also brought along my video camera to film my final goodbyes. All of this happened before I took the pills.

I don't know how many of the dangerous pills I took, but I knew I took enough to do the job. I was going to end all this hurt, all this heartache, for both myself and my family. I started walking in a daze, and before I knew it I was at a landmark in my hometown called Goatman's Bridge.

Goatman's Bridge is a historic bridge that has quite a bit of acreage around it and a hiking trail. I went there frequently for solace—to walk among the trees and stare pensively into the creek that ran softly by. I don't know what drew me to this place at that moment, considering it was a significant distance to walk. But the pills must have driven me there because of a memory, perhaps a memory of a happier time. This was where I would end my life.

I travelled along the hiking trail deep into the woods for about a mile, and then went another hundred yards further into the forest, where I was positive no one would find me until it was too late. I sat against a giant oak tree and contemplated the leaves for a bit. I knew I would never look upon their particular color of green again, and I was okay with that. It did hurt to know I'd miss the beauty of such things, but death was better than another day of horrendous misery.

The pills were beginning to take effect. As I filmed myself saying goodbye, through the screen, I could see the color draining from my face. This was it.

"Momma, don't blame yourself," I said into the lens as I leaned my head against the tree. I held the camera at arm's length and stared directly into it. "One final shot," I murmured. "I'm sorry."

I shut off the camera and lay my head back, awaiting the eternal sleep I craved. I was at peace. I was slipping away, finally... I was....

"Ma'am?"

The voice surprised me so much that my eyes popped open and I felt a surge of adrenaline. This sudden startle from my peaceful float into slumber caused my body to react to the pills and I began to retch. I vomited violently for a few moments before I finally looked into the face of my visitor.

A man stood not even five feet away from me, and looked upon me with a calm that I almost cannot explain. His whole presence was indescribable — peaceful, ethereal, though he looked completely normal. He was dressed in a white T-shirt and denim shorts, he was in his early thirties and his dark eyes twinkled behind a set of wire-framed glasses. He casually leaned against a tree, coolly watching me with a look of steady presence. "What's your name?" he asked calmly.

I was shocked. Not only had I not heard him walk up — the crunch of dead August leaves underfoot would have easily given away his approach — but how on earth did he find me? What was he doing so far off the beaten path, alone, no less? He wasn't dressed in hiking gear, and no one was at the park when I arrived. I also knew without a doubt that I was way beyond anyone's exploring range. I had made sure I was hidden. I just wanted to be left alone. I wanted the pills to do their work. And right then, I wanted that man gone.

"Haley," I answered as I wiped my chin and lay back against the tree with my eyes closed. I didn't want to talk, and I knew I was giving him that impression of coldness, but still he did not move.

"Haley, huh? I like that name," he said. "Where are you from, Haley?"

"Denton," I managed to choke out before another violent retch caused me to vomit more of the pills at his feet. My body was reacting to the poison, and the longer he kept me conscious, the more I was able to vomit the rest of the pills.

I was on my hands and knees vomiting violently, but he did not even seem to notice. Instead he patiently waited until I was done, and then continued asking me simple questions about my life when he saw my eyes begin to droop. Each question brought about more uncontrollable nausea, and I would vomit until tears streamed down my face.

What's your favorite color? Do you have brothers or sisters? What's your favorite song, Haley? These are a few of the dozens and dozens of questions he asked to keep me conscious. He waited patiently as I threw up, then would start the whole routine all over again. He was keeping me involved in conversation to keep me awake, and the longer I stayed awake, the more my body reacted to the overdose. He was getting the poison out of me.

It was then that I realized that this was not natural. Given the circumstances, and the vulnerability of my position, it was obvious what I was doing out in those woods. Any other person would have offered to call emergency help right away. They would have tried to get me to stand up, to get to a car or other source of help, but not this man.

Not once did he ask if I was okay. Not once did he ask if I needed help or what I was doing out in the middle of the woods. Not once did he reach for a cell phone to call emergency help. It was like he knew what was happening. He knew how to handle the situation… and he did. He kept his poise, his calm. His voice was soothing, as he never broke his gentle stare toward me. He leaned against that tree as if he were talking to a lifelong friend about the weather.

Once I realized what he was doing for me, combined with the serenity of his presence, I came to terms with what I was doing. And it was stupid. It was something about looking into his eyes, those dark eyes with the glint—the twinkle of something more than I could understand—behind those glasses. His presence was comforting. Even though at first I wanted nothing more than to be left in peace, I found myself not wanting him to leave.

I was then on my hands and knees in the grass with my finger down my throat. I did not want to die. Somehow this stranger had instilled a new hope in me, and I was determined to get the poison out of me, for my family. I wanted to live. I needed to live. His being there reignited my passion for life!

I raised my head to thank the stranger, but he was gone. He had disappeared just as mysteriously as he had appeared. Not a word, not a sound came from his arrival or departure. He did not say goodbye, just as he had not announced his presence.

I was never a religious person until the occurrence in the woods. That was no man. That was a protective spirit sent by the divine. His purpose was simple: to tell me it was not my time. He kept me from doing the one unforgivable sin, and I thank him for it. I hope he sees now how productive a person I am today. I have told my story to others who are in the same situation. I will never forget what happened that day in the woods or what I learned from that gentle, wise stranger. In the times when I need him most, I just hope I will see him again, standing guard over me.

~H.B. Cunningham

A Loving Reminder

Angels can fly directly into the heart of the matter.
~Author Unknown

should have felt wonderful. On a sunny Sunday afternoon, my husband and I headed for the busy, fashionable mall outside our town. I dressed up—trendy earrings, understated sexy blouse, tailored slacks, matching bag and shoes. We visited a few shops together and then agreed to browse separately and meet at the front entrance in two hours.

I'd visited almost every shop, spending a lot of money without guilt. In both hands, I gripped multiple entwined handles of shiny, smart-logoed, overflowing shopping bags. But my purchases barely veiled my heaviness. At the imported pen shop, we'd had yet another fight. I didn't want to admit it, but they were becoming too frequent. Each time, our unpleasant words escalated, with the anger on both sides surprisingly intense.

Reliving my outbursts, I felt ashamed and helpless and like we were edging toward the big D. Now, despite all the new acquisitions and plush surroundings, I fell deeper into depression.

As we had icily agreed, I arrived exactly on time at the mall entrance near the parking lot and taxi stand so we could get a cab home. We'd supposedly "made up," each saying what we thought we should, as if this would make us feel differently. I already knew from past repetitions that what seemed resolved would only reappear a few days later, sparked by the next most trivial thing.

I dreaded the stony ride home, then unpacking everything that was supposed to have brought us joy, and serving an uninviting cold supper of leftovers. We'd eat without speaking, except for requests to pass the salt, and then disappear into separate rooms, each blaring a TV to cover our resentful thoughts.

Shifting from one foot to the other, I kept looking both ways from the entrance. Where was he? He'd promised to meet me promptly. Now it was much later.

My bags were heavy, so I set them down and propped them against each other. I grew more depressed by the minute and realized I hated the distance and the repeated arguments, wearying in their predictability. I really wanted to regain what we'd had, bask once more in our love. Pacing back and forth, I tried to hold back the tears.

I kept surveying the area for my husband, glancing to the left where the taxi stand was. Appearing as if from nowhere, a man stood at my right.

Startled, I looked full at him. He was tall and stout, towering over me. He wore black slacks and a black shirt open at the collar. In his mid-fifties, he had a large head, somewhat sagging jowls, and dark brown hair. Around his neck, standing out dramatically against the black shirt, a huge gold cross hung on a gold chain.

He peered hard at me. I thought he was going to fight me for a cab or make a pass. Instead, he kept looking at me, and then, with a small smile, he reached into a little black pouch in his hand.

He held out an object. "This is for you."

Automatically, I extended my hand, unafraid. Something small dropped into my palm and, without looking down, I closed my fist. Then he bent closer, his eyes piercing.

"God loves you and so do I." He leaned down and kissed my cheek.

I stood wide-eyed. Regaining a little composure, I nodded.

He smiled more broadly. "Keep thinking that," he said. "Keep repeating that."

My voice breaking, I managed, "Thank you."

I opened my hand and looked down. On a tie tack back, a tiny angel shone up at me. Its gold halo sparkled, and its diamond-cut glass skirt billowed with promise.

I looked up again for him. But he was no longer next to me. Assuming he was walking toward a car, I surveyed the parking lot, but there was no sight of him. He'd just vanished.

I gasped, holding back sobs. How did he know to choose me, a stylish woman looking like she had it all? How did he know that beneath the façade, I felt so lonely and depressed I hardly knew what to do?

The man had sounded so sure in his declaration of God's love for me. Could I believe him? I cradled the delicate angel. Was it really possible? Her wings, like welcoming arms, opened in unlimited love.

How did He know that this was exactly the reminder I needed?

My heaviness lifted and my anger dissolved. I couldn't wait to invite my husband to dinner at our favorite restaurant. This time, I knew, we'd really be able to talk.

He came striding around the corner. I waved and smiled. "Hi, sweetheart. You're just in time for the next cab."

~Noelle Sterne

The Voice of Change

Leave sooner, drive slower, live longer.
~Author Unknown

No one else was in the car with me on the day it happened. Well, almost no one. Speeding on the freeway wasn't new to me. If I have the need for speed, blame it on either the most popular Tom Cruise movie of the 1980s or my parents. My dad brought home a shiny red DeLorean in 1983, and I fell in love with the aerodynamics, the compact, two-seat design, and the idea that it just looked fast. When I turned sixteen, my mom persuaded my dad to buy me a 300ZX (who does that?). After I married, I graduated to a Mustang GT 5.0 that I drove until we started having children. I willingly gave up the zippy sports cars (and speeding tickets), and for the next seemingly endless string of childbearing years, limped along in a Ford Aerostar full of car seats, McDonald's fries, and old bottles of dried-up milk.

When the Aerostar died, it was time for a new car. A sensible girl would have chosen something with four doors, perhaps fuel efficiency, or at least a neutral color. Not me. We replaced the nondescript burgundy jalopy with a fiery red Thunderbird that screamed, "Hey cops! Watch this!" And they did. A lot.

With the exception of the Aerostar years, I averaged exactly one speeding ticket every eighteen months—the legal window I had to maintain in order to attend traffic school to remove the infraction from my driving record. When we bought the T-bird that practice resumed. So it isn't a surprise that I was speeding on the day it happened.

I was a harried mother of three. I'm still harried and a mother of three, but instead of rushing from one school to another or between soccer and baseball practices, I juggle writing schedules, dinners, and my Halloween businesses that require year-round attention. Now, at least, the kids are old enough to get their own food and can even make Starbucks runs for me. But during these years, it was worse because no one else drove. Their father worked out of town, so the details and errands—such as the one I was running that day—were left to me.

At about 4:45 on a warm spring afternoon, I was speeding along the highway trying to get a back seat full of trophies to my son's baseball party. I was the team mom, so the responsibility rested fully on me. And because I didn't have the perspective then that I do now, I thought the world would stop its rotation if I walked in ten minutes late. It wasn't that I didn't plan well; I just didn't plan at all.

With no one else in the car, I blasted the radio and was racing within a half mile of my exit when it happened. The Voice. It was so loud that it muted every other noise. When I heard it, I felt my mortality stand at attention:

Slow down, Dana. Your children need you.

I was startled by the voice in such a way that I obeyed the command and yanked my foot off the gas so quickly my knee slammed into the steering wheel. It wasn't a whisper, more the sound of one commanding from a place of authority—loud and clear, a voice that brooked no argument. Quickly, my eyes darted to the dashboard, where I watched the speedometer drop from 80 mph.

75 mph… What in the world was that? My right foot hovered over the gas pedal as my car began its gradual slowdown.

70 mph… Who was that speaking? Both hands gripped the steering wheel and my eyes continued to watch my speed.

65 mph… Was it my guardian angel?

I know people who've lived in faith far longer than I have, people who've believed in angels and had a much better relationship with God than I did at the time in my life when I was speeding and carrying on without perspective. I was sure God had much better things to do than to send an angel to watch over a person who had only a mild interest in Him. I was wrong, and He decided to prove His love (and existence) to me right there on a stretch of California highway.

Five seconds after hearing The Voice and the moment my speedometer reached 55 mph, my tire blew.

As pieces of rubber cascaded around me and I could hear my pretty red fender being torn to shreds, I used lessons taught in my high school driver's ed class to ease the car slowly off the freeway. I was able to hobble up the ramp safely into a fast food restaurant parking lot.

I'm no physicist, but I can presume that a car experiencing a blowout at 80 mph would react differently from one traveling 55 mph. We've all seen rollover accidents along freeways; many of them don't turn out well.

Why me? I don't know, but it changed me. Why would angels care about one silly, impractical girl when lifelong believers were in need? How was I able to hear the voice so loudly that I avoided catastrophe in my first and only blowout?

I wish I could say that I never speed anymore or that I've had another encounter with my guardian angel. I can't say either of those things, but my walk in my faith changed that day. God really is here, He is real, and He uses His angels to protect even the silly, impractical ones who speed on freeways.

~Dana Martin

Warned and Petted by an Angel

We have two ears and one mouth so that we can
listen twice as much as we speak.
~Epictetus

January 28, 2014, I sat on the couch watching the news. A winter storm watch was in effect over the Atlanta, Georgia area. I laughed at the reported two to three inches of expected snow and all the hoopla about it. Coming from New Jersey, there were winters we had that amount several times a week and we went about business as usual. As a matter of fact, I had just been home two weeks before and a few inches of snow had fallen. I couldn't wait to get back out in the snow.

Now reporters were telling viewers not to venture out if possible. An aerial view of I-20, the major near me, showed bumper-to-bumper traffic. I was glad that I didn't have to travel over the major highway to get to the store and pick up some groceries.

I looked out the window. Snow was steadily but lightly coming down, gently covering everything it touched. Since the store was less than ten minutes away, and I was used to driving in this kind of weather, I felt no need to rush out. So I continued watching the news as I made a mental list of the groceries I needed.

Schools and businesses closed around noon. By 4:30 p.m. I figured traffic should've died down and ventured out. I took a side street, and was surprised to find myself stuck in more traffic and without the ability to turn around.

Finally, after more than an hour, I reached the store. Then after almost an hour's wait in line and with nothing in my cart that I actually went to get, I went back out into the now two inches of snow and freezing rain. The streets had become parking lots. It hadn't crossed my mind that although I knew how to deal with this kind of weather, the people of Atlanta didn't.

A shopping trip that would have usually taken me roughly an hour took me almost four hours, with three spent driving. There were fender benders, abandoned cars, and vehicles that had slid off the roads. Panicked people were walking, standing around, talking on their phones or sitting in their cars waiting for help that couldn't get through. I slowly drove, inching, stopping, easing, and weaving in and out through the maze of honking horns and stranded, angry drivers and their riders.

By the time I got back home, the weather had gotten worse. It was dark, late, freezing cold and I felt as though I had gone fifteen rounds in a boxing ring. Tired and aggravated, I pulled into the garage, opened the door to the house, let my dog out and dragged the bags to the kitchen counter before calling Max back in and closing the door.

After putting the food away and fixing something to eat, I closed the blinds, checked the doors and went upstairs to put on warm pajamas, turn the TV on low and settle into my recliner with a blanket and a good book. Max jumped onto the bed, took his usual place at the foot, and dozed off. I followed suit shortly after, but was suddenly awakened by a voice telling me to shut my garage door. Still half asleep and somewhat disoriented, I sat up in my chair, looked around and chuckled to myself as I thought about how real the dream seemed and how loud the voice sounded.

With heavy eyes, I leaned back into my chair when, out of the blue, Max jumped up, looked towards the bedroom doorway and barked like crazy. I looked over and said, "Calm down, boy. Calm down." But then he jumped off the bed, ran towards the doorway and looked up as if looking at somebody and continued barking madly. Then he did the strangest thing. He stopped barking and, tail wagging, lay down and turned onto his back, the way he does when he's being petted. Then he jumped up and came running to me, barking and looking back towards the doorway. Tail still wagging, looking up and barking frantically, he ran back and forth from me to the doorway. Finally, I checked the alarm system and looked up and down the hall and stairway. Not seeing anything out of the ordinary, I decided to get in bed and call it a night. I was exhausted.

Snuggling comfortably in my blankets, I anxiously watched Max as he continued with this unusual behavior. Then I remembered what seemed like an audible voice telling me to shut the garage door. Thinking it was just a dream, but that maybe I should check anyway, I went downstairs. Sure enough, the door leading to the garage was locked. But when I opened it, to my utmost surprise, the garage door was wide open! Without that voice, I would've never thought to go down and check.

As I hit the button and the garage door slowly came down, Max barked and ran to the edge. He lay on his side and rolled onto his back, silent, but the wagging tail let me know he was enjoying something. Then he jumped up, came to me and faced the closing garage door, barking again. Suddenly the garage door stopped, as it always does when something passes by the sensors. I pushed the button again and the door continued to close.

Max, now calm and quiet, and I, in total astonishment but with indebted thanks, went back upstairs. I settled in bed and Max as usual settled at the foot. We were quite satisfied with our angel encounter. I had been warned, he had been petted, and both of us, along with the house, had been protected just before the power went out.

~Francine L. Baldwin-Billingslea

Touched by an Angel

Renewing My Faith

God in the Cockpit

Peace is not the absence of affliction, but the presence of God.
~Author Unknown

Working in real estate, I'd had the chance to meet and befriend a client who was a property developer. Clarence also happened to be an experienced pilot. He and I had done several business deals together and it was not unusual for him to fly us to see remote parcels of property suitable for development.

One night in late April 1985, I had a dream that Clarence and I were in a plane flying to view some property. A few minutes into the flight I saw engine oil on the windshield of the plane. Looking down in panic, I couldn't see the ground at all. The first thing I saw was the tops of pine trees as they peeked through dense fog, and I knew the plane was going down. Remarkably the next thing in the dream was a clear picture of the actual crashed plane, nose down, as Clarence and I stood back surveying the scene. Miraculously, we had survived.

I woke up really frightened. The image of the plane nose down stayed in my mind. I could not shake the dream. It seemed so real and it had to be a premonition of some sort.

Though the dream continued to bear on my mind, I did not tell my wife. I didn't want to burden her or cause her to worry. I decided, however, that I had to tell Clarence because I did not intend to fly anywhere with him for a while. I truly believed this dream had been a warning, which I intended to heed. I had worried for several days about how to tell him without either insulting him or having him think I was being ridiculous. So one afternoon while he was in the office to see me on business, I finally got up the courage as he started to leave. He was halfway down the hall when I called to him. "Clarence, hold up a minute. There's something I need to tell you." He was standing with one of my other colleagues and he turned back to me. "Yes, Alton? What is it?"

"Clarence, I had a dream the other night that you and I were in a plane crash. It was the most real dream I have ever had. I don't feel good about the dream and I don't think I'm going to be able to fly with you for a while."

Clarence and the other agent started to chuckle. Clarence patted me on the shoulder and said, "Oh Alton, try not to worry. It'll be all right."

Even though he obviously did not take me or the dream very seriously, I felt relieved at having finally told him.

Several days went by and I received a phone call from Clarence telling me about a client who wanted him to build a freight terminal around Daytona, Florida.

"Alton, how about you and I taking the plane down and seeing if we can find something for him?"

I could not believe that after I'd told him about the dream, he still was asking me to fly with him to Florida. I knew then that he really had not believed me or taken the dream as seriously as I did. Not knowing quite how to handle that, I just said, "Well Clarence, I've got a pretty busy schedule for the next few days. Let me look at things and get back with you."

It was really a dilemma. Maybe I was being a little paranoid. He was a good friend and business associate, and he was just asking me to help him find a piece of real estate for a client that I stood to make a pretty good commission from. After serious consideration I decided maybe there was a solution. It had been a while since Eleanor and I had taken any time off — why didn't we drive down to Florida, spend a few days at Epcot, visit my sister Ruth in Melbourne, and then I could drive to meet Clarence in Daytona and check out some properties with him? Clarence went ahead and flew down, and we found a suitable piece of property. Later, I drove him to the airport feeling good about avoiding this flight and what I feared was sure disaster.

About 10:00 p.m. I got a call from Clarence's wife. She wanted to know what time he had left Daytona—she was beginning to worry because she thought he should have been home by then. Cold panic set in. It had been four hours since he'd left Daytona and yes, he should have been home by then. I tried to play it down and not frighten her, so I told her that he'd probably run into some delay at the airport after I left and to give me a call if she had not heard from him in an hour. Turns out there had been a report of bad weather, and he had decided to land at a small airport and complete the trip once the threat of danger had passed. He was fine and I felt relieved knowing now that he had avoided the crash I had dreamed about.

Although the deal closed on our first trip, there were still details like surveys, soil samples and permits. So one morning Clarence called and wanted to know if we could fly down to take care of the things. Feeling confident the danger of the plane crash was behind us, I agreed. Tuesday morning, about 5:15, we left Covington, Georgia and headed for Daytona. Around 5:30 a.m., after we had reached about 5,000 feet, Clarence leveled out the plane. He turned on the cabin lights and we had some of the coffee and sandwiches his wife had made us for the trip. Once settled, he turned the cabin lights back out. That's when I saw it—oil all over the windshield. Just like in the dream. We watched as the oil pressure fell.

We searched for an emergency landing field, but below us was a complete covering of dense fog. We could see no landmarks, no lights, nothing. We turned back towards home to try to get out of the fog. Minutes later the oil pressure dropped to zero and the plane shook so violently that we feared it would break apart. Then the engine locked up, the propeller stopped turning, and the silence in the cabin was deadly. Both of us, however, seemed strangely calm.

"Clarence, remember the dream I had—we've been in these same seats before. And although we crashed, remember we both walked away. Let's just stay calm and try to think of what to do next."

We checked the altimeter, calculating at what point we would hit the ground. This all took less than five minutes—but time seemed to stand still. When we got to about 1,000 feet we saw a break in the fog. All I remember seeing was pine trees. Again, just like I saw in the dream. On its glide path, the plane cut down about eight of those trees and came to rest on its nose in a clearing the other side of those pines. I smelled the strange odor of fresh cut pine and gasoline as it gurgled out of the tank. For the first time, I felt fear.

We managed to get out of the plane and made our way over to a log, where we sat to assess our injuries. We looked back at the plane to the exact same scene I'd first seen in my dream.

I believe God sent me that dream as a warning and a message. I thought I could avert the crash by driving to Florida that first trip. But with that crash, He made it perfectly clear that He, and not I, was in control of my life—in fact, all life.

Several weeks later, a friend asked me if Clarence had been the one piloting the plane. "Well," I responded, "he was the pilot when we took off, but he and I both were passengers when we landed."

~Alton Housworth

Safety Net

Faith is the vision of the heart; it sees God in the dark as well as in the day.
~Author Unknown

aid off. What an awful phrase. It strikes fear in the hearts of most American families that live paycheck to paycheck. I thought it would never happen to us. I was wrong.

My husband's company was involved in a hostile takeover. When the new owners came in, they began laying off employees, group by group. Bruce's turn came about three months into the layoffs.

We immediately put our beautiful California home on the market, thinking it would take us a few months to get a respectable offer. But the house went into contract on the second day. A generous cash offer.

The buyers, a sweet old couple, were anxious to move in right away, so Bruce and I moved most of our belongings into storage.

We wanted to save as much of Bruce's severance pay as possible. There was no telling how long it would take for him to find another job. But we assumed, with his qualifications and experience, that his job search wouldn't take long.

Our church family offered to let us park our camping trailer on the church grounds until the school year ended. That was about six weeks away. "What an answer to prayer!" I told my church friends. "By the time school's over, we should be packing to move to Bruce's new job."

I was teaching at a local community college, so most of the time the only space I needed was a table and a chair to read and grade papers. The trailer was fine for that work.

"This'll be great, Bruce," I said, looking out over the heavily treed church property. "Just like camping."

Bruce shot me a dubious look. "We'll see."

Our pastor invited Bruce to move his computer into the church office so he could be connected to the Internet.

Each day Bruce worked on his résumé and sent out inquiries to appropriate companies. And in our trailer, I prepared my music history lessons and graded quizzes. At night, we prayed and prayed that God would provide just the right job.

The days grew longer and warmer, and with that warmth came the annoying bugs that any camper faces: mosquitoes, spiders, ants, even ticks. I began to sorely regret that we had agreed to let our buyers move in right away.

The bugs and the hot weather drove me inside the air-conditioned church building more and more often. I got used to going in and out of the three inside corridors off the church lobby. The first one led to the main office. I went in there daily to check on Bruce's progress. Close to that doorway, maybe ten or so feet, was a wide staircase that led downstairs to the classrooms. It was nice and cool in the lower level and that's where I did my college work when it was unoccupied. The third corridor—separated from the stairwell by a wall, was the one that we usually exited through to get to our trailer.

By mid-May, Bruce and I grew uneasy. In spite of his excellent résumé, he wasn't getting any bites from employers. In our discouragement, we asked ourselves many questions: Where are the jobs? Where should we move? God, have you forgotten us?

I felt as if our prayers were hitting the ceiling and going no further. "Lord, why are you allowing us to go through this trial? My head knows that You care for us, but my heart feels as if You've abandoned us. Please help us!"

One evening, Bruce stayed late in the church office. I came through the usual back entrance to see what was delaying him. When I came into the office, he was just shutting down his computer.

"Dinner's ready," I announced with a whine in my voice. This extended "camping" experience was wearing thin on my nerves.

"Give me two minutes," Bruce said. "I just have to check all the doors and shut off the lights."

"I'll turn off the lights in the lobby." When I flipped off the light switches, the interior of the church was darker than I'd have imagined. Black as a cave.

I put my hands out in front of me to feel where I was going. Except there was nothing to feel because the lobby only had furnishings on the north end. I think I traveled about fifteen paces. Where was the wall that led to the south exit? I took another step.

My foot met nothingness. Panic jolted me.

It's an amazing phenomenon when the brain registers imminent doom. It seems to be able to think a thousand thoughts simultaneously.

In a fraction of a second, I knew I'd turned prematurely and missed the south-end corridor. I knew I'd stepped blindly into the stairwell. I knew that I would not be able to catch myself and that the fall down those dark stairs was going to hurt me. The least I'd do was break my wrist. The worst: crush my skull.

My body shot forward. I didn't even have time to scream as I threw out my arms and tried to clutch anything. But, of course, there was nothing to grab.

Then something I can't explain in scientific terms happened. A force kind of like a wall of cotton stopped me mid-flight, pushed me back into a vertical position and settled my haunches down onto the same stair I'd just blindly overshot.

How does one overcome momentum? By the application of an opposite force. But no one had grabbed my arms, or stepped in front of me to catch me.

I sat quietly for about thirty seconds, waiting for my thumping heart to settle, and trying to make out what had just happened to me. Bruce was still on the other side of the church, so—even if he could have seen in the dark—he wouldn't have been aware of my near-death experience.

When I heard Bruce come out of the office and shut and lock that door, I stood up and moved quickly away from the stairwell. Later, in the trailer, I told him what happened to me in the stairwell. He shook his head in wonder.

It's so easy in bleak times to imagine that God has turned His back, or doesn't care what you're going through. But my wonderful rescue showed me that God never ceases to watch over His children. I did not have to see a heavenly being when I fell into that dark stairwell to recognize the invisible, but certainly real, rescue.

~Dena Netherton

Love Lifted Me

Prayer is the principal means of opening oneself to the power and love of God that is already there, in the depths of reality.
~Bishop James Albert Pike

grew up in a very small town. If you saw someone sitting on the porch, they didn't have to know you in order to wave and smile. If a person became ill, it wasn't uncommon for neighbors to babysit, bring soup, and feed the children. When they mowed their lawn, they would mow yours too. When someone baked cookies, it was often enough for all the neighborhood children who played together daily. It was like one big happy family, a community of caring people.

At a very young age I wanted to dedicate my life to God. But I first needed to know that He was real. So I prayed. I had a talk with the Lord, and I told him that I could listen to everyone else speaking about him, but I knew that I would make a better witness if I knew him for myself. I needed to know that God was real.

That same week I decided to go swimming, thinking nothing else about the conversation I had with God. When I got to the swimming pool, I was very shy. I ran out to the pool and jumped in, hoping that everyone else didn't notice. I flapped around in the water. I splashed and splashed, pretending to swim. While in the water, I noticed a guy from my class staring at me. He was playful and asked how I was doing. I thought he was handsome and liked his attention.

I got out of the pool for the fifteen-minute break the lifeguards had announced, and sat talking to friends and my next-door neighbor. When it was time to get back into the pool, the guy from class told me that he noticed I was a very good swimmer. He said that he saw me dive off the deep end of the pool.

I explained to him that I could not swim, and that I had never been in the pool's deep end. He didn't believe me. I told him I wasn't teasing and could not swim. He smiled at me as if I was joking, picked me up over his head, and threw me into the deep end of the pool. I saw him turn and look back as he walked away from the pool's edge.

The water seemed to grab me. It was cool and warm at the same time. The more I reached for something, anything to grab, the more I realized nothing was there to grasp. All of a sudden I knew, without a shadow of a doubt, that I was drowning. I struggled and I fought that water until I was too exhausted to fight any more.

I kept swallowing the chlorinated water. I drank so much water that I could not feel it going down my throat anymore. My body became totally relaxed and I said to myself, "Wow, I could live like this." Later, having talked to a nurse, I learned that I couldn't feel the water going down my throat any more because I was almost dead.

All of a sudden, the water became a pool of extremely bright light. The water rumbled and shook. Gazing upward, I saw how beautiful the sky looked. My body was relaxed. A huge hand of light came from underneath the water of light. A voice that sounded like thunder shook the water. As the hand of light rose up out of the water, I too rose with it. I heard the thunderous voice say, "NOT YET!" I rose to the top of the water and my next-door neighbor pulled me out of the pool. An old song by James Rowe called "Love Lifted Me" came to mind, and I think of it every time I tell this story:

Love lifted me
Love lifted me,
When nothing else could help
Love lifted me.

That day God proved to me, without a doubt, that He lives.

~Sheila Ross Felton

An Ordinary Miracle

If you have worry, you don't have faith, and if you have faith,
you don't have worry.
~Jack Coe

"Can we go out for lunch after church, Mom?" my seven-year-old son, Jordan, asked.

"Sorry, but we can't today, bud," I said.

He looked down at his feet and sighed. "No extra money this week?"

I felt the always-present lump in my throat grow bigger at his words. As a single mother of two, money was a constant concern for me, and it made me sad that my young children were already aware of my troubles. I longed to protect them from it, but Jordan was too perceptive. He read my emotions, and all too often he carried a burden he was too young to bear.

I patted his shoulder and tried to smile. "Maybe we can grab some pizza next weekend."

He shrugged. "Yeah, maybe."

I dropped Jordan and his sister off in the children's church and then headed for the sanctuary. I sang a few hymns with the rest of the congregation and then the pastor stood up to give his sermon.

"Do you trust God to meet your needs?" the pastor asked. "I mean, really trust Him?"

I thought about his words and decided that I did trust God.

"Do you worry about your finances?" the pastor continued. "Because if you worry, you aren't trusting God to meet your needs."

If I worry? It was practically the first thing on my to-do list every morning.

The pastor shared several real-life stories of people who had nothing and God took care of them. I thought about the many times in my own life that I'd had more bills than money, but somehow, my children and I never went hungry.

"God works miracles every day, but we have to trust Him," my pastor said. "God does His best work when His people trust that He will take care of them."

I bowed my head and asked God to help me trust Him to provide for my children and me. In that moment, I felt more peaceful than I had in more than a year.

My pastor wrapped up his sermon and then the offering plates were passed. Most Sundays, I didn't contribute anything. After all, I had nothing to spare.

But I'd decided to trust God with my finances. For the first time in months, I reached for my purse. I had sixty dollars, but fifty was earmarked to fill my gas tank on the way home from church. I grabbed the ten-dollar bill from my wallet and put it into the offering plate.

Ten dollars might not sound like much, but besides my gas money, it was all the money I had.

I'd stepped out on a limb and trusted God.

The kids and I left church and headed for the gas station. I pumped exactly fifty dollars of gas and then the kids and I went inside to pay. (This was in the days before most gas stations implemented the "pay before you pump" policy.)

"Pump four," I told the clerk behind the counter. I reached for the fifty-dollar bill in my wallet and came away with a ten. But I'd put the ten-dollar bill in the offering plate at church. And then I realized what I'd done. I'd accidentally put my gas money in the offering plate.

And what was I going to do now? The gas was already in my tank, and I had no way to pay for it.

I'd trusted God with my finances and look where it had gotten me.

I fought tears as I told the clerk, "I don't have enough money to pay for my gas."

She looked at me, confused. "Your dad already paid for it."

"My dad? My dad isn't with me."

"Oh, I'm sorry. Is he your husband?" She shrugged, embarrassed. "He just looks a lot older than you."

"There's no one with me. Just my kids and me."

The clerk's confusion grew. "A man came in and paid for your gas. He handed me fifty dollars and said it was for pump number four."

I ran outside to thank the man, but there was no one around. I went back in and asked the clerk what the man looked like.

"Oh, just a nice older man," she said. "He was pretty ordinary-looking, nothing special about him."

"He might have looked ordinary, but he was definitely special," I said. "He performed a miracle for me."

The clerk looked skeptical. "By paying for your gas?"

"No," I said tearfully, "by teaching me that God is worth trusting."

~Diane Stark

Precious Gifts

The only gift is a portion of thyself.
~Ralph Waldo Emerson

enjoyed playground duty when I worked at an elementary school in Southern California. Children often came up to me for a hug or to hold my hand and walk with me. One day I noticed a little girl leaning against the building during recess sucking on her finger. When I looked at her, she would look down or turn her head. I made a point of smiling at her every day. Eventually I won her trust and she held my hand when I reached out to her.

Amelia was quiet. I learned she was new to this country and still learning the language. She communicated her feelings with her big brown eyes. And she was shy. She watched children hug me, but holding my hand was her limit. I was satisfied that at least she was no longer leaning against the wall during recess.

On the last day of school she was waiting for me at the playground. She stood smiling and with one arm behind her back. She looked at me and crooked her finger for me to come closer. I knelt in front of her. She brought her arm from behind her and held out a small glass dog.

"This is for you," she said. I noticed a small chip on the right ear of the glass dog, which only made it more precious. When I thanked her, she gave me another precious gift. A hug. Then she ran off to play with the other children.

I transferred to another school the next year, so I never saw Amelia again. The glass dog had a special place in the china closet. Every time I saw it, I thought about Amelia and felt her hug.

When we moved from Southern California to Northern California several years later, I didn't notice the glass dog was missing until long after I finished unpacking. Apparently it was left in a box that was thrown out. I was left with only the memory of Amelia's gift.

A few years later, on my way out of town to attend a lecture, I stopped at a small antique shop. I was looking at a display of glass figurines and thought about the little glass dog. I described it to the storeowner and asked if she had ever seen one like it. She told me they were vintage carnival prizes and had seen something similar in a box she was unpacking before I came into the store. She asked me to wait while she got it.

She returned holding a glass dog like the one I had lost. Tears filled my eyes. I held it and thought about that shy little girl who finally gave me a hug. When I looked more closely, I saw a small chip on the right ear. I knew I held the glass dog Amelia had given me.

I pulled out my wallet and the storeowner shook her head. "You can have it. It's not a saleable item because of the chip." I smiled. That chip was the very thing that made it priceless to me. I clutched the glass dog to my chest and thanked her, amazed at the circumstances that brought the glass dog back to me. I tucked the tissue-wrapped glass dog into my tote.

Traffic was light so I arrived at the lecture hall early enough to sit and read more of the speaker's latest book, which I had brought along to be signed. A short time later, a young woman sat down next to me. We started talking and discovered we both had lived in the same area in Southern California during the same period of time. I no longer worked in education, but she had recently become an elementary school teacher. We also shared a common interest in antiques.

I told her the story about the glass dog and how thrilled I was to be reunited with it. I unwrapped it to show her. She picked it up, saw the chip and blinked back tears.

"Why are you crying?" I asked. She dabbed her eyes and looked at me.

"I was that little girl who gave you the dog. My name is Amelia."

I looked into her dark eyes as she spoke and saw the little girl I remembered. A hint of shyness remained in her smile.

She leaned back in her seat and recalled that time in her childhood. "I had a hard time adjusting to school and learning English when we came here from Mexico. You were the first person at school who made me feel loved."

She pointed at the glass dog. "My older brother won that at a carnival. It was sitting on the windowsill in our living room. I took it when I left for school on the last day to give to you. I pushed it up the sleeve of my sweater so my brother wouldn't see me carry it out of the house. It slid out and dropped onto the sidewalk on my way to school, but I didn't notice that the ear chipped."

We talked about the incredible coincidences that had taken place within the last few hours. But I wondered if they were mere coincidences or part of a well-orchestrated plan by a higher power to remind two people of the precious gifts they had given each other.

~L.A. Kennedy

The Voice

The most incredible thing about miracles is that they happen.
~G. K. Chesterton

Nothing tastes as bad as the Indian Ocean. Not turpentine. Not rotten eggs. Not even cod liver oil or mud. Especially when you are in the middle of it, choking and swallowing large portions, and mercilessly drowning in it.

And that's where I was—although not really in the middle of it, but only a few miles from shore off the coast of Mogadishu, Somalia in 1974. Struggling to breathe and stay afloat, and fighting desperately for my life. And slowly, inexorably drowning in the beautiful, sunlit waves of an inhospitable sea.

My ordeal began when suddenly, and without warning, a surge of stomach cramps hit me. Seconds later the first wave of surf struck and I was sent spiraling to the cold depths below. But I quickly resurfaced and was ready to do battle with this monstrous element. For I was young and in the prime of health and physical condition. And being young and cocky, I felt indestructible and was scared of nothing.

Serving on Marine Security Guard Duty in East Africa, I was one of a group of young marines assigned to protect the U.S. Embassy in the capital of Somalia's tiny, poverty-stricken nation. This was many years before that poor country made headlines and saw other young Americans embattled and struggling for their lives there. It was a time when there was still infrastructure, a centralized government, numerous businesses and even occasional tourists. There were even friendly nightspots to wine, dine and dance the humid evenings away, as well as a fair number of Italian farmers and Americans and Europeans of various business interests and occupations with whom to socialize and enjoy the yearlong sunny, sandy Indian Ocean beaches.

But there were no sunny beaches or friendly tourists for me this morning. And no one three miles away on shore—even with a good set of binoculars—would spot me writhing and wrestling with the sea. Nor were there any nearby swimmers or sea vessels to come to my aid. I was totally alone.

Having resurfaced, and with barely time to take a breath, another swell—larger than the first—appeared from nowhere and forced me under again. At the same time, another wave of cramps—this one also worse than earlier—came upon me. As I was sent twisting below the surface, I felt my body grow slack and begin to lose what I always had assumed was a boundless strength and vitality.

A whole minute passed before I resurfaced. Somehow another swell failed to roll in and punish me. So, although I was exhausted, I started for shore. Then, and again without warning, another wave slammed against me with even greater weight and force. I was sent below the glaring surface a third time, coughing and retching on the brine I had already swallowed. But I was also struggling not to gasp for air while submerged, for I had only exhaled a tiny breath before again submerging.

What were only seconds seemed like hours this time. But I had little to contemplate or to reflect upon except the stark realization that I wasn't an atheist and did believe in God. And now would be a good time to pray.

But I had no time to pray. No time left to reflect upon my brief, uneventful life. Let alone time to ask God—whom I seldom prayed to—for divine intervention. I was drowning and about to die. I had swallowed a sea of saltwater and despair, and was physically depleted and spiritually drained.

Then, unexpectedly and not knowing how, I was once more above the surface, coughing up water and gasping for air. But I was barely afloat, and unable to move a single muscle. The end would come soon now, and I had no idea why it already hadn't. Then ultimate despair turned into ultimate terror: out at sea, not more than thirty or forty yards distant, another gigantic wave was heading towards me. And at a hurtling pace! It was at this moment I heard The Voice.

But no, it was more than a voice. Gentle in tone, and powerful and confident in inflection, it was at the same time a soothing whisper and a mighty clarion: both comforting and commanding. It said, "Relax, let go of yourself. And fall back upon the waves and lie still. I will save you!"

I did as I was told and let myself become limp and ceased further exertion. Suddenly, I was on my back, stretched out and calmly floating upon the tossing surface. Then a tide—of a momentous size—loomed above me… but only for a second. The next instant I was riding its crest and being ferried towards shore.

During this not unpleasant ride to shore, I had a sensation of floating on a cushion of air or reclining in a soft bed of flowers. Overhead, all I saw was a perfect-looking noonday sun as well as some scattered, friendly-looking clouds. But in my mind all I heard and kept rehearing was The Voice that spoke to me: its firm, gentle words, and nothing more. And then I was delivered to the shore and crawled out, where I sprawled for an unknown period until my strength and senses returned to me.

This was over thirty years ago, and much has happened in my life since then; some things bad, but many things good. And though I have no physical evidence of the event—no film or tape recording or eyewitness, and sometimes even forget that it actually happened (as I often forget to be a prayerful person)—I know that it did. Especially on lovely sunlit days and whenever I am near the ocean. I also know that it really happened because I am still alive.

Someone or some thing spoke to me in angelic tones one day when I was drowning in the Indian Ocean. It told me that I would be saved. And I was.

~Patrick P. Stafford

A Miraculous Prediction

Doubt sees what currently is and no more. Hope sees what can be but is not yet. Faith sees what will be as if it were now.

~Rex Rouis

"Come here, Mom! Quick!"

My nine-year-old son, Collin, never came in the house quietly, so I was not overly concerned when he barreled in that night yelling. I doubted I even needed to leave the couch. I rarely had in the evenings lately.

I was not given a choice. Collin rushed over in front of me and helped pull me up. "Come on, there's a baby kitten on the back porch! It's so cute." The next thing I knew, I was in the back yard in my pajamas.

Sure enough, there was a small, fluffy white kitten in the bushes by our back deck. She was just a tiny thing, and I could not help but think she was cold, lost, and most likely hungry. I am not sure if it was my maternal instinct, or the fact that I was feeling just as lost as that little cat, but I knew we had to feed her. I sent Collin back in the house for a can of tuna and a bowl of water, and put both on the ground in a well-hidden spot near the bushes.

"Do you think she will still be here in the morning?" Collin asked hopefully.

I just sighed. As usual I was exhausted. "I'm not sure, honey.

She's just a stray." "Go to bed and we will check on her first thing in the morning."

I had not had a good night's sleep in months, my depression and hopelessness consuming the quiet hours. But that night, I have to admit, I snuck out onto the back deck several times to see if the little kitten had eaten the tuna.

The past year had taken a real toll on me emotionally. I had just experienced two miscarriages in eight months, after years of infertility. And I was worried about my son. Collin had been praying for a baby brother or sister for years and took the losses particularly hard.

The next day, Collin and I looked for the kitten many times. Both of us seemed equally taken by the little creature, probably because life had been so hard lately and we needed a distraction. She never showed her face that day, but once it got dark, she came out again. And she did the same thing the next evening, and the next.

That tiny white kitten quickly became my new "pet" project. She was not friendly, but she would come to our back door for food.

Honestly, I needed a project, someone or something to nurture. I found myself at the grocery store, buying cat food and treats, even a few cat toys. I quickly walked past the baby aisle to get these necessities, trying to ignore the feelings of desperation I had every time I saw bottles and diapers during my shopping trips.

Collin soon decided it was too cold for our little Snowball—original name, I know—to sleep outside in the elements. So he built her a little house from scrap plywood and covered the bottom of the house with carpeting so she would stay warm. And then he added an old beach towel to "make it soft." He carefully placed this bed near the back door of our house.

"Do you think she will sleep in it?" I could tell Collin wanted Snowball to be comfortable and warm. "I don't know how animals can sleep outside in the winter."

Deep down, I wanted protection for this little kitten as well. I wanted to protect something. I had not been able to save my unborn babies. The doctor could offer no reason for my losses. "It just happens," he told me. "You can still have more children." But I didn't believe him, not anymore.

We never saw Snowball in the little house when we checked. But after several nights, Collin made an interesting discovery: white, soft fur on the dark-colored beach towel. Obviously, our smart little Snowball had found her new home!

I continued to nurture this little kitten and gain her trust. Each night, I would sit out on the back deck and tempt her with cat treats. And each night, she came closer and closer to me. It took weeks, but finally she let me pet her briefly. I felt my heart gently opening a little more to this sweet kitten each day. I felt more alive, a spark of my old self slowly returning.

And then a massive cold front hit, and the temperature was predicted to drop into the 20s at night. My first thought was of Snowball. She needed to come inside and stay warm. That night, I sat shivering in the doorway out to our deck after I had lined the way into our house with kitty treats. My husband was not impressed, as I was letting all the cold air inside, but I was bound and determined to bring Snowball into the house. And at least I was off the couch, doing something productive instead of staring aimlessly at the television.

It took almost an hour, but she finally came inside. From that point on, we knew we had her. I was finally able to tame her enough to get her in a cat carrier to take into the vet for shots. She fit into our family perfectly, and we wanted to make sure she was well cared for.

Then we got the news. The vet had discovered our little Snowball was very sick and would not recover. We had no choice but to let the vet put her down.

Needless to say, Collin was devastated, and so was I. I had bonded with Snowball too. I was the one who sat outside in the cold night after night, taming her, gaining her trust. I was not sure how we would deal with this loss, how I would deal with yet another loss.

A few nights later, I prayed with Collin. And we felt closer, more like a family after sharing our experience with Snowball. It was like God had brought her to us as a little angel to provide healing.

"You know, Mom. I think God took Snowball from us because He's going to send us a baby," he said confidently. "I think she was here to help us and now that she has, I am finally going to have a brother."

I just looked at him. "Maybe so, honey." I did not believe this for a minute; my faith in that area was all but gone. I had zero hope of ever having another child; I wasn't sure if I even wanted to try, the losses just being too devastating. I did not give this comment another thought for many, many weeks.

Nine months after we lost Snowball, Collin was the first one to hold his baby brother, Caleb.

Sometimes healing can come from unexpected places, like the back porch. And sometimes our child's faith is stronger than our own.

~Denise Valuk

Heaven-Sent

You may ask me for anything in my name, and I will do it.
~John 14:14

A recent back surgery had been more difficult than I had anticipated and, as a result, I had a long list of errands and responsibilities that I had not tackled yet. Now that I had improved somewhat, it was time to prioritize those responsibilities and handle one item each day. Today I was helping Dad, who had his own problems with mobility and other health issues. He had stopped driving and he depended on me to get him from place to place. Today we had to go to the bank to correct some information. This particular location was a real nuisance and it wasn't the first time we'd had problems with paperwork there. This bank branch often had a full waiting area of customers and staff that seemed overwhelmed by the heavy volume of work.

This day was no different. From the entrance, I could see the bank was jammed to capacity with customers. By their slumped shoulders and tense faces, I sensed things were not moving quickly and my heart sank when I noticed not one, but two long lines snaking around the customer service area.

It pained me to see the look on my own father's face as he walked toward the end of the line. Back and foot problems made it difficult for him to stand in one place too long. I was in no better shape myself. My own health issues left me feeling unsteady too.

My pastor sometimes speaks about calling on God's favor in times like this. One Sunday, he even joked about how, when entering a crowded parking lot, he sends a petition to Heaven asking for a space, and often one will appear. I wasn't so sure about the efficacy of such a prayer. Honestly, it sounded a bit like mumbo-jumbo to me. I mean, doesn't our Good Lord have better things to do than find parking spots for us? But desperate times call for desperate measures and as Dad and I took our places at the end of the line, I quickly sent up my own petition: "God, please show us some favor today and help us get through this transaction quickly." Just then, I watched as a uniformed security guard left his post and approached us.

"Follow me," he said with authority as he maneuvered us past the lines straight to the front counter. He even brought a chair for Dad so he could sit during his transaction. It didn't take long before all the corrections were made and we were happily on our way out the door. As we neared the exit, I passed by the security desk only to find it empty.

I approached another employee. "I'd like to thank the security guard for helping us," I explained. "Can you tell me where he went?"

"Security guard?" he questioned. "He's not in today. He called in sick."

On the car ride home, Dad and I wondered aloud about the true identity of the uniformed man who helped us. Was he just another customer, some random person, or maybe even a figment of our imaginations? We tossed around these ideas, yet couldn't agree. But there was one thing we could agree upon. We really had been shown some favor that day, because whoever that man really was, he had been Heaven-sent right when we needed him most.

~Monica A. Andermann

Pilgrim's Proof

Believers, look up — take courage. The angels are nearer than you think.
~Billy Graham

t was October 2nd. We were traveling in England, having just picked up our little blue rental car, and heading west on the M4 motorway. Irrationally, I grumbled about the color. I had envisioned a red car. Also there was an odor — probably cleaning fluid. We'd have to stop and air it out.

I kept pace with the other cars in the middle lane. Lorries lumbered along in the slow lane on my left, and other cars sped past me in the fast lane on my right. Suddenly our car lurched to the right. I corrected left, and it lurched again almost into a big lorry. I corrected again. Then our vehicle began waddling like a drunken duck, disregarding my efforts to steer. It swung around and cut across the fast lane into the cement median — narrowly missing a red car passing us. Banging into the median, we spun around full circle.

I thought we were going to die. But still, I prayed, "God help us! Please, God, help us."

We ground to a halt. "Are you okay?" my husband asked.

"Yes. How about you?" I answered.

At that moment my door opened, and a young man offered his hand to help me out. Another young man was helping my husband out of the passenger side. My helper reached in and switched off the ignition. He gave the key to my husband. "A souvenir," he said.

"The lorry driver has gone down the road to the call box to request an ambulance. I know that you are all right, but you'd never get a taxi in the middle of the M4," he told us. "The driver of the car that passed you on the right has stopped about a mile down the road. He thinks he's having a heart attack, but he isn't. He'll be all right."

Just then another car pulled up and an enraged driver jumped out. Glaring at us, he yelled about the hazard of having our car in the middle of the motorway. He shouted at my husband, "You're big enough! Move that car."

I held him back, worried that the physical exertion added to the trauma of the accident might be too much for him. Our two helpers, however, immediately lifted the car to the edge of the motorway. Satisfied, the angry man sped away.

Our car was a sorry sight. The windows were blown out, and the tires were mere shreds of rubber hanging from the rims of the wheels. The motor hung sloppily off the front of the chassis. Broken glass covered the road, and our suitcases had been thrown several yards ahead.

My helper spoke again. "The police will ask you some questions, but there'll be no trouble because there was no other vehicle involved. The ambulance should be here soon."

In seconds the two emergency vehicles arrived. The constable asked me what had happened. I told him as much as I could. He nodded and said, "Yes, well there was no other vehicle involved."

Hearing him echo my helper's words, I asked, "I suppose you got a statement from the two men?"

He looked confused. "Who? I thought there was no other vehicle?"

Our helpers were nowhere around, and my husband was getting into the ambulance. The policeman indicated I should go too.

The ambulance drivers asked us some questions of the sort that check for rationality—such as "Do you know where you are? Do you know what day it is?" We passed the test.

They took us to the nearest hospital to be checked over. As we had nothing more serious than minor scratches, the nurses were more concerned about our accommodations and found us a bed and breakfast called Pilgrim's Rest. A taxi took us there.

I paced around the bedroom in a daze, trembling and wondering if I were really alive or if I had died in that crash and was in some sort of limbo. I touched the furniture and the curtains, the windowsill—there was a Bible on the sill. I flipped through it, not looking for any Scripture in particular. Some words caught my eye, as if they were written in gold. "Your journey has the approval of the Lord." I slammed the book down. Goose bumps prickled the back of my neck.

I considered our itinerary. It included three traditional pilgrimage sites: Glastonbury Abbey, the shrine at Walsingham, and Canterbury Cathedral. And here we were at Pilgrim's Rest. It was a pilgrimage.

The next day, the rental company sent us a replacement car—a red one.

We later learned that October 2nd on the church calendar is Guardian Angels' Day. Although I am a practicing Christian, I always assumed that angel stories were a literary device—a beautiful way to tell of God's truth. I never believed that there were supernatural beings that flitted in and out of our lives, hovering over us, guarding us.

For about two years, people gave me books about angels and "angel on your shoulder" pins. I took it all as part of the current angel fad. Then one day I was reading Billy Graham's book, *Angels: God's Secret Agents*.

I asked my husband, "When we had our accident on the M4, what do you remember about those two young men who stopped to help us? What sort of car were they driving?"

We went over the scene together. There was our little blue car being carried to the side of the road by the two men. There was the angry man's car. Then there was the ambulance and the police car. That was all.

"They had no car," my husband said. It was impossible but true. They had arrived in the middle of a busy motorway at the moment we had stopped spinning. They had information about the lorry driver and the driver of the red car that passed us. They knew what the policeman would say, and on announcing the arrival of the ambulance, they disappeared as suddenly as they had appeared. And it happened on Guardian Angels' Day. What more proof did we need?

~Diane Jones

A Rose
Without a Thorn

I believe we are free, within limits, and yet there is an unseen hand, a guiding
angel, that somehow, like a submerged propeller, drives us on.
~Rabindranath Tagore

wish I had known that I had the world in the palm of my hand
when I was a kid. Such confidence deserted me amid childhood
bullying and the robbery of my self-esteem every time someone
slayed me with an insult, mockery, or a racial slur. I survived it
somehow. And when a knight in rusty armor came along and promised me the world, I believed him. I was thrilled that a half-handsome
guy saw me as more than a punch line for a joke.

I was cowed by his temper from day one, and I obeyed his commands. I believed him when he told me no one else would want me
because I was so unattractive and boring. I did what he wanted and
became a mother before I graduated high school. While everyone
else squealed about college plans and graduation parties, I was home,
bedridden in pre-term labor, swollen from head to toe. Teen pregnancy
was taboo in the 1990s and we didn't have our own reality show yet.
My family was mortified and my friends abandoned me. I still managed
to earn my diploma, thanks to a sympathetic school counselor who
brought my final exams home to me in bed.

At eighteen years old, I went into labor. I screamed and writhed,
and rightfully so. It was too late for anesthesia, and this child was in a

hurry! I had never experienced such horrid pain. I felt as though my childhood was literally being ripped out of me with every excruciating push. With every second of agony, I lost faith in myself, in life, in humanity. I felt like I was being punished for the pain my foolish irresponsibility had caused my parents, and I secretly hoped for death during the ordeal. My selfish thoughts were sharply interrupted by my baby's first cry.

I did the "right" thing by marrying Mr. Wrong. I was introduced to a worse form of bullying called spousal abuse. I never imagined I'd have even more of a reason to loathe living until the first slap burned my face like fire. Four tearful years later, I had son number two, again after pre-term labor. By that time, abuse was joined by infidelity. I carried on.

In September 1998, I was six months pregnant with my third son. Despite my inner angst, I was elated to be carrying another gift from God. My children were the last string of hope I had left to separate me from my cruel reality. My faith in anything holy had dwindled to almost nothing but a mother's love. I believed God was mad at me but gave me these darlings as a way of saying, "Here, be a good mom, prove yourself worthy, and I will eventually forgive your misdeeds." Another sweet little baby would be there to coo and celebrate the mere sight of my face. I couldn't wait to meet him.

My newfound bliss was slaughtered by a jolt of pain at 2 a.m. that sent me to the bathroom only to hemorrhage. I ended up in an ambulance headed to the nearest emergency room. I was placed behind a dirty, stained curtain on a bed with no pillow. I was bleeding so much that it somehow ended up in my hair. The room was spinning, and voices sounded muffled. My parents came and got my older son, and our baby stayed with my husband at the hospital. I was comforted by the sounds of his happy gurgling and humming, totally oblivious to the life-and-death situation of his mom and younger brother. Before I knew it, everything in front of me went black.

I woke up in a trauma room, drifting in and out of consciousness. I kept hearing voices shouting that I was losing too much blood and my blood pressure was dropping dangerously low. I could still hear the happy sounds of my baby boy somewhere in the room. I had the worst headache of my life. I could think of almost nothing else but the jackhammer inside my skull. Then, all of a sudden, the pain stopped.

I felt a cool, soft touch against the sides of my head. I was suddenly able to hear and think clearly. I opened my eyes and saw a nurse hovering over me from behind. She appeared upside down from that angle.

"Hello, Neesha. My name is Rose. I want you to try and relax, okay? I am right here, and I'm going to do everything I can to help you." Her voice was so comforting.

She even paid me a random compliment that I found quite odd, considering the circumstances. "You have such a pretty face," she said. I wrote it off as a tactic to keep me calm and appreciated the effort. She held my hand and talked me through the delivery as I pushed and pushed a baby that was already gone.

When the doctor delivered the news that my son was stillborn, I demanded to see him, yelling that it wasn't true. They brought him to my bedside lying lifeless on a towel. I'll never forget his lovely face. I closed my eyes and cried until the rest of the world was drowned out by my grief. After a blood transfusion, I was cleaned up and placed in a private room to recover. When I saw my doctor again, I asked her if I could please speak to Rose, the nurse who was at my bedside. I wanted to thank her for all she did to keep me calm and comfortable during the horror.

The doctor looked at me puzzled and said, "I'm sorry, there is no Rose on the staff that I know of." She called out a few other names, but none sounded even close. I told her I specifically remember that she wore lavender scrubs, my favorite color. But my doctor told me the staff color in the ER was green. I just stared at her blankly before insisting this amazing person was there with me and deserved a proper show of appreciation. The doctor suggested I had hallucinated after such tremendous blood loss and trauma.

I beg to differ. I know I had a personal encounter with an angel. And my faith in life and all things good was restored. I carried on until

I built up enough courage to leave my abuser and start a new life with my two sons and the memory of the third. I went from a hopeless nobody to single mom to college student to university graduate to professional journalist to the happily remarried woman and mom I am today.

~Neesha Niaz

Meet Our
Contributors

Monica A. Andermann lives on Long Island with her husband Bill and their latest addition, a cat named Samson. Her writing has been included in such publications as *Guideposts*, *Sasee*, and *Woman's World*, as well as many other Chicken Soup for the Soul books.

Lorraine Bruno Arsenault is a yoga teacher and author of *The Long Run Home*, poetry in *The Healing Muse*, and "In the Light" in *Chicken Soup for the Soul: Miraculous Messages from Heaven*. Lorraine holds a B.A. in Philosophy. She's a member of the Downtown Writer's Center and lives with her family and rescue dog near Syracuse, NY.

Francine L. Baldwin-Billingslea has been published in over twenty-five anthologies, including the Chicken Soup for the Soul series, Whispering Angel, Thin Threads and Silver Boomer, as well as *The Rambler*, *Mused* and *Sasee* magazines. She has authored an inspirational memoir titled, *Through It All and Out on the Other Side*.

Marla Bernard is a passionate victim's rights advocate, writer and public speaker. She holds a Masters of Arts degree with honors from Baker University and is a professor for a national university where she has written several criminal justice courses. She recently published a true crime novel entitled *Through the Rain*.

Michele Boom turned in her teacher chalkboard to be an at-home mom. While juggling two toddlers and a traveling husband, she began to write. Her work appears in regional magazines across the U.S. and Canada. She is also a contributor to *Chicken Soup for the Soul: Parenthood*. Visit her at mammatalk.blogspot.com.

Kitrina Brian is a stay-at-home mom, homeschooling her two young children. She enjoys learning, exploring and finding educational experiences with her kids in everyday life.

Christine Brooks is a freelance writer who lives in western Massachusetts with her very opinionated dog, Clancy. She has published several essays in magazines across the world and one book, *Postcards from the Road*. Christine received her Bachelor of Arts degree, with honors, from Western New England University in 1999.

Susie Brunton is an aspiring writer, currently working as an administration manager. She has a wonderful husband, two beautiful twins and two equally beautiful stepchildren. Susie enjoys traveling, reading and spending time with her fabulous friends. She plans to continue writing inspirational content.

Jill Burns lives in the mountains of West Virginia with her wonderful family. She's a retired piano teacher and performer. She enjoys writing, music, gardening, nature, and spending time with her grandchildren.

May Carlson received her Bachelor of Science degree from Northeastern University. She maintained a successful career in finance and is working on a collection of stories based on her journey as a single mother. She hopes to document her spiritual life to enhance and empower the lives of others. E-mail her at maycarlson@comcast.net.

Danny Carpenter is a Texas pastor, author/writer, Vietnam veteran, proud father of two daughters, and grandfather of three great kids. He enjoys golfing, strumming the ukulele, and family trips.

Brenda Cathcart-Kloke is a retired school district administrative assistant in Thornton, CO. She enjoys spending time with her family, oil painting, reading, and writing short inspirational stories.

Christina Ryan Claypool is an Amy Foundation Writing Award-winning journalist and speaker. She's a graduate of Bluffton University and has a master's degree in Ministry from Mount Vernon Nazarene University. Her inspirational novel, *Secrets of the Pastor's Wife*, will be released soon. She enjoys time with her husband, reading, and chocolate.

Kat Crawford, author of *Capsules of Hope: Survival Guide for Caregivers*, is known as The Lionhearted Kat. She is one of the Leadership Team for Omaha Wordsowers Christian Writers. Kat shares encouragement on her blog, *From the Eyes of a Joyful Widow*. Learn more at www.lionheartedkat.info.

Barbara Crick, a graduate of the Institute of Children's Literature, has been writing since third grade when a teacher told her parents she showed promise. She has won several awards for her poetry through the Poetry Society of Colorado. Barbara lives with her disabled husband, her greatest fan. E-mail her at bjcrick@gmail.com.

H.B. Cunningham is a freelance writer and content administrator from a small town in Texas. Aside from writing as a hobby, she has been a news writer for CBS, and has published a memoir.

Lorri Danzig holds a master's degree in Jewish Studies focused on aging. Her "Let It Shine Journeys" program for elders approaches aging as a journey of deepening wisdom and expanded possibilities. Her works of nonfiction and poetry are published in professional journals and anthologies. E-mail her at lbdanzig@letitshinejourneys.com.

Laury L. Davis grew up close to the shores of Lake Erie in Northern Ohio. She currently lives with her husband and three children near Memphis, TN, and enjoys traveling, mission work, and writing. Go to laurydavis.com for more info on her book *In Pursuit of Happiness: Stewarding Freedom as a Modern Christian Woman*.

Linda C. Defew became disabled while working full-time and raising her son and daughter, which led to going back to college, where she discovered her love for writing. Now, living a mile from their nearest neighbor, she and her husband raise dogs and chickens, and grow acres of wildflowers every spring.

Sylvia Diodati is a writer, composer and pianist in Toronto. She believes in destiny and divine intervention, hoping to inspire and entertain with her stories and creative works. Her greatest pleasure is spending time with family, her husband and young daughter, and cherished friends! E-mail her at sylviadiodati@rogers.com.

Roberta Marie Easley likes adventure and stories that are well told.

Laurie Carnright Edwards is a freelance writer, substitute teacher, and ministry partner with pastor husband Dale Edwards. She is also the proud mom of two adult children. She enjoys living in the wilds of New Hampshire. Laurie holds degrees from Berkshire Christian College and Gordon-Conwell Theological Seminary.

Karen Ekstrom is a frequent contributor to the Chicken Soup for the Soul series. She and her husband David have five children, two dogs, and four cats. They live in Texas on a working cattle ranch... all of which gives her lots to write about in her hysterical mommy blog, FlunkingFamily.com. E-mail her at kcekstrom@yahoo.com.

Terri Elders, LCSW, lives near Colville, WA, with her dog Natty and three cats. Her stories have been published in nearly a hundred anthologies. She now has two dozen stories in the Chicken Soup for the Soul series. She co-edited *Not Your Mother's Book... On Travel*. She blogs at atouchoftarragon.blogspot.com.

Karen Trotter Elley's inspirational essays have been published in newspapers across the country. She and her husband Michael live in the Nashville, TN area where Karen is busy writing her memoir and seeking publishers for her inspirational children's book and a paranormal romance. E-mail her at karen.elley@gmail.com.

Kate Fellowes is the author of five romantic suspense novels and numerous short stories and essays. Living near the shore of Lake Michigan, she and her husband share their home with a variety of companion animals. A graduate of Alverno College, she blogs about work and life at katefellowes.wordpress.com.

Sheila Ross Felton is a fifty-seven-year-old mother of two sons, ages nineteen and twenty-five. She volunteers with abused women and children and in homeless shelters, homeless veterans who were fighting addictions and has volunteered in rural areas where people were struggling with poverty. In her spare time she takes classes.

Peggy Purser Freeman, the eighth child of a sharecropper, is author of *The Coldest Day in Texas* (TCU Press), a finalist for The Writers' League of Texas Teddy Children's Book Award, presented by First Lady Laura Bush. Her latest work is *Crusin' Thru Life: Dip Street and Other Miracles*. Peggy writes for several Texas magazines.

Marilyn Ellis Futrell has always had an interest in writing but began writing in earnest after the loss of her nineteen-year-old son, John Robert Woodfin, in 2005. She has an avid interest in science, consciousness, spirituality and the interplay between the three. She is currently writing a book on after-death communication.

Heidi Gaul lives in Oregon with her husband and four-legged family. She loves travel, be it around the block or the globe. In addition to contributing to Chicken Soup for the Soul anthologies, she is active in American Christian Fiction Writers and Oregon Christian Writers. She is currently completing her second novel.

Robyn Gerland is the author of *All These Long Years Later*, a book of short stories, published this year, and a contributor to various magazines and newspapers. She is the past editor of the glossy, *Hysteria*. As a graphic artist, her work has been shown in several Canadian cities; London, England; and Sydney, Australia.

Marie Gilbert writes paranormal and science fiction. Her blog, *Gilbert Curiosities*, chronicles her ghost investigations and steampunk events. She is senior writer for *Biff Bam Pop!*, and her first book in an apocalyptic series, *Roof Oasis*, can be found on Amazon.com and Amazon Kindle.

Gina Gutzwiller has studied law at the University of Fribourg in Switzerland in both French and German, and is currently training to become a lawyer. She has been telling stories ever since she was a child. Gina's story, "Always Watching Over Me," is her first to be published. E-mail her at gina.gutzwiller@yahoo.de.

Dr. Shari Hall, a Yale/Columbia graduate who formerly worked at Walter Reed in D.C., is an international recording artist who recently released her second album, *Faith*. She is a mother who enjoys sharing her story and inspiring others to live a healthy, passionate life. E-mail her at sharihallinfo@gmail.com or visit her website sharihall.com.

A retired medical secretary, **Susan Hawthorne's** true passion is writing, both fiction and nonfiction. She has written numerous short stories—three included in anthologies—and is editing her fantasy novel, *Legacy of the Medallion*.

Gail Hayden grew up in Florida and now lives in the beautiful Mount Morris Park Historic District in Harlem. She has been a business journalist and now freelances.

Carol Goodman Heizer, M.E.d., resides in Louisville, KY. She is an eight-time published author whose books have sold in the U.S. and overseas. Her work has appeared in several Chicken Soup for the Soul books. Her previous works may be purchased through Amazon.com, CreateSpace, and in bookstores. E-mail her at cgheizer@twc.com.

Marijo Herndon's stories, ranging from humor to inspiration, appear in several books and publications. She enjoys writing at her home in New York, where she lives with her husband Dave and two furry kids, Lucy and Ethel.

Nancy Hill is a Portland, OR writer and photographer. She's written features for national magazines, fiction for literary journals, and published children's books illustrated with her photographs. She's now working on an anti-war novel. She has two sons and a Collie. She has a master's degree in writing. E-mail her at nancyowho@gmail.com.

Nancy Hoag graduated with honors from the University of Washington while raising three children. She's now a grandmother and Habitat for Humanity volunteer with four-plus years on the road in an RV with her husband in order to build HfH homes nationwide. Nancy has seen nearly 1,100 stories published and four nonfiction books.

Alton Housworth was born on his family's farm in rural Georgia during the Depression. At the age of seventeen, he joined the United States Marine Corps and served during the Korean War era. He later became a successful real estate broker and land developer. He lives with his wife of sixty years in the metro Atlanta area.

Georgia A. Hubley retired after twenty years in financial management to write full-time. Vignettes of her life appear in various anthologies, magazines and newspapers. Once the nest was empty, Georgia and her husband of thirty-six years left Silicon Valley in the rear view and now hang their hats in Henderson, NV. E-mail her at geohub@aol.com.

Jennie Ivey lives in Tennessee. She is the author of several works of fiction and nonfiction, including stories in many Chicken Soup for the Soul books. Visit her website at jennieivey.com.

Jeanie Jacobson is on the leadership team of Wordsowers Christian Writers. Her stories share God's greatness. She's currently writing a Christian fantasy series. She's active at her church, including the praise dance team. She loves visiting family and friends, reading, hiking, and gardening.

Diane Jones received her Bachelor of Arts (1974) and Master of Education (1983) degrees from the University of British Columbia. She has raised five children — grown up with their own families — so she now lives with her husband and cat. She enjoys volunteering, traveling, languages, and writing, especially for children.

Teresa Keller has been a Family Services Specialist for the past twenty-five years for a local Department of Social Services. She has served six years in the U.S. Army, which is one of the things she is most proud of. She is married and has two sons and one stepson, five grandchildren and three step-grandchildren.

L.A. Kennedy writes from her studio in Northern California. Her stories have appeared in three previous Chicken Soup for the Soul books, Guideposts publications and various magazines. Also an artist, she created clay, paper mache, floral and fabric projects for magazines and holiday items for retail stores. E-mail her at elkaynca@aol.com.

Vicki Kitchner recently retired after teaching Exceptional Student Education for thirty years. She and her husband divide their time between North Carolina and Florida unless they're off on an adventure, such as backpacking around Mont Blanc or floating down the Colorado River in a dory. E-mail at her at Vicki@hikersrest.

Author and psychic **Gregory A. Kompes** is included in more than a dozen anthologies, among them *Chicken Soup for the Soul: What I Learned from the Dog*. He holds a B.A. degree in English Literature from Columbia University, an M.S. Ed. from California State University, and is pursuing an MFA in Creative Writing at National University.

Catherine Kopp received her B.S. degree from Framingham State College and Master of Education degree from Lesley University. She has been teaching elementary school since 1973. Catherine teaches fifth grade in Denver, CO, where she lives with her husband Jim. During her free time, she enjoys writing, reading, yoga, and gardening.

This is **T. Jensen Lacey's** ninth story to be published in the Chicken Soup for the Soul series. She has published sixteen books, including a young adult adventure series *Growing Season* and *Growing Season 2: Dolphin Summer*. She is available for writers' workshops and speaking engagements. Learn more www.TJensenLacey.com.

Julie Lavender is married to David and they have four children. She is a homeschooling mommy and her favorite thing to do is spend time with family. Julie writes religious news articles for her local newspaper, and this is her second story in a Chicken Soup for the Soul book.

Suzanna Leigh was born in the UK and began acting at twelve. She went on to co-star with Elvis. She is bringing out *King Travels with Elvis* in 2015 as well as *Footsteps in Paradise*, in which she chronicles her spiritual experiences throughout her life.

Jaye Lewis is an inspirational author who lives near Whitetop Mountain in Virginia. By her side is her service dog Dixie Mae Doxie, a ten-pound Dachshund, who has changed her life. Visit both of them at www.facebook.com/jaye.lewis.7 or www.facebook.com/DixieMaeDoxie?ref=hl.

Jane Lonnqvist is a former special education teacher who went on to be a program coordinator at the local senior center. She loves writing, painting, crocheting and reading. She is a facilitator of a writing group that publishes a yearly book, with proceeds to the Fitchburg Senior Center. Jane plans to continue to write and fundraise.

Sharon Cairns Mann has a B.A. degree in English and M.A. degree in Communication. She is a professional writer and psychotherapist.

Sharon lives in Colorado and enjoys family, writing, mosaics, and hiking.

This is **Dana Martin's** sixth story in Chicken Soup for the Soul. Martin received her Bachelor of Arts degree from California State University, Bakersfield and now runs two successful haunted house attractions when she isn't writing or editing. This story is an account of a truly amazing and life-changing experience. Enjoy!

Annette McDermott is a self-proclaimed displaced country girl, freelance writer and children's author. Her features and stories have been published online and in magazines for children and adults. She has also been published in *Chicken Soup for the Soul: It's Christmas!* Visit her website at www.annettemcdermott.net.

Though her career is in music, **Cynthia McGarity** has an international following for her blog, *God's Daily Message... for the terminally dense.* She's a Master Teaching Artist for The Young Americans and The Walt Disney Company. Her latest project, the *Branching Out in Faith* app, is available in the Apple Store. God is the greatest!

Kathleen Swartz McQuaig is a writer, speaker, teacher, wife, and mother who loves to encourage others. After earning her master's degree in Education and living in military communities stateside and abroad, Kathleen and her family settled in south central Pennsylvania. Visit her at www.KathleenSwartzMcQuaig.com.

Harriet Michael is a writer whose work has appeared in numerous publications, including magazines, devotionals, and anthologies. Her e-books on prayer are sold through Lulu.com. Born in Africa, the child of missionaries, she and her husband have four children and one grandchild. You can follow her blog at www.whatHehasdoneformysoul. blogspot.com.

Randy Joan Mills is a retired special education teacher who was born and raised in Canada, but now lives in Idaho to be near her children and grandchildren. She loved teaching her incredible students, but now divides her time between her other passions: her family, genealogy, and traveling, especially to Ireland.

Jackie Minniti is a former teacher and the award-winning author of *Project June Bug*, a novel about a student with ADHD. She is a columnist for *The Island Reporter* in St. Petersburg, FL, and is a previous contributor to Chicken Soup for the Soul. Visit her website at www. jackieminniti.com.

Marya Morin is a freelance writer. Her stories and poems have appeared in publications such as *Woman's World* and Hallmark. Marya also penned a weekly humorous column for an online newsletter, and writes custom poetry on request. She lives in the country with her husband. E-mail her at Akushla514@hotmail.com.

Dena Netherton is a blogger, novelist, a classically trained musician and an educator. She studied at Oberlin College Conservatory, the University of Michigan and the University of Northern Colorado. Dena and her husband live in the Colorado Rocky Mountains.

Neesha Niaz has a B.A. degree in Communication from the University of Houston-Clear Lake. She is a professional writer/editor and journalist in the Houston area. Neesha is the mom of two boys, an avid reader of science fiction, loves to cook, and writes short stories in her free time. Visit her at www.NeeshaHosein.com.

Kimberly Nichelle is a native of Birmingham, AL, who currently resides in Atlanta, GA. She is a freelance writer, aspiring film producer and screenwriter. She published her first book in December 2010, which is used to raise awareness against domestic violence. She plans to continue to inspire others with her screenwriting.

Randi O'Keefe blogs at foreignquang.blogspot.com. Her articles have appeared both in print and online publications. She won second place in a short story contest and her reflective piece "Trollin' for Luv," was published in the anthology *Dolls Remembered* in 2009. She is happy to admit that she completed NaNoWriMo in 2010.

Shirley R. Redmond holds an M.A. degree in Literature. She has been married for forty years to her husband Bill. They have two adult children and two grandchildren. Shirley has sold numerous magazine articles to a wide variety of publications, as well as several children's books and two inspirational romances.

Denise Reich is an Italian-born, New York City-raised writer. She writes regularly for *Shameless* magazine and has contributed to numerous Chicken Soup for the Soul books. She can usually be found taking photos, painting, dancing in media events, or cheering at concerts and baseball games. Coincidentally, her favorite team is the Angels.

Donna Reames Rich is an RN and freelance writer who has been published in a wide variety of online and print publications, including *Brain, Child*; *Long Story Short*; *Nursing* and *Mothering* magazines, *The Harris County Herald, Harris County Journal*, and *LaGrange Daily News*. She has three daughters and is working on a memoir.

Johanna Richardson, always a lover of the written word, dabbles with writing for her own pleasure and is a voracious reader. Her life has been blessed by a wonderful husband and family. She is an RN, has a master's degree from the University of San Francisco, and is a Peer Volunteer for the National Alzheimer's Association.

Mark Rickerby is a writer, screenwriter, singer, voice artist and multiple Chicken Soup for the Soul contributor. His proudest achievements are co-authoring his father's memoir, *The Other Belfast*, and releasing a CD of songs for his daughters, Marli and Emma. For more info on Mark's projects, visit www.markrickerby.com.

D. Riley is a teacher, freelance writer and editor, and avid reader. She loves to spend time with her family enjoying sports, films, music, and the blessing of everyday conversation.

Liz Rolland currently resides on a small farm with her husband, two daughters, two rescued Akitas, and assorted wildlife. She has written three mystery novels set in her hometown of Nyack, NY, and plans to publish the first titled *Blind Angel* this year.

Sioux Roslawski is a third grade teacher in St. Louis, a dog rescuer for Love a Golden, a member of the infamous writing critique group the WWWPs, and a freelance writer in her spare time. She wishes she could have said "thank you" to her birth mother. Learn more at http://siouxspage.blogspot.com.

Award-winning author and editor **Paula L. Silici** firmly believes that angels really do exist, and that they have guided and protected her all her life. She lives with her husband Frank near Denver, CO. E-mail her at psilici@hotmail.com.

Darlene Sneden is a writer and editor who lives in her dream house in Montclair, NJ. Married to her high school sweetheart, Darlene is known as Mom to two wonderful young adults. She blogs about her newly emptied nest at adventuresofamiddleagemom.com.

Rev. Jim Solomon, a former businessman, has helped over 1,000 families and individuals across the nation experience life-change through counsel and care. He lives with his wife and two children in Newtown, CT, serving as Pastor of New Hope Community Church and chaplain to the Newtown Police Department.

Patrick P. Stafford lives in Northridge, CA, and works full-time as a journalist, copywriter, editor and poet. He has written for AccessLife.com, *Wheelin' Sportsmen*, *Amateur Chef* magazine, *Healthcare Traveler*, and

Northern Virginia Magazine, and has sold poems, articles and editorial pieces both online and in print publications.

Diane Stark is a wife and mother of five. She loves to write about the important things in life: her family and her faith. She is a frequent contributor to the Chicken Soup for the Soul series. E-mail her at DianeStark19@yahoo.com.

Noelle Sterne's *Trust Your Life: Forgive Yourself and Go After Your Dreams* helps readers reach their secret desires. Her new book guides dissertation writers in overcoming vital but often neglected nonacademic issues: *Challenges in Writing Your Dissertation: Coping With the Emotional, Interpersonal, and Spiritual Struggles.*

Natasha Stoynoff is a New York Times bestselling author. She has been a news reporter/photographer for the *Toronto Star*, *TIME* magazine, and columnist/feature writer for the *Toronto Sun*. She's covered celebrities for *People* magazine for nearly two decades. Natasha lives in Manhattan and is working on her second screenplay.

Ashley Thaba lives in Botswana, Africa. Her love for God and desire to be obedient to whatever He calls her to do has taken her on a journey of adventures all over the planet. She wrote an amazing book about the near death of her son and his miraculous recovery. E-mail her at ashleythaba@gmail.com.

Patti Ann Thompson is an award-winning freelance writer, author and speaker. She has been published in *Guideposts*, the Chicken Soup for the Soul series and she released her first book, *Seeing God Through New Eyes*, in 2010. She resides in Shawnee, KS with her husband Larry. You can visit her website at www.pattiannthompson.com.

Denise Valuk lives and writes from San Antonio, TX while homeschooling three boys. Writing experience includes *Guideposts* and *Mysterious Ways* magazine. Learn more at www.denisevaluk.com.

Anne Ullenboom Van Humbeck was born in Germany and immigrated to Canada with her husband and baby daughter in 1956. They farmed in Manitoba. Prodded by her children, she has written and self-published her life story upon retirement. She now enjoys writing short stories.

Robin Veldboom is a photographer, proud mom of three girls, and nana to two adorable grandchildren. She has been married to the love of her life for thirty-four years, and would like to thank her daughter Elizabeth Veldboom for her help writing the story in this book. See more of Lizzie's writing at www.mercycrown.wordpress.com.

Donna Volkenannt is a writer and creative writing teacher who believes in angels. First-place winner of the 2012 Erma Bombeck Humor Award and top ten finalist for the 2014 Erma Bombeck Human Interest Award, Donna lives with her husband and grandchildren in Missouri, where she's working on a novel. E-mail her at dvolkenannt@charter.net.

Jan Walker is a freelance writer, editor, digital artist and photographer based in Florida. She is a passionate advocate for inspiring and promoting creative expression in children and the elderly, and she enjoys teaching others to realize their untapped creative potential. E-mail her at walkerworkscreative@outlook.com.

Sharlene Walker has a master's degree in metaphysics. After living in Europe for several years, she currently resides in Burlington, Ontario, close to her two children and five grandchildren. Her proofreading sister is always on call. As a Reiki Master Sharlene practices on all living creatures.

Terri Webster began writing when she privately wrote in her journals as therapy to ease the pain and hardships of being a single mom. This grew into a passion to write with a purpose. She published *Markers for Single Moms* in 2013, and has two more in the works. She enjoys the outdoors, traveling and being with family.

Mary Z. Whitney has been featured in over seventeen Chicken Soup for the Soul books. She also writes for *Guideposts* and *Angels on Earth* magazines. Her latest publication is an inspirational children's book entitled *Max's Morning Watch*. She has also published *Life's A Symphony*. Both of her books are available at Amazon.com.

Dallas Woodburn has written fiction and nonfiction for a variety of publications including the *Nashville Review*, the *Los Angeles Times*, and *Louisiana Literature*. Her short story collection was a finalist for the Flannery O'Connor Award for Short Fiction. Connect with her at writeonbooks.org and daybydaymasterpiece.com.

Cynthia Zayn lives in the Atlanta area, and is the author of *Narcissistic Lovers: How to Cope, Recover, and Move On.* She has taught in public and private schools throughout the United States and Mexico City, and now works as a freelance editor for community magazines while pursuing a full-time career as an author.

Karen Vincent Zizzo, M.A., is an author and inspirational speaker whose passion is to inspire people to overcome obstacles in their lives. She shares very personal messages of faith, hope, love and the power of prayer through her Ask and You Shall Receive series of books, CDs and workbooks and at www.karenzizzo.com.

About Amy Newmark

Amy Newmark was a writer, speaker, Wall Street analyst and business executive in the worlds of finance and telecommunications for more than thirty years. Today she is publisher, editor-in-chief and coauthor of the Chicken Soup for the Soul book series. By curating and editing inspirational true stories from ordinary people who have had extraordinary experiences, Amy has kept the twenty-one-year-old Chicken Soup for the Soul brand fresh and relevant, and still part of the social zeitgeist.

Amy graduated *magna cum laude* from Harvard University where she majored in Portuguese and minored in French. She wrote her thesis about popular, spoken-word poetry in Brazil, which involved traveling throughout Brazil and meeting with poets and writers to collect their stories. She is delighted to have come full circle in her writing career—from collecting poetry "from the people" in Brazil as a twenty-year-old to, three decades later, collecting stories and poems "from the people" for Chicken Soup for the Soul.

Amy has a national syndicated newspaper column and is a frequent radio and TV guest, passing along the real-life lessons and useful tips she has picked up from reading and editing thousands of Chicken Soup for the Soul stories.

She and her husband are the proud parents of four grown children and in her limited spare time, Amy enjoys visiting them, hiking, and reading books that she did not have to edit.

About Gabrielle Bernstein

Gabrielle Bernstein is the New York Times bestselling author of *May Cause Miracles* and *Miracles Now*. She appears regularly as an expert on NBC's *Today* show, has been featured on Oprah's *Super Soul Sunday* as a next-generation thought leader, and was named "a new role model" by *The New York Times*. She is also the author of the books *Add More ~ing to Your Life* and *Spirit Junkie*. Gabrielle is the founder HerFuture.com, a social networking site for women to inspire, empower and connect.

YouTube named Gabrielle one of sixteen YouTube Next Video Bloggers, she was named one of Mashable's 11 Must-Follow Twitter Accounts for Inspiration and she's featured on the Forbes List of 20 Best Branded Women. Gabrielle has a weekly radio show on Hay House Radio. She has been featured in media outlets such as *The New York Times Sunday Styles*, *ELLE*, *OWN*, *Kathie Lee & Hoda*, *The Dr. Oz Show*, Oprah Radio, *The Queen Latifah Show*, *Anderson Live*, *Access Hollywood*, *Marie Claire*, *Health*, *SELF*, *Women's Health*, *Glamour*, the cover of *Experience Life* magazine and more. For more on Gabrielle's work, visit www.Gabbyb.tv.

Thank You

We owe huge thanks to all of our contributors. We know that you poured your hearts and souls into the thousands of stories that you shared with us. We appreciate your willingness to open up your lives to other Chicken Soup for the Soul readers and share your own experiences, no matter how personal. As I read and edited these truly awe-inspiring stories, I was excited by the potential of this book to inspire people, and impressed by your unselfish willingness to share your stories. Many of you said this was the first time you were sharing your angel story, so we thank you for letting our readers be your confidants.

We could only publish a small percentage of the stories that were submitted, but every single one was read and even the ones that do not appear in the book had an influence on us and on the final manuscript. Our editor Kristiana Pastir read every submission and pared the list down to several hundred semi-finalists. She was aided by Ronelle Frankel and Mary Fisher on our publishing team. After I chose the 101 stories, Kristi chose many of the wonderful quotations that were inserted at the beginning of each story, which we think add so much richness to the reading experience. Our assistant publisher D'ette Corona worked with all the contributors to make sure they approved our edits, and she and editor Barbara LoMonaco performed their normal masterful proofreading job.

We also owe a very special thanks to our creative director and book producer, Brian Taylor at Pneuma Books, for his brilliant vision for our covers and interiors.

~Amy Newmark

Sharing Happiness, Inspiration, and Wellness

Real people sharing real stories, every day, all over the world. In 2007, *USA Today* named *Chicken Soup for the Soul* one of the five most memorable books in the last quarter-century. With over 100 million books sold to date in the U.S. and Canada alone, more than 200 titles in print, and translations into more than forty languages, "chicken soup for the soul" is one of the world's best-known phrases.

Today, twenty-one years after we first began sharing happiness, inspiration and wellness through our books, we continue to delight our readers with new titles, but have also evolved beyond the bookstore, with wholesome and balanced pet food, delicious nutritious comfort food, and a major motion picture in development. Whatever you're doing, wherever you are, Chicken Soup for the Soul is "always there for you™." Thanks for reading!

Share with Us

We all have had Chicken Soup for the Soul moments in our lives. If you would like to share your story or poem with millions of people around the world, go to chickensoup.com and click on "Submit Your Story." You may be able to help another reader, and become a published author at the same time. Some of our past contributors have launched writing and speaking careers from the publication of their stories in our books!

We only accept story submissions via our website. They are no longer accepted via mail or fax.

To contact us regarding other matters, please send us an e-mail through webmaster@chickensoupforthesoul.com, or fax or write us at:

Chicken Soup for the Soul
P.O. Box 700
Cos Cob, CT 06807-0700
Fax: 203-861-7194

One more note from your friends at Chicken Soup for the Soul: Occasionally, we receive an unsolicited book manuscript from one of our readers, and we would like to respectfully inform you that we do not accept unsolicited manuscripts and we must discard the ones that appear.

Chicken Soup for the Soul

Changing your world one story at a time®

www.chickensoup.com